"This is an exploration of race in America by two young women who are earnestly challenging their own assumptions and encouraging the rest of us to do the same. If you're a young person who wants to be part of our national conversation on race but don't know where to start, this book is an engaging launching point."

—Cecilia Muñoz,
former director of Intergovernmental Affairs under
President Obama and senior vice president of the National Council of La Raza
(now UnidosUS), the nation's largest Hispanic policy and advocacy organization

"This is a critical book for current times where we are seeing a resurgence of nationalism, racism, sexism, and authoritarianism globally. Better communication and understanding, particularly among the next generation, is the key to humanizing the unfamiliar and countering identity politics. Kudos, Priya and Winona, for your vision, your journey, and the honesty and respect with which you tackle diverse stories from across the country. The fact that you are teenagers makes me doubly hopeful! This book should be on top of our lists."

—Yasmeen Hassan,
global executive director of Equality Now

"While we know a lot about racial literacy, the work that Winona Guo and Priya Vulchi have accomplished in *Tell Me Who You Are* brings life to this concept. They are magical in weaving in the stories of everyday folks' racial traumas and triumphs and force us to question the way we see the world. They encourage us to stop assuming we understand racial, gender, sexual, age and ability biases and open our eyes. They implore us to be more than spectators or witnesses, ignorant of the broken racial promises right in front of us and speak to that loss. This work is a call for not just talking about social justice but doing random acts of justice every day. Be careful. If you want your racial justice neatly packaged into the 'saying the right thing' or 'avoiding the wrong thing to say,' go elsewhere. But if you want to become fluid in how to keep the racial justice promises we make to people who are different in this society, read on."

—Howard Stevenson, Ph.D.,
director of Forward Promise, Racial Empowerment
Collaborative, and Constance E. Clayton Professor of Urban
Education and Africana Studies, University of Pennsylvania

"From the moment these two remarkable young women took the TEDWomen stage as high school seniors to talk about their commitment to have a real conversation about race, I knew their work would be a game changer in the conversation about race in this country . . . and *Tell Me Who You Are* is just that—the outcome of an extraordinary journey from the wealthiest neighborhoods to the poorest reservations and communities to find out more about who we all are."

—Pat Mitchell,
former president of CNN Productions
and the first woman president and CEO of PBS

"In *Tell Me Who You Are*, Priya Vulchi and Winona Guo do exactly that—tell us who they are, how they have come to thinking so carefully, so deeply about race, and how they want to create change. This book is at once hopeful, raw, and brimming with curiosity, engagement, and youthful energy. Through the conversations these women have with people from all walks of life, we see that the key to any kind of progress begins with letting people tell us who they are. If you want to have richer, more fruitful discussions about race, gender, all the things that comprise our identities, this book will give you a necessary vocabulary. All you have to do is turn the page."

—Roxane Gay,
*New York Times*–bestselling
author of *Bad Feminist* and *Difficult Women*

"Brave. Bold. Insightful. This book not only offers insight into how we think and do race, it is a testament to what this generation can do to fundamentally transform our world. The reader can't help but feel the energy, passion, and commitment of these two brilliant young women."

—Eddie S. Glaude, Jr.,
James S. McDonnell Distinguished University Professor,
and Chair, African American Studies, Princeton University

"I'm truly astonished by the vision, audacity, and leadership of Winona Guo and Priya Vulchi to compile these amazing stories from over 150 Americans. These girls are the antidote to the notion that this generation is apathetic. In fact, they are our thought leaders and have proven to be dynamic change-makers! It takes enormous courage to confront the cracks in our humanity and hold space for such diverse stories. *Tell Me Who You Are* is exactly what our country needs right now. In these divisive times, two young women have managed to create a tangible catalyst for compelling and necessary conversation, by doing something truly radical: Listening. Deeply."

—Monique Coleman,
actress, global youth advocate, and CEO of Motivated Productions

# WINONA GUO AND PRIYA VULCHI

# TELL ME WHO YOU ARE

## A ROAD MAP FOR CULTIVATING RACIAL LITERACY

A TarcherPerigee Book

tarcherperigee

An imprint of Penguin Random House LLC
penguinrandomhouse.com

First trade paperback edition 2021

Most TarcherPerigee books are available at special quantity discounts for bulk purchase for sales promotions, premiums, fund-raising, and educational needs. Special books or book excerpts also can be created to fit specific needs. For details, write: SpecialMarkets@ penguinrandomhouse.com.

Library of Congress Cataloging-in-Publication Data

Names: Guo, Winona, author. | Vulchi, Priya, author.
Title: Tell me who you are : sharing our stories of race, culture, & identity / Winona Guo and Priya Vulchi.
Description: New York : TarcherPerigee, [2019] | Includes bibliographical references and index.
Identifiers: LCCN 2018050286| ISBN 9780525541127 (hardback) | ISBN 9780525541134 (ebook)
Subjects: LCSH: Race discrimination—United States. | United States—Race relations. | Group identity—
    United States. | BISAC: SOCIAL SCIENCE / Discrimination & Race Relations. | POLITICAL
    SCIENCE / Political Freedom & Security / Civil Rights. | EDUCATION / Students & Student Life.
Classification: LCC E184.A1 G945 2019 | DDC 305.800973—dc23
    LC record available at https://lccn.loc.gov/2018050286

ISBN (paperback) 9780593330173

Printed in Italy
4th Printing

Book design by Pauline Neuwirth

For our beloved parents,

who (eventually) let us

take a year away from school

# CONTENTS

"In our traditional way of life, we believe that

I don't tell you who you are. You tell me who you are,

and that is who you are."

–a Cherokee saying shared with us by Ahyoka
from Tahlequah, Oklahoma

# INTRODUCTION

*K*ids start developing signs of prejudice and stereotyping at three or four years old, and yet, after over a decade in both private and public schools in the United States, we don't remember ever having an honest conversation about race. All we got, instead, were pastel pink signs on our classroom walls that declared, "Here, in this room, we will not discriminate based on race, gender, religion . . . or any other reason."

Despite this lofty ideal, however, we've been told something very different.

"Don't associate with black people."

"Your queer friends are ruined."

"That short skirt means you deserve to be raped."

"Don't be the racism police."

"Injustice is a fact of life."

Priya was repeatedly told to bleach her skin. Winona was frequently asked why her eyes were always closed in photos. For over a dozen years, we both remember looking in the mirror in the morning, recalling the White girls at school who didn't remember our names, thinking, over and over again, "I am so inferior."

After years of silence, Eric Garner's death in July 2014 prompted a surprising group conversation in our tenth grade history class. It was the first time we remembered *any* teacher initiating a discussion about race—and he was a self-identifying WASP—a "White Anglo-Saxon Protestant" and "straight man of privilege." He inspired us to disrupt the comfortable patterns of silence in our lives—first through class conversations, and then through the shockingly unheard stories we collected outside of school.

Once we started learning, we couldn't stop. We approached friends, teachers, peers, and hundreds of strangers all around our hometown of Princeton, New Jersey. Our first public interview was at a Starbucks windowsill, when we asked a young woman: "What does the word 'race' mean to you?" No one had asked her that question before, and she described, waving her hands in at least fifteen different directions, how she felt being told that she would never make it to college being Latina—and then being the first in her family to do so. She thanked us profusely for simply listening. Others whispered their fears for their children of color; some cried loudly while describing the psychological impact of their past experiences on their lives today. It felt like being on the end of a fire hose, which made us wonder why stories about race had been ignored, suppressed, or unshared for so long.

Once, the principal of an elementary school pulled us aside and said, "You're going to have to explain what 'race' is, because these kids have no idea." Then we asked the fourth grade class, "Who here has experienced or seen racism?" Almost all of their hands shot up.

We cofounded CHOOSE as a platform for racial literacy. We shared all the stories we heard on our website and social media. We started speaking at schools. We sent out surveys. We designed multiple iterations of classroom materials for K–12 educators. We self-educated through a reading list much longer than for any of our classes. We gave language to not only our traumas but also our many privileges—from being able-bodied, to having parents who love us, to having teachers who assumed that we, as Asian Americans, were capable, to living near and with access to so many resources that enabled our work. Of everything that happened in the next four years, perhaps the most impactful to our work were the mentors who always stood by our side. One mentor, Princeton University Professor Ruha Benjamin, tweeted this: *Racial literacy is not about acquiring the words to have a 'conversation on race'—which too often stays at the level of anecdote and sentiment. Racial literacy is developing a historical & sociological tool kit to understand how we got here and how it could've been/CAN BE otherwise."*

We realized that our anecdote- and sentiment-driven model was not enough. Our focus had been on raising consciousness toward racial inequity— *why* we all need to talk about race—without giving the tools of *how* to break it down. We wanted to accomplish both. We began to understand that our anecdotes would require a larger "historical & sociological" context. So we created a model: stories, paired to research, to close what we called "the heart–mind gap of racial literacy." In our first TED Talk, "What it takes to be racially literate," we described the heart part of the gap as "an inability to understand each of our experiences, to fiercely and unapologetically be compassionate beyond lip service," and the mind portion as "an inability to understand the larger, structural ways in which racism operates." We also began including fun facts with every interviewee's story—the design was inspired by our team member Marie Louise James's work—in order to further humanize people beyond race.

Together, the stories and statistics we found pulsated with truth and power. Everything we'd been told previously—like, "there's no racism in *Princeton* of all places!"—felt like a cover-up. The town of Princeton, with its Ivy League association and upwardly mobile citizens, had adopted a culture of silence and denial about race. What about the rest of the America?

We were due to start college in fall of 2017—Winona to Harvard and Priya to Princeton—but we kept feeling like the work was far from complete. In junior year, we had published, using our heart–mind model, a racial literacy textbook called *The Classroom Index*, funded primarily by Princeton University's Department of African American Studies. When it was covered in national media like *Teen Vogue* and ordered by schools in more than forty states, we felt that we had to do better. For one, the stories we had collected came mostly from central New Jersey and New York City, and we knew those voices could not represent the vast experience of Americans. We believed our idea for an effective racial literacy tool kit could impact communities near and far from Princeton, people in and out of the classroom. We knew there was much more we could do to contribute to the world—now, rather than four years later. So we fundraised our senior year of high school to take a year off before college and to hear for ourselves the diversity of voices across the nation. Later, as TED Residents in New York City, we would research and write this book.

We started off in Anchorage, Alaska, in July 2017 and finished in Charlottesville, Virginia, in February 2018. During our travels, we collected over five hundred stories. We asked everyone, *How has race, culture, or intersectionality impacted your life?* The responses were astonishing. These identities had so significantly shaped the lives of the people we spoke to

Intersectionality refers to "the overlapping systems of advantages and disadvantages that affect people differently positioned in society." This means that race cannot be examined in isolation from other social classifications like class, gender, religion, and sexuality, identity markers which can often produce new forms of domination, too. Read more in Chapter 3.

that it often felt as if we had asked them simply, *Tell me who you are.*

In a restaurant in the Mississippi Delta, Black servers told us that some of the White customers in the room had previously refused to be served by them—in 2018! We stayed with a philanthropist in Park City, Utah, who introduced us to friends affiliated with the Academy Awards, then lived with a young transgender man and his girlfriend in Tulsa, Oklahoma, who were struggling to put together enough money for a small wedding. In downtown Montgomery, Alabama, we read public markers that announced the city's history of slavery, while Confederate flags waved on the highway a mile away. While we had previously scheduled many of our interviews, many also came from strangers we tapped on the shoulder—strangers ranging from a homeless man sitting in a tunnel to Alexander Rodriguez entering a shiny black SUV. One of our first interviewees was a White man who condemned President Barack Obama for "throwing his White mother under a bus and pretending to be Black for political expediency," while among our last was a White man who worked at a women's correctional facility and condemned color-blindness. We had long conversations on a yacht in Point Loma, San Diego, as well as in broken-down reservation houses in some of the poorest places in our nation. We frequented spaces exclusively with other people of color, and also stayed in nearly all-White rural communities like Troy, Idaho (in a log cabin built by hand by our hosts!). From Honolulu to Chicago to Omaha to Los Angeles, we did not find a single diverse town or city that was not physically separated by race in its housing and resources. It was astonishing to us how we became conscious of these divides now, but growing up, like most other youth in Princeton, we had no idea that "Black and Hispanic neighborhoods" existed, that slavery had existed in our town square, and that to understand the intergenerational legacy of that injustice would have dramatically altered how we understood the divided lunch tables, clubs, and classes at school we saw every day.

When we started this trip, we thought we already fundamentally understood racial division in our country. The astonishing complexity and intensity of division we witnessed proved we didn't. Communities were not just divided *everywhere*, but also divided *in every way*. We learned how impossible it is to treat a racial group as one monolith. In a meeting that lasted an hour and a half, a band of Keetoowah Cherokee elders spent more than an hour of that time talking about inter-tribe prejudice. In St. Paul–Minneapolis, a Hmong writer told us that, rather than being perceived as an Asian-American "model minority," she must "write to write [her] people into existence." We learned how much intersectionality matters. A gay Black man in D.C. left his queer community because it didn't accept his Blackness, while a gay Chinese woman in DeLand, Florida, was ostracized from a Chinese community that didn't accept her queerness. In Philly, a trans woman lost nearly all her relationships after she came out, and when she had to use a wheelchair after being shot twice and stabbed seven times in a trans hate crime, trans community gatherings were no longer physically accessible to her and so she lost them too. We learned how strongly race shapes even communities of racial justice activists. In Charlottesville, Virginia, Heather Heyer's mom guiltily described how she felt that her daughter's death after a protest got so much attention, because she was White. We saw that many were frustrated. Many just wanted "to communicate, live together, and love each other better." Yet, at least a dozen people told us, separately, that they knew a race war was coming.

Our heads throb and our hearts hurt when we think about the stories we have heard. Many are tragic. Many are hopeful. Most detail lives we have never imagined and still cannot imagine.

The stories leave us feeling disturbed. Touched. Tired. Energized. Sad. Optimistic. Angry. Compassionate. More than anything, they leave us urgently wanting to make sure these stories are heard. As we have traveled, we have learned that racial literacy never stops. We—including the two of us—can all learn more about who we are.

We are so excited to share this extraordinary breadth and depth of the U.S. American experience. This book chronicles our journey of racial literacy so far: a journey of two eighteen-year-old young women of color traveling, alone, to all fifty states, listening to strangers talk about the most vulnerable parts of their hearts, from Anchorage to Charlottesville. We believe this literacy tool kit can help catalyze generations of change, through over a hundred intimate interviews, paired to systematic context.

Hundreds of people breathed life into this book. From the courageous people who shared their stories, to the tremendous activists and educators we have learned so much from, to the families who opened up their homes to us, to the students who spent hours transcribing each interviewee's words, to the parents, teachers, doctors, librarians, CEOs, nonprofit leaders, professors, and one "spice hunter" who helped us edit everything, truly a team worked together to make this book possible. Our team, further described in the acknowledgments, transcends many boundaries of age, geography, or background. We often think that if every person we've met on this trip got together in one (very large) room, it could be the most diverse gathering in American history.

Two disclaimers:

First, this book does not reflect a complete or representative picture of race in

America, and it is not meant to. This book reflects a personal journey. We planned every part of this trip ourselves. For safety reasons, our destinations depended largely on whether we had a trusted contact to host us. The two of us were too young to rent cars, and we mostly interviewed in places accessible by rideshare apps, public transportation, or foot. We wish we could've included many more voices, or spent much more time in each community, but we were constrained by time (our gap year) and space (our page limit). Even out of the five hundred plus stories we heard, we could share little over a hundred here; out of a hundred and eighty days of travel, we could only share ten moments in our chapter introductions. These moments, oftentimes describing a place we visited, are truthful to our experiences yet also both subjective and incomplete. Our methodology—from who we were able to find as hosts, to how willing strangers were to talk to us, to what questions we asked—has been heavily shaped by our own individual identities and experiences. Much more academic analysis could be added to support each story. (And while some footnotes might be relevant to more than one story, we've only included them alongside the first relevant story.) Many more statistics and vocabulary terms are also important to know. This book simply reflects much of what we have learned so far, and we have much to learn still.

Second, the people you'll "meet" are much more complex than can be encompassed in one or a few pages. Our longest interview was four hours, which meant over fifty pages of transcription. We (painfully) cut those pages down to one or two. We eliminated parts in context of what would be included elsewhere. Some facts may have also changed since our interview was conducted. Remember: each story is not the full story. At the same time, we tried our best to be accurate and fair, to convey all essential details of a story, and to retain the interviewee's personal voice. We can't say we agree with every perspective we included, but we nevertheless urge you to open-mindedly consider them all, and to trust that they have been shared with honesty. If you'd like to keep reading more, to view photographs with engaging fun-fact illustrations, or to find other content that brings each story further to life—check out our social media (Facebook: chooseorg; Instagram, Twitter: choose_org) and website (chooseorg.org).

Millions of Americans—both White people and people of color—still don't come close to fully understanding people outside their mostly homogeneous immediate communities. Dr. Martin Luther King, Jr., once wrote that the "great stumbling block in the stride toward freedom" was not the obvious racist but "the White moderate who is more devoted to 'order' than to justice." In fact, three out of four White people in America don't have a *single* friend of color, and the average White American has 91 percent White friends. For all of us, White or not, seeking to learn exclusively from the people we know and are comfortable with would only widen our heart–mind gap. Looking around at both ourselves and others, we realized that, as much as we all like to believe we are open-minded and progressive, *many* of us have not truly broken out of our racially divided bubbles. We have not learned from and formed friendships across the true diversity of our nation. We have remained too aloof from the pursuit of justice.

We, and so many people we know, have the privilege and resources to do *something.* The two of us have been told that we are too young, too bold, too uneducated, too aggressive, too insignificant; particularly as Asian-American females fighting for racial equity, we've been told we should stay silent. We find that opinion not only misguided, but also not an option.

What does that *"something"* look like for you? We hope that the stories throughout this book will inspire some new ideas, and the last chapter of this book, "Let's All Get to Work," contains a formula for action in your daily life. Americans—moms, dads, teachers, entrepreneurs, scuba divers,

Wall Street executives, archaeologists, policymakers, humans—we *can* all reframe our work and lives toward racial literacy. Educators, try connecting book chapter themes and words from the index to your existing lesson plans, perhaps photocopying stories and stats for your students. Students, maybe form a reading group to discuss takeaways from this book, and transform those takeaways into concrete action plans for your school or district. Parents, you could read a few stories to your children each night before they sleep. Anyone could gift this book to a friend who might be touched by its stories, or who could benefit from some racial literacy. Any person who is part of a community can help ensure that the voices within that community are heard. We *can* prevent some of our racial pain before it seeps into our younger generations. We *can* heal the communities we are already part of so they are defined not by division but by honesty and justice, by love and liberation. If we *can* do it, why don't we? As we both discovered in our travels, racial division is not a problem that only affects some. It is not a reality detached from our daily lives. The topic speaks to the very nature and future of our nation, our communities, and all our humanity. This is all of our responsibilities. As we do with ourselves, we challenge you to get to work.

# A BRIEF HISTORY

Main source: *Racial Domination, Racial Progress* by Matthew Desmond and Mustafa Emirbayer

*T*he racial categories that we're familiar with developed only two hundred years ago, primarily by England and Spain. Otherwise cut off from the rest of the world, England kept on invading Ireland, labeling the people as savages—in fact, the cruel saying "the only good Indian is a dead Indian" first circulated in England as "the only good Irishman is a dead Irishman."

A little less than two thousand miles away from England, Spain, loyal to the Catholic Church, was offering the Jewish and Muslim people under their rule three choices: "leave, convert, or die." While many Jews and Muslims converted to Catholicism to escape persecution, church leaders questioned their sincerity, leading to the 1478 Spanish Inquisition, during which "interest in *religious purity* morphed into an obsession with *blood purity*."

In both England and Spain during this time, **nationalism** (the creation of "a 'people'" within "artificially created borders") and **capitalism** ("social relationships in the countryside [transforming] into relationships based on the exploitation of agricultural labor for sake of profits") began to rise.

To satisfy Europe's growing sense of nationalism and hunger for capitalism, the **Age of Discovery** began—"or, from the standpoint of the Indigenous people of Africa and the Americas, the 'Age of Terrorism.'" When Christopher Columbus "discovered America"—aka happened upon an island in the Bahamas that was already inhabited—the Americas were populated by approximately 50 to 100 million Indigenous people.

With Christopher Columbus's lead, the Spanish colonized the Americas; the English followed a century later. **Colonialism** "occurs when a foreign power invades a territory and establishes enduring systems of exploitation and domination over that territory's Indigenous populations." From 1600 to 1900, 90 to 99 percent of America's Indigenous peoples died "as a direct result of European colonization."

With the rise of nationalism, capitalism, and European discovery of the "New World"—which, again, was only "new" from a European perspective—a different worldview was desired to make sense of it all. Through colonialism, "race" became a key element of that worldview.

To further their capitalist interests in the "New World," the English needed a labor force.

So, indentured servitude started. Indentured servants were often kidnapped. They included

# OF WHITENESS

Irish, impoverished English, Indigenous, and African people. (Note how the English and Irish are identified as people from two separate nations, whereas Indigenous and African people, all from different nations, are considered as two monoliths.)

Indentured servitude evolved into chattel slavery. Among all other indentured servants, why were Black people singled out to be enslaved? It couldn't be Native Americans, because their numbers were reducing rapidly, they could escape their captors more easily since they were familiar with the land, and they were already relied upon as trappers in the lucrative fur trade business. It couldn't be the "savage Irish" because, upon escaping, Irish slaves could "blend in" with their English captors.

Africans, however, "could not blend in." Furthermore, Africans were not accustomed to the American landscape, making escape from captivity more difficult; they were also immune to Old World diseases, unlike Natives, and many were already farmers. "Africans soon came to be seen as 'the perfect slaves'" and originally *not* strictly because of their Blackness.

Thus, Whiteness and Blackness were born: "twins birthed from the same womb, that of slavery." The White race began to be formed "out of a heterogenous and motley collection of Europeans who had never before perceived that they had anything in common."

Whiteness remains the dominant category today—other races are compared and contrasted relative to it. Whiteness positions itself against ideas of, among others, Blackness, Indigenousness, Asianness, and Hispanic-ness. This is why people of color, rather than White people, will frequently be identified by their race. Whiteness has become the norm.

## WHAT IS RACE?

Main source: *Racial Domination, Racial Progress* by Matthew Desmond and Mustafa Emirbayer

- Race is a symbolic category based on *phenotype* (such as height, hair texture, eye color, and skin tone) and *ancestry* (including tribal, regional, and national affiliations). Race is not natural: it's a well-founded fiction, a social construction rather than a biological truth.
- In the United States, the current racial taxonomy has five major groups: 1) Native American and Alaskan Native; 2) Asians and Pacific Islanders; 3) African Americans (Blacks); 4) Hispanics; and 5) Whites.
  ▶ Is there a biological basis for this taxonomy? *No.* In fact, there is "8.6 times more genetic variation *within* traditionally defined racial groups than *between* them." Furthermore, "people might speak different languages, uphold different traditions, worship different deities, [and] enjoy different kinds of food," yet they are still homogenized under one racial category.
  ▶ This taxonomy has changed dramatically and continues to change over time.

## NOTE TO THE READER

**The Four Dimensions of Racism:** Our racial reality today can be described in four dimensions (according to trainings by Race Forward: The Center for Racial Justice Innovation). As you read the stories in this book, think about which of these dimensions are being described.

- **Internalized racism:** "The private racial beliefs held by individuals."
  ▶ These can be both conscious and unconscious, held toward oneself or toward others.
- **Interpersonal racism:** "How we act upon our racial beliefs when we interact with others."
- **Institutional racism:** "Racial inequities within institutions and systems of power."
  ▶ Example: "School systems that provide unequal opportunities for people of different races."
- **Systemic racism:** "Racial bias across institutions and society."
  ▶ Example: "The racial wealth gap reflects the cumulative effects of racial inequities."

# CHAPTER ONE

# RACE IMPACTS EVERYTHING

As Yaari spun onstage, singing in an almost-forgotten language, the room vibrated with her rage and pain. Traditional blue Inuit tattoos protruding from her mouth like fangs, her black eyes stung the scattered audience, and her limbs wailed *Hear me, hear my people* as she danced to an Alutiiq drum. We sat, stunned, as she narrated Saint Lawrence Island Yup'ik stories.

We were at the very start of our journey: a day ago, we had landed in our first state, Alaska. We realized that we had never met anyone who identified as a full-blooded Indigenous person before. In school, all mention of Native Americans stopped after the Trail of Tears. Priya remembers a kid shouting once, "No way! You're Indian?! I thought they were extinct!!" Even when we had followed the typical tourist itinerary through downtown Anchorage, we saw White people everywhere.

Yet, suddenly, here we were watching Yaari dance, and her emotion pierced us. After she got off the stage, we hurriedly approached and asked her for an interview. She opened her mouth, stretching the five double stripes of her inky blue tattoos . . . and popped in a stick of bubble gum. "Follow me," she said. We followed her to a large room at the back of the Alaska Native Heritage Center. There, a handful of Alaskan Natives sat behind information and artifact booths. They looked bored. An older man stared at his glowing phone while a red-haired woman absentmindedly ran her fingers alongside the ridges of her wooden sculptures.

"They'll answer your questions," Yaari calmly said to us. "I'm sorry, but I don't feel comfortable talking about anything political on behalf of the Heritage Center. Plus, there's a big tour group coming in about thirty minutes."

She left. In front of us, the man put his phone down and the woman stood up. They told us their names: Alfred and Darlene. The glass window behind them framed a view of luscious trees standing tall behind a pond that reflected their spiky silhouettes and the icy blue sky. As Winona pulled out her phone to snap a photo, a bird swooped by, its feet grazing the water.

A tourist walked up to Darlene's booth. "Beautiful sculptures," we overheard him saying. "What a great display of Eskimo culture." Darlene made a familiar face—the one we make before answering the *Where are you from?* question for the hundredth time—but we didn't understand what was wrong.

Leaning over to look at the panoramic photo Winona took, Priya muttered, "Wow, this place feels so out-of-worldly. I mean, it's crazy that it's a part of America!"

Alfred chuckled, and then said, "This place is more American than any other part of America. We are more American than any other American. We were here *first*."

Those words were our foundation to understanding how race and racism inescapably impact everything around us. Even the very *existence* of the United States demanded their presence.

Some people never realize how poor their vision is until they get glasses—once you slide those shiny frames onto the bridge of your nose, the world looks completely different. An increased clarity about how our country was built upon race, that the concept of race was *constructed* to divide us, will leave you similarly flabbergasted.

Before European colonization, scholars estimate the Americas' Indigenous population to have been anywhere from 50 million to 100 million people. After colonization, by 1650, the Native population declined to less than 6 million. There was the genocide of Native Americans, and the abuse of the Chinese and Irish who connected vast stretches of this country with their backbreaking labor. There was the theft of African bodies and souls, dragged here in shackles. Our country's success, in large part, rests on an enormous price of Black and brown and yellow bodies.

While visiting Alaska, we began to recognize that race—this ubiquitous thing that controls our lives—goes deeper than the ground we walk on (whiiiiich was most likely obtained by a violated treaty with the Indigenous peoples who lived there). Race goes well beyond our history. We began to notice how, when we visited the Anchorage drugstore, the "skin color" Band-Aids lining the walls weren't meant for Priya's brown skin; how, on the sidewalk, we passed by a carefree, singing

White biker and then, one block away, an officer calling a Latino biker to a stop; how, in the TV show we watched later that night, the one Asian-American character didn't say a word; how taking a selfie together was nearly impossible because our phones can't handle our different skin tones (thanks to the technology only being tested on White folks); how almost all the artwork that hangs on the government buildings we visited were of White men; how the women who later did our stage makeup and hair tried to make Priya's skin lighter ("brighter") and Winona's eyes bigger ("more visible"); how our university campuses are dominated by colonial-style housing; how *every single* city we've been to had racially divided neighborhoods; how people have told Winona her playing of the *erhu* "doesn't feel as civilized as Western instruments"; how doctors more easily ignore the pain of Black women—who are three to four times more likely to die from pregnancy—and how, growing up, we were taught that White was right.

The list goes on. From our televisions to our artwork to our health care, race is a cancer that impacts every part of our lives. It often determines anything from where we live, to whom we know, to how we walk through the world.

Thinking about it all, our heads spin, spin, spin, like Yaari spinning on that stage in Alaska, her feet thumping loudly, urging people to *stop* condoning Indigenous invisibility and to realize the Saint Lawrence Island Yup'ik people are still alive. We think of Alfred and Darlene, who corrected that tourist by saying, "Actually, *Eskimo* is a derogatory term given to us by the Russians who invaded this land. It means 'raw meat eater,' so you're *technically* an Eskimo too, young man." We think of how frequently the word "Eskimo" was used in our history textbooks, and how Wikipedia still uses it to describe the Yup'ik people. We think of how Alfred cried, telling us how he's afraid that our generation will forget his story.

The truth of the world—that race is inextricable with everyday life—is heavy. But, if we all cared and dared to *share* the weight of that truth, perhaps we can hold it high enough and long enough for things to change. Perhaps if we started by simply recognizing that race impacts everything, that everything is impacted by race, our vision would begin to clear.

# Alexa, Justin P., and Jennifer L.

**CHICAGO, ILLINOIS**

My favorite author is Raymond Carver.

I own a seven-year-old beagle.

I love the show <u>Atlanta</u> with Donald Glover.

The best thing I know how to make is Japanese curry!

I have a twin brother.

I am a slam poet.

*Jennifer:* Growing up, I was surrounded by the Vietnamese community. My mom raised me by herself. It was me, her, and my sister—for a while, we actually lived in a shelter. Being from a family that didn't have much, if we wanted to get anywhere, we'd have to walk. So, for a lot of my younger life, I only stayed in my tight-knit Vietnamese neighborhood. I didn't know what anything other than Vietnamese culture looked like until high school. At that point, I'd never really talked to a White person before.* Can you imagine?

I got a lot of my views from my very conservative dad. He wasn't really around, but in the short period that he was, he would say stuff like, "Don't hang out with Black kids 'cause they're dirty." Now when I look back I think, okay, this makes a lot of sense, because he hadn't really met a Black person before to know or feel otherwise.

I really tried to reflect my dad's views myself because I thought, "This is what Dad would want—if he decided to ever come back." And so when I went to a majority Black, Asian, and Latino school, I just remember saying the most awful things to the Black kids. I'd say, "Don't hang around me. I don't want to be around you." I'd ask my teacher, "Can we split up the classroom? I don't want to be close to them." I didn't even know what segregation was, and I was out here being the advocate for it! Looking back, I'm just like, *why* was I like that?

When I was seven, my mom was dating this White guy, and in the car he'd say, "Oh, so weird, you've never heard of this, and this? You've never done that?" It was a rude awakening that what he knew was what it meant to be American, and what I was living wasn't it. I thought when I went to high school with all these rich White kids, a complete 180 from my old neighborhood, I could finally live like a real American. But there was this divide, I didn't fit in. My freshman year, I experienced my first racial slur. A lot of my early high school days became a lot of crying.

My sophomore year I had a moment of self-reflection. It was a moment for me to realize my privilege as an Asian American. I don't have to face police brutality, because of my light-skinned privilege, and nobody's going to question that I'm not smart, because usually Asians are the model minority**

---

* As of 2010–2014, Milwaukee ranked as the most racially divided large city, followed by New York City, and then Chicago. As of 2015, on average a White resident in Chicago lives in a neighborhood that is 71.5 percent White, and on average a Black resident lives in a neighborhood that is 64 percent Black.

** In addition to invalidating and treating all Asian Americans as a monolith, the "model minority" myth is harmful because it has been used as a "racial wedge" by White Americans to minimize other oppressed groups' struggles against racism (particularly Black Americans). The myth perpetuates a false narrative that every American has an equal opportunity to "make it" as long as one works hard.

second to being White. I became more vocal, more educated on race, and I now lead the Asian Student Alliance at my school. Right now, my biggest challenge is finding ways to continue being an ally••• to others.

At my school, we have Asian students, but usually they're rich Asian students who've been growing up in this White culture all their life. I was kind of angry at ASA for a long time. I'd think, "Why aren't we more like the Latinx Affinity Group? Why aren't we celebrating one another more?" I had to learn that not every person who comes to ASA is going to be another Jennifer. Not everyone necessarily identifies with being poor•••• or wanting

to flex your culture all the time to feel seen. Not every person wants that.

I'd never taken time for myself when I was younger to be anything besides the smart kid. My mom's always told me, "Go be a doctor for that financial security," and I see that my friends back home are still stuck in that. There's just this extra layer of privilege and understanding that I have going to a private school, even though I'm on scholarship, because I feel like I don't have to fill that smart stereotype••••• to be happy. It's hard seeing my sister, though— she still says the n-word no matter how many times I tell her not to. She's sixteen, and I see her stuck in the same spot that I

••• A definition of *ally:* "Someone who makes the commitment and effort to recognize their privilege (based on gender, class, race, sexual identity, etc.) and work in solidarity with oppressed groups in the struggle for justice. Allies understand that it is in their own interest to end all forms of oppression, even those from which they may benefit in concrete ways. Allies commit to reducing their own complicity or collusion in oppression of those groups and invest in strengthening their own knowledge and awareness of oppression."

•••• Overall, Asian Americans have a higher median household income than Whites. Yet 12 percent of Asian Americans live at the poverty level, compared to 10.4 percent of Whites, and it varies widely by factors like ethnicity and generation of immigration.

••••• A stereotype is an over-generalized perceived notion about a group of people. The idea that all or even most members of a race can share the exact same characteristics is false and damaging. While racial stereotypes are usually negative (an example: the association of Black Americans with the blackface Jim Crow minstrel clown), even so-called positive stereotypes like "all Asians are smart" or "all Black people are good at sports" or "all Hispanic people work hard" are inaccurate. What stereotypes do you consciously or unconsciously subscribe to? Do you ever find yourself saying to a person of color, "You must be good at [insert stereotype here] because of [insert person's race or ethnicity here]"? Through reading the diverse stories of individuals in this book, we hope you will begin to deconstruct and actively challenge stereotypes in your daily life.

was. Another thing that's the result of being educated: knowing not to turn to violence immediately. So when I go home and I tell my sister, "This is something that happened today," something offensive, she'll tell me, "You're so White, Jennifer, that's so White, you just beat their ass."

I wish I was more patient with my family and with people from my old neighborhood. I'm trying to give back, give back, give back, you know? I'm trying to give back all that I've learned, and even if they don't understand the first time, I'm trying not to give up on them and to keep pushing these conversations.

The conversation for White people has always been, "Yes, but what about me," to insert themselves and make themselves relevant. It should be, "Yes, and how can I support you?" or, "Yes, and what do you need from me?"

*Alexa:* When I moved here, I didn't really realize where I was, or the fact that I wasn't going back to Mexico, and that I wasn't going to see my family again. In fact, I had to say bye to my grandparents forever because they passed away a couple of years ago, and I couldn't ever visit them.

I feel like I've blocked out a lot of what happened in my first school, but I remember that there was one day where this kid had a big roll of money. He said, "Oh, it's toy money, it's not real money," and he gave me a couple hundred bucks—like *actual* hundred dollar bills. I took it home,

and my parents said, "What is this?" And I said, "My friend gave it to me." So my mom called the school and turns out that the kid got the money from his dad, and his dad was a gang member, a drug dealer.

After that, she realized that I had to get out of there. My teachers would also tell my mom, "She's really bright and she likes school, and we don't have enough resources right now to support what she wants to do, what she might be one day."

I went to another school in the West Side of Chicago called Pulaski International School of Chicago, and I got into their gifted program. It was also mostly Hispanic people, there were some Black people, and there were, like, two White people in total. Those were the first White people I met for sure. There was a lot of code-switching••••••— I would use the n-word, 'cause I didn't even know what it meant. My friends would use it all the time too. I straight up thought it was a name for a friend.

At one point I realized that maybe I am a little bit different. A lot of these kids were Mexican, or just Hispanic in general, but they were dark-skinned, and I was light-skinned. They would start calling me *güera*, which means blond White person, or *gringa*, all the time. That would really hurt me

←

•••••• **Code-switching occurs when one alternates between different languages, dialects, or ways of speaking among different groups of people.**

because I was actually from Mexico and these kids, they were born here. I knew that I was Mexican, and I knew who I was, but one day I just thought, "Am I not? Am I White? Why are these kids calling me White?"

They were calling me rich too, and it started opening my eyes to this connection between color and socioeconomic status. I thought, "Wait, this doesn't match up: my parents are struggling—my mom can't get a job, my dad is working at a restaurant, and we have this tiny house that we're renting."

I ended up moving because I was getting bullied too much for being light-skinned and born in Mexico.

On the first day of my next school, I see all these White faces, but I just automatically assumed that they were all Mexican and light-skinned like me. I went up to them and started speaking Spanish, and they're like, "What the . . . ?" And I say, "Wait, where are you from?" And they're like, "I'm Polish." And I'm like, what is *that*?!

Now, at home, going to a good school or getting an education is equated to being White. We're too colored for the kids in our school, and then we go back to our families and we're too White for them. It's like you can't have it any way.

I am a woman, but I'm also Mexican, and I'm also undocumented. Yeah, women earn seventy-eight cents to a White man's dollar, but that's only *White* women. Hispanic women, they earn *fifty-six* cents to a White man's dollar. Fifty-six cents! And we don't talk about that. People are

like, "Women were allowed to vote in 1920," and it's like no, girl, whatcha talking about?! That's White women only!

I applied to a private boarding high school. In the application I remember it asked what my citizenship status was, and for all other schools I'd written that I'm a noncitizen. They all said that it would be harder for me to get in because of that, so I decided to say that I am a citizen. I got in, and I got a full scholarship, all $60,000 worth. They would fly me out—my books were covered and everything.

When I told them I was undocumented, the guy that I interviewed with said, "You were honestly the best interview I had, and I'm going to fight for you to get in." They had meetings but, at the end, they decided that I couldn't go.•••••• It was heartbreaking. It broke my parents' hearts too. They didn't know what else I was qualified for but would never be allowed to do.

I've learned and grown and realized where I am in society—not just in a victimized way, but also in the way that I do have privilege. Yes, those kids made fun of me and it sucked, but maybe there's a

---

•••••• **For public schools, under the Supreme Court decision in *Plyler v. Doe*, children of undocumented workers have the same right to attend public primary and secondary schools as do U.S. citizens and permanent residents. They are also required under state laws to attend school until a mandated age.**

reason behind that. There *is* anger about my skin tone because, based on that, I get treated better. It's not okay that they made fun of me, but it makes sense and there's a reason behind it, and now I know that. And I do know, even if I am undocumented, there are so many other undocumented kids that are not in the position that I'm in now. They don't know that they could get into college, and I'm lucky enough to know that I can. It might be harder, but I know that I can.

It's important to validate people's experiences. I have an amazing White friend who, when I talk to her about my experiences, doesn't tell me I'm wrong or say "yes, *but*." She might not understand but she's listening and she hears me and supports me and appreciates what I'm sharing. It feels great to have that. If someone tells you they don't get heard enough in their honors science class, say, "Okay, I understand, maybe I don't see it enough because it's not affecting me, but if you're saying it's happening, then it's happening, and I'm going to do what I can to be the megaphone for your voice."

*Justin:* I grew up in the southwest side of Chicago in a neighborhood called Brighton Park. It's predominantly Latino, predominantly low-income immigrant families. As long as I could remember, me and my twin brother were always top of the class. Everyone knew us as the smart kids.

I didn't have any non-Latino friends. I hadn't met my first White friend until high school. Everyone that I knew kind of shared a very similar reality—your family came here, now you're first generation, now you're just trying to make it through life.

It took me a while to really understand the privileges I have as a light-skinned Latino in my neighborhood. I was thought of as this more well-spoken kid, so every time the teacher would come around, they'd pay more attention to me, and I'd be this perfect straight A student. The moment the teacher would leave, I'd start to say the n-word and yell out different Latino race jokes again. Before I even knew what code-switching was, I was doing that.

Getting straight As where I'm from and getting straight As at some other school across the city are two different things. I grew up with the gang culture. My goals started small. I told myself that I'm going to be the top of my class in my neighborhood high school. And then what? Fast forward four years from that, and you're lookin' at schools like Yale and Wesleyan—this is a whole dream that I never even thought possible.

Some of my best friends are now dropouts from high school, some of them have joined gangs. I call them my best friends because none of us are comparing our socioeconomic status, our academic success. But in this private school I'm in now, there's a culture where everybody asks, "So what is your ACT score?" That's just something I don't do with my childhood friends. I think there's two different cultures we're talking about here: I'd spend eight hours a day in this private school, wealthy, predominantly White culture, and my reality back home was this Latino, low-income, immigrant culture. You only have a few students making that jump. The first part isn't part of the dream until you *show* kids like me that we can make it.

It's not even about skin tones sometimes—I'm darker skinned than some people in my family, yet I'm the Whitest. I remember trying to explore that, knowing why they thought I was White, but they couldn't give me the reasoning. I had to ask, "Is it the way I speak English, is it the school I go to?" And of course they're like, "Yeah, yeah, that's it." Like, even me coming downtown is not something my family or my friends do. My Chicago isn't the nice architecture down here, it isn't the North Side for me, my Chicago is the Orange Line, the lines where you have the working class going on the train.

I remember we had a soccer game down south, near where I live. We're driving our bus over there, and so the moment we get into my 'hood—I know it, I already know it, me and my brother aren't saying anything, and they start talking about it, like, "Oh wow, it's so crummy down here, wow, this is so sketchy, who even lives down here?" My bro's like, "We live down here," and so they're like, "Tell us more about it, like, oh, do you ever hear gunshots?" And you're like, "I don't know what to tell you, gunshots just happen." They were like, "Do

you ever drop down to the ground!?" And I'm like, "No, you just continue doing whatever the hell you were doing." And they then talk about the drug dealers, all this stuff that isn't their reality, like, "Wow, that's so exotic, blah blah."

Here was my journey: in freshman year, you're like, I'm not going to be accepted here. Sophomore year, you get exhausted having these very aggressive arguments with kids, hearing racial slurs and stuff. In junior year, you kind of don't care and form your clique with the people of color, feeling like you're forced there because the other side won't accept you. Senior year, you're kind of in your own lane. I'm going through that now.

Recently, another student was trying to start a club around these difficult race conversations, and I was thinking, "Oh, wow, this is interesting" . . . and then at the bottom of the post they wrote, "If you come to this club, you can't say something's racism, if it's not." I was like, okay, well, that's part of the problem! How do *you* decide, when you maybe can't experience it? White people are so worried about being uncomfortable for one moment, while we're uncomfortable all the time. You really do get exhausted talking about this. I remember I stopped sitting in the lunchroom because they had divided the table, and they had put me on one side and said, "This is the Mexican border, and you can't cross it to sit with us." I didn't know what to say. I just left.

# Queen Esther

I make the best pound cake in the world.

I've got six brothers, and before I hit puberty, I used to honestly believe that I was a boy too.

I learned how to read when I was three.

*People are caught* up in the fantasy of the Whiteness of country music. It's just White, White, Whitey White White, and it's something that they think belongs to them. Well, it doesn't.

I came up with Black Americana in 1996 or '98 and everybody asked me, "Shouldn't you be singing R & B? I mean . . . you're *Black*." But no, believe it or not, I'm a Black country singer, and I sing Black Americana. The phrase seems like an oxymoron. But Americana is just Black, Black, Blackity Black, and no one is willing to say it or acknowledge it. To me, the genre is all-encompassing because it acknowledges that the foundation of all American music—blues, bluegrass, swamp grass, and everything else—is African music traditions. There isn't anything in popular American music that can't sit in that tree that is Black Americana.

The banjo came from West Africa, built like an *akonting*, which is from Senegal and Gambia, played with the same downstroke technique as that classic 1840s banjo. Until the 1840s, we were the only ones who played banjo. But then Joel Sweeney came along and commercialized it. But it belonged to us.

There are so many things that were invented by slaves, but slaves weren't allowed to claim their own inventions so their owners—the White colonizers—could say that they created them and get the patent and get the money and get the historical credit. A popular filament in lightbulbs was created by a Black man. Jack Daniel's whiskey was created by a slave named Nearest Green. Green taught him top to bottom how to do this, and Jack Daniel and his whole family and everybody knew it. Green never got any money for it, though. He's never gotten acknowledgment, never even gotten praise for it, until very recently in 2016.

So many tools your gynecologist uses came from this guy, J. Marion Sims, from South Carolina. He didn't believe Black people could feel pain. After he failed miserably as a general practitioner, he went to plantations and used Black women to experiment on to solve this pressing vaginal problem in the nineteenth century. He had a makeshift hospital with eight beds and he essentially butchered Black women with no anesthesia until he got it right. Their Black bodies were not their own.* One was seventeen years old, with thirty surgeries. Because of them, we have the field of gynecology. Who knew?

———————————————————→

* **Black women were denied rights to *their own bodies* in many other ways. In the context of enslaved Black women giving birth, Dorothy E. Roberts writes, "Here lies one of slavery's most odious features: it forced its victims to perpetuate the very institution that subjugated them by bearing children who were born the property of their masters."**

Your refrigerator, the traffic light, the Super Soaker, the technology behind caller ID, potato chips—there's a jillion and one things that we use every day that Black people invented or advanced that people either don't know or don't care to know. People really want to believe the narrative, "Well, African Americans just haven't done anything." They need to believe that because if they knew the truth, if they knew that if it weren't for the Black, the African infrastructure, that built up this country and created its first-world status, this country would just be a backwater because no one would've been there to pick the cotton or the tobacco or chop the sugarcane. I mean, it actually boggles my mind. Now in Texas, and in other parts of the country, you've got people rewriting textbooks** because they're just not *comfortable* with the idea of slavery. So they're calling slaves "migrant workers," "volunteers"—they're just rephrasing and falsifying history.

When I'm dealing with White people—especially Americans—I wanna

** As of 2015, public schools in Texas adopted a new history curriculum. It barely addresses slavery, frames the Civil War as a debate regarding states' rights, and doesn't mention the KKK or Jim Crow (a racial caste system that *legally* restricted Black rights in every part of life, primarily in the South from 1877 to the 1960s).

understand their propensity for Whiteness. Whiteness is a marketing ploy which was created to be juxtaposed to Blackness, to create Blackness. The idea was to erase the African captives' history, their culture, their language, their religion, their everything, and just leave this stripped-down husk of a person. A Black person.***

I'm from the Low Country—that's an area in the South encompassing Georgia, South Carolina, and some of Florida. I'm also two generations removed from slavery. My father's mother's parents were slaves. And I know that both my father and his mother were born on plantations, so it's a constant reminder for me that this stuff didn't happen so long ago. Maybe that's why my African roots are really strong in me. Stronger in me than most people. I was in church every day of the week, started singing spirituals and field hollers as soon as I could stand. Those roots made me stick out like a sore thumb when I came to New York City to sing. People were like, "Why is a Black girl singing country music?" The further north I went, the more *Southern* I became, the more frustrated I became that nobody seemed to realize that me holding a banjo and singing country music was not

*** Here Queen Esther also quoted Zora Neale Hurston: "I feel most colored when I am thrown against a sharp White background."

me *straying* from my Blackness, but me *reclaiming* it.

Jimmie Rodgers said that country music is just "the White man's blues," and it basically is. It was called hillbilly music before it was called country music. Hillbilly music was sold to poor working-class White people. That was the pitch. There was this sentiment, this yearning for this image of the South that was green and lush, free of slaves. That is where they wanted to belong. It was a magical wonderment. The record label gave them that sound, they nurtured it and eventually marketed it as "country." At the core of country music, right down to the banjo that they can't stop playing, is the African blues-based tradition. It just happens to be a White guy playing instead of a Black person.

I don't think that people understand what the African captives did, what slavery meant, how pervasive and all-encompassing it was, and how it established America's first-world status. This country wouldn't be what it is without my ancestors. This country's music would not exist. This country in and of itself would not exist. That's the biggest takeaway of all, and I don't know how to explain the enormity of that. It's something as simple as: You owe Black people for everything.

# Justin E.

I'm a soccer player—all day all the way.

I'm a cultural anthropologist.

I have one more semester left before I graduate.

Living in Los Angeles is the end game.

*The first time* I realized who I was, was in middle school. I was wrestling in the yard with a friend in my predominantly White neighborhood. A White person drove by, lowered his window, and called me "nigger." So, being Black has defined me. I grew up knowing my ancestors were part of the slave trade, and that defined me too.

But I saw a different way when I went to Senegal, West Africa,* to study for a bit. Senegal has an island which was one of the last slave ports. They'd keep slaves on islands off the coast of Africa so they couldn't run away back to their homeland. What was interesting was viewing some Africans' perspectives on slavery and who they now are. It seemed, when I was talking to them, that the whole slave trade was something that happened in their history. It wasn't something that *defined* them now.

In the United States, on the other hand, Black people are only introduced in our history as slaves. That's all we are.** When White people first see me, I realize that they're only gonna see a Black face. That is, until I open my mouth. Once I start talking, I crush all stereotypes.

I could talk forever about this stuff. I can talk with my grandma, because she's my grandma. But with older employees at work? I'm talking, and they say they get me, but I look at their faces and know they don't get it. White students need to know about the experiences of students of color, but the

---

*   Notice how Justin didn't just say "Africa," as if it's a country (it's a continent). There is more genetic and physical variation within all populations of sub-Saharan Africa than there are among any other populations on the globe. This means that, biologically, it is likely that a woman from the Congo would have more in common with a woman from Germany than she would with a woman from Botswana. The false idea that race is instead biological has led to abuses like the U.S. eugenics movement in the early 1900s, which sought to eliminate "undesirable" traits (largely in poor, disabled, uneducated, or minority populations) through forced sterilization.

**  Post Traumatic Slave Syndrome, coined and developed by Joy DeGruy, "is a theory that explains the etiology of many of the adaptive survival behaviors in African American communities throughout the United States and the Diaspora. It is a condition that exists as a consequence of multigenerational oppression of Africans and their descendants resulting from centuries of chattel slavery. A form of slavery which was predicated on the belief that African Americans were inherently/genetically inferior to Whites."

people who aren't gonna listen are the ones who need to be changed. Only a White person, I've learned, can talk to another White person and get farther than I can get. Because either they're gonna stop listening to me, I'm gonna get angry, or both.

Sometimes, it's easy just to think about giving up, telling them to fuck themselves and to stay away from you. But you can't do that because they run the world. So you just gotta keep telling them and keep waking them up. It's all baby steps, you know?

The oppressed shouldn't have to do it all. The oppressor needs to help out. White people need to talk to other White people about what is what. Y'all gotta teach each other—like, *right now*.

## Nick

**PORCUPINE, SOUTH DAKOTA**

I have met the president of the United States.

I was a commercial fisherman in Alaska.

I was arrested at Standing Rock.

I have four kids.

MINNESOTA VIKINGS

RESIST

*Like the* Black Panther Party, the American Indian Movement protected their neighborhoods by policing the police. They documented police brutality against Native communities. My mom's Native American and my dad's Jewish. The first lawsuit from the American Indian community was filed by my Jewish grandpa, bringing my two worlds together.

My very first memory was when I was about three and a half years old and I was at a protest for political prisoners. My parents were organizing the rally because there were a lot of Natives in prison for petty theft charges. I was this little guy, so they had me tucked away in the car. I remember looking out the window and my mom was on a stage and she was talking, and my dad was doing something backstage, like plugging cords in. Then, suddenly, my heart quickened. I saw a whole bunch of police officers in riot gear. They attacked the crowd, there was smoke everywhere. A window was open in the car I was in, and something flew in. I found out later that it was a canister of tear gas. I just remember clawing to get out, not able to breathe, and then quickly passing out.

I was so terrified of the police from then on. Once, my dad was pulled over for this routine traffic stop, and I was so scared

that I started digging myself *under* the backseat to hide. Like, completely *underneath* the seat. They had to *unbolt* the seat and remove it to get me out.

I know what it means to be part of the Oglala Lakota Nation; we have our own language, ceremonies, culture, history. When I asked my Jewish grandfather what it meant to be Jewish, he said, "Throughout history, Jewish people faced persecution, and we survived. Jewish people have a responsibility to stand up in solidarity with people being persecuted today. The act of doing this is what actually makes you Jewish."

So, I attach myself to the sense of service and fighting back—it's my whole identity. We were one of the last tribes to resist, so resistance connects me to my identity. The Indian wars were supposed to be over in the early 1800s, but Indian wars continue today in many different forms. For example, seven of the eleven poorest places in America are Indian reservations in South Dakota. Natives make up only 9 percent of the population in South Dakota, but are 30 percent of male prisoners; with women, it's 52.48 percent. We have to change the harsh realities and outcomes for our communities.

I always felt that the American dream was the American lie.* The American

---

* Over five hundred treaties were made with American Indian tribes, and around five hundred treaties were also broken. Nick asked, "Isn't the Constitution supposed to be the backbone of American democracy?"

dream is not real because it is built on our backs and integrated in our land. Most Americans today have no understanding of that. Most think, "The Indians just *went away*." Like, *poof.* To me, this is the final stage of colonization, when people say that it never happened. I think that's how racism is perpetuated. Every Native person has to end up being a *historian* and constantly remind people, but why is that our responsibility? This is the *shared* history of this country.

*All* people of color have a shared history of struggle. I don't believe in the pure sovereignty of Indigenous communities unless it also has an equity lens, just as I don't believe in the sovereignty of the African-American people or the Asian-American community if it doesn't have an equity lens. Without the equity lens,** we will continue to be divided, we will continue to divide our struggles from the whole. We have much more to gain when we work together toward a more equitable world.

** One definition: "Racial equity is the condition that would be achieved if one's racial identity no longer predicted, in a statistical sense, how one fares."

Just remember, every piece of ground that you walk on was at one time occupied by Indigenous people, whether you're on the East Coast or the West Coast or wherever. Acknowledgment of that is important. You should also acknowledge that there are millions of Native people left, and they need your help. You need to ask yourself, "Is it morally, ethically right for us as Americans to be so prosperous when the first people of this country are in such poverty? Are we really about justice, democracy, and equity if we don't collectively start dealing with the challenges that exist in Native communities? Are those only Indian people's challenges, or are they our collective responsibility?"

We Indian people are not going anywhere. We've already been to the bottom. You've tried to murder every one of our people, sterilize our women, take away our land, remove our children from our homes. No matter what you try, you're never going to get rid of us. Indigenous people are part of the past and present of this country, and damn right we're part of the future.

# Vic

**SEATTLE, WASHINGTON**

I love Blood Orange, a Black artist.

I make jewelry and other things out of recycled materials.

I come from mountain people, the Teochew.

I really love durian, I could eat it for every meal.

*My optimism about* White people is part of my privilege. In high school, I knew how to be respectable, eloquent, do the right things, and say the right things at the right times. I was very careful, very nervous. I was always well spoken.

I've faced a lot of denial of my experience as a woman of color. When White people meet me—I think because I'm an Asian cis woman—they think, "Oh, this one is safe. This one will be my sidekick."

I wonder if gentrification is happening in Beacon Hill—a neighborhood just south of Chinatown*—because White people are more comfortable with Asians than they are with Black people. Jazz was at the center of the central district here. There were a ton of artists, like Duke Ellington and Langston Hughes and Ernestine Anderson, but they weren't allowed to perform, live in, or stay in a hotel in certain areas, so they would stay here, in Chinatown. Do y'all know about single resident occupancy rooms, SROs? These hotels were designed specifically for immigrants, people who arrived in the United States and couldn't afford to live elsewhere, so they crowded together in one room. It was all men, because immigration from China only allowed men,** so it was like a little bachelor hang pad. There's a history of many people of color, of different ethnic backgrounds, concentrated in this one area because of blatant segregation. A lot of people have poured love into this area.

Anyways, I was really grappling. I had no clue about positionality,*** about where

---

* Chinese people were "prohibited by law to testify in court, to own property, to vote, to have families join them, to marry non-Chinese, and to work in institutional agencies." To survive, they banded together in communities that we today call "Chinatowns." While Chinatowns are mostly made up of Chinese Americans, Vietnamese Americans and other Asian ethnic groups also reside there.

** America's *very first* immigration law banned females from China. When Chinese men came to the West Coast to build U.S. railroads, most voluntarily but some kidnapped, their wives couldn't come with them. The reason was that if Chinese women came, then there would be Chinese-American babies and families—and by that time, the Constitution extended citizenship to anyone born in the States. White Americans only wanted Chinese immigrants for their labor, not to welcome them as citizens.

*** The concept of positionality was introduced by philosopher Linda Alcoff in 1988. It discusses how gender, race, class, and other important parts of our identity are "markers of relational positions rather than essential qualities."

to find my voice. I didn't want to be anyone's sidekick! I wanted to be loud! I wanted to be heard!

I realized I had to stop sugarcoating things for White people. My framework shifted. I used to see it as my responsibility to educate everyone, and then I realized that it's my right to speak truth, but not my responsibility to educate. For example, we had to analyze *Apocalypse Now* in class; it's a film about the Vietnamese–American War, and it's *ugly*. In the film, I felt like the Americans were treating Vietnam like a Disneyland for killing people. But the White people in my class didn't even *flinch* when a Vietnamese person was being shot. Didn't. Even. Flinch. However, when a pig died in the film, all the White girls were like "*gasp* oh my god, I can't look at this!" Later, when I wrote my essay analyzing all of the film's racism, my teacher called it a "rant," so I just slid back into my shell.

You see, I was caught in White respectability politics. I think that's something a lot of Asian people fall into. They think they can change things through academia, through being respectable, by being extra compassionate to White people. I now realize it's based on policing the emotions of Black people, mainly, and other people of color. I now think that the real change comes from organizing the community. Research papers and big words aside, what are you *doing* to shake things up?

# Melina

**DENVER, COLORADO**

I've lived on three continents.

I won a pie-eating contest.

I like skydiving.

*My journey* in thinking differently started in the required Power, Privilege, and Oppression class at Colorado College. I was meeting the class with so much resistance. I can remember ticking off that list of stupid things White girls say—like "yeah, but my best friend's Black," or "yeah, but when I'm at my boyfriend's Sunday dinner, I'm the only White girl and that's really awkward for me." I am constantly remembering the emotional labor that my classmates had to invest in order to battle my insistent color blindness.** I think about the patience of my professor. It helps me find compassion for people who are in different places in their journey, because I was in that place one time, of really having no idea.

* Melina's journey parallels studies like Janet E. Helms's Model of White Racial Identity Development, which begins with the "Contact" stage: "one encounters the idea or actuality of Black people . . . one will enter Contact with either naive curiosity or timidity and trepidation about Blacks and a superficial and inconsistent awareness of being White."

** Among other characteristics of Helms's stage 2, "Disintegration": "one must markedly alter one's real self in order to be accepted by significant others in one's environment," potentially resulting in feelings of "guilt, depression, helplessness, and anxiety." One's prior conception of the world is challenged. Stage 3, "Reintegration," can involve avoiding or expressing fear and anger toward people of color.

Later, I found myself on the other side. My professor was talking about a value in our culture of light or White skin, and a student said that that was changing because now we value tan skin. I raised my hand and said, "No, that's a class privilege: it used to be that fair skin was an indication of your class status, because you didn't have to be in the fields working in the sun. Now, having tan skin as a White person is an indication of your class privilege, because you can go on vacation, or you can go to a tanning bed." In that moment, I thought, *"Oh, I've started to switch in my journey,*** *to now having some capacity to be able to teach other White folks."* And when I went to a heavily shame-based training later, I felt lucky to be far enough along in my journey to where I was open to hearing things, and able to connect with other White people to continue this journey together.

I've come to realize how I can have a role in all of this: helping other White people**** on their journeys to dismantle systems of

*** Stage 4: "Pseudo-Independence": acknowledging White responsibility for racism, learning how to grapple with new intellectual and emotional learning.

**** Stage 5: "Immersion/Emersion," often involves seeking out other White people with similar identity journeys and regaining positive emotions toward self that help fuel later activism.

White supremacy. I educate other White people, resource communities and activists of color, and provide marshal or action support. I see activism as intentional work toward social change for justice and equity. Not just equality, but equity. I struggle a little bit with calling my journey one of racial literacy, because that limits people to thinking either you're literate or you're not literate, and once you're literate you're done learning. I really want to challenge myself and others to think about all of this work as a journey with no feasible destination. • • • • •

I talk about *systems*, because dismantling patriarchy is a part of my life too. I call this The Big Three: patriarchy, capitalism, and White supremacy. They're all connected, and together, they create a system of power that's been built up over generations. Capitalism quantifies the value of people. Patriarchy differentiates value of people based on gender. White supremacy differentiates value of people

------------------------------------------→

• • • • • Melina reaches the final stage of Autonomy. She "abandons cultural and institutional racism as well as personal racism," becomes "increasingly aware of how other forms of oppression (e.g., sexism, ageism) are related to racism," and still thinks of it "as an ongoing process . . . continually open to new information."

based on race. All three quantify people as being worth more or less. They feed each other. I question whether you can dismantle one without dismantling the others. I suspect there are absolutely communities and cultures that thrive without those three, but I think part of our struggle in identifying those is that the entire history of this planet has been impacted by colonialism, in almost every corner of the globe.

My partner, a White cis man, is invested in the local Denver comedy scene, and it's been going through some turmoil because female comedians were experiencing sexual harassment. I've been supporting my partner in trying to dismantle the patriarchy there—going to community discussions, reviewing posts, things like that—but I find all the support that I give him utterly exhausting. It triggers my own incidents of being a victim of sexual assault. Any exhaustion around dismantling White supremacy is different, because I don't experience that same triggering emotional labor. One is "I have to do this, because it's my job as a White person who has all these privileges," versus, "I don't have to do this, but I'm choosing to, when I have the energy, because I'm a woman and I do want patriarchy dismantled." The way I describe it to my partner is, "*Conversations around gender are my gift. Conversations around White supremacy are my responsibility.*"

I've experienced economic struggle as a child; however, my White privilege*••••• meant that that struggle was never life-changing in a way that kept me from being able to benefit from determination and hard work. What's hidden is that I didn't live in a community where I had to fear for my life, where if my family experienced homelessness, there wouldn't be a place for me to go. I didn't live in a community where I was an outsider. I *did* live in a community where systems were set up for my success. My teachers believed in my success, my school believed in my success, my community believed in my success. And I can't separate our history of slavery—that my great-great-grandfather benefited from the ability to own land, which led to my great-grandfather being able to own a farm, which led to my grandmother having the capacity to send my mother to college, which meant that we valued education in our family, and that I knew how to access Pell grants and scholarships and resources. None of that can be separated. So the small inconveniences from some economic hardship that I experienced were just small inconveniences. It means that I'm frugal and really careful with my savings. But I benefited from my privileges more than I struggled with my marginalization.

For me, it's been a journey in gaining racial literacy and dismantling my own White supremacist behavior. Am I going to be a person that's like, "Oh, oppression, yeah that sucks," or am I going to be a person that is actively fighting against these systems? I hope to help people learn that you don't have to be an activist to do the latter. Having a thoughtful conversation with your family at the dinner table is dismantling White supremacy. So is questioning your own motives and listening for understanding before responding first. So is educating yourself to be mindful of not exploiting any positions of power you hold—whether that's in the workplace, or in a family. Instead of seeing activism solely as career or volunteer work, we should see how we can be activists in our spheres of influence,

•••••• A definition from Francis E. Kendall of White privilege: "Having greater access to power and resources than people of color [in the same situation] do," usually in a way that is both unearned and unquestioned. Alluding to Peggy McIntosh's well-known essay, "White Privilege: Unpacking the Invisible Knapsack," an article in *Teaching Tolerance* adds, "White privilege is both unconsciously enjoyed and consciously perpetuated. It is both on the surface and deeply embedded into American life. It is a weightless knapsack—and a weapon. It depends on who's carrying it."

in whatever we do. You're a cook—you cook for the revolution. You're an artist—you design for the revolution. You're in a position of power at an organization—you work to make your hiring processes more inclusive.

The more privilege you have, the more responsibility you have to do it. I know it's a really hard thing for people to do. Power feels good, privilege feels good, it makes life easier. I think it starts with acknowledging our collective humanity. We deny little White boys their humanity when we indoctrinate them into a system of taking what they want, of exploiting, of raping not just women, but systems, and the earth. I think about my earliest memory of being touched by a classmate in sixth grade, about how the teacher didn't do anything, and yes, I have a lot of frustration and anger about not being supported, but also, what was denied for that boy? When nobody said, "This is not acceptable, this is not the way you treat people, or women," it robbed him too of being better, doing better. And it robbed me of my dignity. Everybody loses in that moment. Everybody loses when The Big Three are allowed to continue.

# Rylee, Marley, and Parker

**HONOLULU, HAWAI'I**

took Hawaiian
for four years
in high school.

I make bangles
out of shells and
want to start
selling them.

I can't cook.

I love the ocean.

I love to bodyboard.

I dance hula.

I think my sisters are hilarious.

I watch dancing videos
more than I should (it
takes up a lot of time).

*Rylee:* We get asked questions like, "Do you live in huts? Do you wear coconut bras? Do you ride dolphins?" It's totally weird. Someone assumed I was Black and I went, "Oh no, I'm Hawaiian," and his friend was like, "You're Hawaiian? You just look like a tanned White person," and I was like, "Yo, what?"

*Parker:* A lot of stereotypes are also about abusive spouses, broken marriages, laziness, and overweight guys. But at the same time very "Aloha!" and very friendly—but the naïve, dumb sort of friendly, you know?

*Marley:* Someone once asked me if I rode a dolphin to school. I was like, "We have cars!"

*Rylee:* Something that irks me—like, really irks me—is the fact that any culture can cry cultural appropriation* (which is not a bad thing, it's what I push for), but anyone, anywhere is allowed to throw on a lei or wear aloha shirts, and it's just like, "Yo, what the fuck?" Like, oh, we can call anyone else out for culturally appropriating, but since Hawai'i is now a part of the United States, we can't call that out? We were our own people before you came and made us a state!

*Parker:* Yeah, we were overthrown and illegally annexed. The language was cut off. You couldn't dance, you couldn't do anything in terms of our culture. You had to be American, American, American. Eventually, the government gave Hawaiian people homestead land. The idea was that if you had 50 percent of Hawaiian blood then you could live on the land for very cheap, but the government put us on land that was very dry, land that no one would want to live on anyways. What's it called when you get stuff back for . . . you know how certain Native American tribes were given back almost, like, stipends—you know what I mean? Reparations!** Yeah, there's none of that. We got a "sorry." After what seems like a century, we got a fucking "sorry."

*Rylee:* I don't feel like most Hawaiians think of themselves as American. It's a common misconception because being

---

* Vernon François, a celebrity hairstylist for many Black celebrities, says, "For me, cultural appropriation is when an aesthetic of one culture is borrowed by another and is celebrated in a way that was never done for its originator."

** Reparations "serve to acknowledge the legal obligation of a state, or individual(s) or group, to repair the consequences of violations—either because it directly committed them or it failed to prevent them."

from Hawai'i does not make you Hawaiian—it's not like people who might refer to themselves as "Californians." Being Hawaiian is a race. We're Indigenous. Being from Hawai'i does not make you Hawaiian. It makes you local, yes, but it does not mean you have Hawaiian blood.

*Parker:* I'm proud to be Hawaiian. I'm proud of how people down here are very open and are willing to help. You walk down the street, people smile at you, they wave at you, people say aloha. I don't know, the vibe down here is just more relaxing and easygoing. There's more love to give.

*Rylee:* Usually, everyone is auntie and uncle. Like, "Hello, Auntie! Hello, Uncle!"

*Parker:* Yeah, so the equivalent of that would I guess be ma'am and sir on the mainland?

*Rylee:* Also, always a kiss on the cheek. The party you go to? You kiss everyone hello. It's just how it is. In American culture, there's this thing called "personal space," but we don't know what that is!

*Parker:* Yeah, people find it weird, and when we try to kiss them hello, they're like, "Whoa, I don't know you!"

*Rylee:* Oh, and if I can add one thing: It's not pronounced "Hawaaaaii." It's "Hav-ai-i!"

**SAN FRANCISCO, CALIFORNIA**

I climbed to the summit of Mount Kilimanjaro two years ago.

When I was a kid, I wanted to be an astronaut.

I like colorful clothes.

I threw out the first pitch at an A's game once.

*The* *New York Times* posts a list of "52 Places to Go" each year. Well, I'm Black, I'm female, and I usually travel* alone. So, I look at this list, and I'm thinking, *"I could not go to any of these places."*

I went to the Czech Republic in 1999. Eastern Europe had started to open up. It got weird; I had people asking to take my picture. I realized that I was the only Black person that they'd seen! I ended up leaving early because I didn't feel like I could enjoy my time without being this object. Later, when I went out with some of my friends, they got mad on my behalf and were like, "All right, we're going to start charging people!" They were hoping that that would be a turnoff, but people whipped out their wallets and were like, "How much again?" We were mortified.

Before I went to Australia, everyone was like, "Australia's amazing, the weather is amazing, blah blah blah." But it was so hard. If I opened my mouth and identified myself as an American, *then* I would be treated well. But if people just saw me, I'd get treated totally different. Once, when I was out in the botanic gardens, this guy came up to me, he was a tourist, and he was like, "Can you take a picture?" And I was like, "Yeah, give me your camera," and then he was like, "No, no, I want you to hold this thing I got, and I want to take a picture *of* you." He thought he'd found an Aboriginal person.

When I went to East and South Africa, it was a little different. I'm Nigerian, and first generation, so I felt a sort of sense of belonging. Walking around, people thought I was from there. It wasn't until then that I realized the burden I carried growing up in a space where I was outnumbered. Because, in the United States, even if people don't point at me and take pictures of me, I feel their eyes on me. I feel the legacy of Jim Crow, of slavery—I always say that it was only a policy change, we didn't actually change the people. So, in Africa, it was interesting because I was able to walk around and experience moments where I felt . . . well, *free.*** But even that didn't last: sooner or later, I'd run into the legacy of Apartheid, the legal racial segregation and discrimination in South Africa.

---

* Have you noticed how most hotels don't offer shampoos that work with Black hair? Or how the "main highlight at a resort is lying out poolside in the sun"?

** "It is a peculiar sensation, this double-consciousness, this sense of always looking at one's self through the eyes of others. One ever feels his two-ness—an American, a Negro; two souls, two thoughts, two unreconciled strivings . . . ." —W. E. B. Du Bois

Ed
HONOLULU, HAWAI'I
My favorite place to travel is China.
I can stay calm in the middle of a storm.
I find a way to make that "no" a "yes."

*I am the* grandson of a slave. My grandfather was freed when he was ten years old, but once you're free, where do you go? And how do you make a living? How do you get educated in South Carolina in those days? Somehow, my grandfather went to school. He then went to college and tried to be a teacher. But he had nobody to teach. All the kids were working in the growing season,* and the parents couldn't afford to pay him.

My grandfather was a slave. His son was a musician. I am a meteorologist.** Who would've known? Who would've known that a little African-American boy would want to be a weatherman? When I was in the fourth grade, my teacher wrote on my report card, "Edward cannot do math." When my mother saw that, she was angry. She went up to the teacher and said, "My son is fully capable." She said, "Don't you ever write that on his report card again." In high school, the counselors thought I shouldn't go to college, and my mother had to intercede again. She said, "No, he's going to college. He's gonna be a meteorologist." And I did. Thank God for my mother, right?

You don't see many Black people in science. You don't see many Black people in meteorology, but we're needed desperately. When I lived in Fort Worth, Texas, there was this storm that actually went through Dallas. It was bad. Real bad. People came home and there was nothing left, their houses were gone. The only thing remaining was the sidewalk.

I asked my colleagues, "Wait, are you helping the African-American and Hispanic communities impacted? Is anyone paying attention to them?" They said, "Oh. No." They were only covering the damage in the White communities—it wasn't even on their radar, it didn't even *occur* to them, that they should go to the places where Black people were living and help out. So, I encouraged them to. Especially in places where you have flash flooding and other things, you must prepare the locals every year. They need to know what to do, they need to know what the signs are, and where they'll hear the warning—if it will be the radio, TV, or a siren. A siren means you have minutes. Recognizing the warnings is the difference between living and not living. So, I pushed my managers to go out into the Black and Hispanic communities, for the first time, and inform those people too. When they finally did, my reaction was, "What took you so long?"

I have a big responsibility as, what feels like, the only person of color working in weather.

---

* Emancipation is often framed as the U.S. government finally righting its wrongs once and for all—but once freed, African Americans were then neglected, and systems of oppression redesigned. For instance, about 1 million of the 4 million formerly enslaved people died or suffered from illness (60,000 died from a smallpox epidemic) between 1862 and 1870.

** As of 2018, African Americans made up 2 percent of the American Meteorological Society and less than 5 percent of the National Weather Service.

# Chef Tu

**OAKLAND, CALIFORNIA**

I aspire to sing like Babyface.

I work at San Quentin State Prison and teach inmates how to cook.

I love Oprah and I love Ellen. I would cry if I met them.

*I'm from an* island of Vietnam, so the food that I cook is very different. The way that I look is very different. The way that I speak is different. Non-Vietnamese customers have told me that my food "doesn't taste authentic." Actually, "authentic" has become my new least favorite word. I always wonder, is it because of the way I look? Or is it that me being Vietnamese doesn't match with your notion of being Vietnamese?* A place like Vietnam, the Portuguese were there, the British were there, the Japanese were there, the Chinese were there, the South Asians were there, the Cambodians were there—all those cultures make up Vietnamese culture and show up differently, depending on the region, depending on who you speak to. Vietnamese food is always evolving. So, when people tell me that they don't feel that I'm "Vietnamese enough," I'm like, what the hell?

I've always gotten upset with those applications that ask you, "What do you identify as?" I always had trouble filling out the bubbles. Like, am I more Vietnamese? Am I Cambodian? I have Chinese in my blood, my mom's half French, who am I not embracing? With food, though, I feel liberated from that thinking. Food has complicated roots, and food forms cultural bridges. That's why I love it. When I'm cooking, people can usually identify with something. In Jewish culture, they have kreplach, kreplachs are another version of wontons, wontons can be connected to Italian tortellini, which can be connected to Japanese *gyoza*. Every culture has bread. Every culture has a stew where there's vegetables, seafood, tofu, meat, whatever. Everybody wants to eat delicious food.

My parents have their palate, and these century-old recipes, and they make them "American" when they come here. We used to live next to a Mexican-American grocery store, and my mom would buy *chayote*, which is a traditionally Mexican pear-looking squash, and it isn't super huge in Vietnam. We'd eat it and cook it in Vietnamese ways. I remember standing in the kitchen asking my mom when the food was ready, tasting things. I learned how a carrot tastes, how an onion tastes, as they get cooked longer. She taught me my palate.

I think one of the biggest forms of love anyone can show is handing down recipes. It's an acknowledgment, and it's a responsibility. By passing down recipes to me, my parents are also saying, "This is our family story, keep it alive." My parents were refugees of the Vietnam War.** They got out right before the fall of Saigon. When they hand those recipes over, I always feel the weight of how they're a tie to my homeland, and I feel humbled and . . . beyond honored.

←————————————————————

* There are fifty-four ethnic groups in Vietnam.

** It's estimated that as many as 1.5 million people fled the Vietnamese War. "Estimates for deaths vary from 50,000 to 200,000."

Vineela and Tyler G.

LOS ANGELES, CALIFORNIA

I love dramas.

I played college baseball.

Me and my mom have the same tattoo of my grandma's name.

I love romantic comedies.

I've lived on three different continents.

I want to skydive before I die.

*Vineela:* It was really hard for me to have a normal high school experience because of my mom's restrictions. I couldn't stay out late, I couldn't have sleepovers. I tried to bond with girls by doing what I thought was normal, but they weren't normal for my mom—they were out of her comfort zone, because that's not how she was raised. She was like, you need to be eighteen to dye your hair, you need to be twenty-one to date. If I didn't stick by my mom's rules, she'd say, "Oh, you're trying to be American" or "You're trying to stray from your roots," but it's not like that at all! I just wanted to change my hair! At the time it didn't seem like that big of a deal.

*Tyler:* I was born and raised in the wonderful city of Las Vegas, aka Sin City, where we met. Both my parents are White. My dad comes from a very small town in Pennsylvania, and he was very small-minded, raised by a very small-minded family. But I wanted to be my own person and treat people fairly. Vineela's mom didn't want her to do any sleepovers, change her hair, or date *me*. But you get older, and you want to have your own experiences and thoughts. That's how we become these sort of rebel children, not listening to our parents.

*Vineela:* When we met, we talked for hours. It was really easy and really unexpected. The person that I dated before was Asian. I didn't expect to have so much in common with someone who was White.

*Tyler:* I had never talked to, dated, hooked up with a girl that was not White. Actually, we didn't hook up *once* the first few times we hung out. We were just having really, really in-depth conversations about life, talking about our upbringing, and our backgrounds. Before I left for L.A. to pursue acting, I knew it was getting serious. So, because family is very important to me, I insisted on meeting her mom.

*Vineela:* Yeah, I didn't really have an option.

*Tyler:* And her mom refused to meet me.

*Vineela:* Yeah . . .

*Tyler:* Her mom kept on saying, "I'm not ready." She told her, "Well he's White, he dropped out of school, he was a baseball player, he wants to be an actor . . ."

*Vineela:* But, after a while, my mom said okay. We went to get Thai food. And she shows up in a flannel shirt—

**Sharing soul stories (including stories about your identity or cultural/racial background) can bring you much closer to people than always sharing ego stories (stories about more superficial things like your résumé).**

*Tyler:* Flannel shirts are my *thing*. Like, I'm always wearing them.

*Vineela:* So my mom did it on purpose, because she was like, "Oh I thought this could be the ice breaker, that I'm also wearing a flannel shirt."

*Tyler:* Our lunch turned into, like—

*Vineela:* It felt like my mom was on a date with Tyler.

*Tyler:* Yeah, Vineela didn't speak once.

*Vineela:* I sat at the side, ate my food in like two minutes, finished my Thai tea, and they're just sitting there chatting away—they barely touched their food.

*Tyler:* Her mom was talking about her favorite movies and actors. She wanted to know about my acting style, my methods, et cetera. She started saying stuff like how she was impressed that I was brave enough to pursue my dream—

*Vineela:* You should've seen my face when she said that. She would never say that to *me*!

# CHAPTER TWO

# THE PAST IS THE PRESENT

*I*n Arkansas, an elderly woman we were interviewing leaned in and whispered, "You know what they say . . . We're not so bad . . . Thank God for Mississippi!" In Alabama, a couple exchanged looks and said between nervous laughter, "Yeah, thank God for Mississippi!" In Georgia, we heard the same thing. Louisiana—Same. Exact. Thing. Pretty much every day before January 18, 2018, we were thanking God that we weren't in Mississippi.

And then we arrived in Mississippi.

Mississippi has the highest state population of African Americans in the United States. "The soil is very rich here, so it was turned into the profitable crop of cotton. And where you had cotton, you had a lot of slaves. And today, where you had a lot of slaves, you have a lot of African Americans," a White professor from the University of Mississippi, Dr. Andrew Mullins, told us. "When I was twelve years old, an eighty-year-old Black man stepped off the sidewalk for me to pass," he continued. "That mentality persists. It's hard to overcome a hundred and fifty years of slavery, and then another hundred years of second-class citizenship, in thirty-five years. We tried to keep a majority of our population uneducated, and now we're paying the price." Mississippi has both the lowest education rate and the poorest population in the nation.

Our first day there, our host, Hunter, drove us halfway to Clarksdale, Mississippi, for a gas-station rendezvous with a woman named Mrs. Tatum, who would then drive us the remaining distance to Cleveland, Mississippi. We had never met Mrs. Tatum before—she was our mentor's colleague's friend's mother-in-law—so when we waved goodbye to Hunter and slipped into her white Toyota, we were a bit nervous. "Y'all can call me *ME-me*," she immediately said, her deep Southern accent engulfing each word. Meme's hair was almost as white as her car, and her wrinkles were almost as deep as the dents in it. Her thin lips glowed a slick bubble-gum pink color. "Welcome to Mississippi."

Sitting in the front passenger's seat, Winona thanked Meme for driving us. Priya watched Hunter's car exit the gas station and swerve back onto the main road. He was gone.

"All righty, the drive to Cleveland's 'bout an hour," Meme said. "Buckle up, y'all."

The drive was full of rain, and the sky was a continuous gray block. We've always been told that a dark, heavy cloud looms over this state—remnants of its racist past—so it seemed fitting that there would literally be a cloud looming over us today.

Forty minutes later, we pulled into a parking lot and peered through the car window at our final destination: Cleveland Central High School. The school was pancake-like: a flat, long building made of brown brick. A bell rang inside, and students with brightly colored backpacks streamed in and out of the front doors. We remembered how our mentor, Annah, had told us half a year ago that "you two cannot *not* visit this school; it *just integrated this school year.*"

School segregation did not end in 1954 with the *Brown v. Board of Education* ruling. As of 2015, nearly 180 U.S. school districts were involved in active desegregation cases, forty-four of them in Mississippi. In 2016, the federal court ordered the historically White Cleveland Central High School to consolidate with the historically Black East Side High School. In 1969, fifteen years after *Brown v. Board of Education,* Black high school and middle school students had been allowed to enroll in any of Cleveland's schools, but that only diversified the district's historically White schools, not its historically Black ones. East Side High* remained almost all Black until 2017, when its students were all transferred to Cleveland Central High. Today, the integrated school is about 70 percent Black and 30 percent White. Just as Mississippi's high-poverty and low-education rates are linked to deep-rooted and legal racism, its racially divided schools are too.

As we interviewed in Cleveland Central High, though, we felt an unfamiliar freedom to talk about race. It was as if people knew that dialogue was inevitable and were ready to delve right into it. Former principal Randy Grierson said, "I've been called a cracker, a White motherfucker, but I shake it off. History's

→

* East Side High was turned into a middle school.

watching this school, and I'm not going to let it fail."

Within these school walls, you can't hide under the pages of a history textbook, claiming that racism's an outdated issue. Slavery has been outlawed, and Jim Crow segregation too, but we haven't shaken ourselves free from that history's legacy yet. Do you think it's a coincidence that the state with the highest population of African Americans suffers so much? As Roniece, whom we interviewed the following day in Tennessee, said, "That Whites-only sign is still kind of hovering over that water fountain."

After interviewing at Cleveland Central High, Meme treated us to "a true Southern lunch"—grits, hush puppies, fried catfish, and fried greens. After eating, we snuck into the back kitchen to interview the restaurant staff. Jaymia, an African-American waitress, said, "More than once, White customers refused to be served by me." The White manager, Amanda, told us that her family doesn't accept her Black husband. "He's never been to my mama's house, and I don't know if he ever will . . ." Amanda and her family don't talk anymore. Meme told us how years ago, before integration, she "went to Cleveland High, and there were less troublemakers then." She added that she "grew up in a plantation home, and the only Black people I interacted with growing up were the sharecroppers on our farm."

Cleveland Central High School's challenge as an institution in its first year of desegregation is not exclusive to the Mississippi Delta. While we've made much progress, racism is still alive and well, and it's evolved** astonishingly to match the times.

In this chapter, we hope you realize how—while you may "thank God for Mississippi," because, by contrast, your state might *appear* so much better—the cloud of racial inequity hangs over every part of our nation. In many ways, the past is *still* the present, and it's up to us to change things. After all, history's watching.

---

** Police across the country kill "more Black citizens today than were lynched at the height of U.S. segregation."

# Susan

CHARLOTTESVILLE, VIRGIN

My daughter, Heather, had the best laugh I've ever heard.

I used to wear my hair super super long.

I always wear jewelry.

I've been remodeling my trailer for the last five years.

*So in my* mind, when a twenty-year-old driver drives into a crowd, it's for the purpose of *silencing* the counterprotesters. Well, you don't silence *my* child.[*] You don't tell my child to shut up, and you certainly don't murder my child and think you're gonna get away with it. That gives me the empowerment to pick up Heather's baton now and run with it.

We didn't have money to bury Heather. Even to cremate somebody is at least three thousand dollars, and we didn't have it. We lived paycheck to paycheck. I knew Heather didn't have money in her savings to cover any such thing—we took her last paycheck and bought clothes for her dad, her stepdad, and myself to wear to the funeral.

So, a friend of theirs from childhood started a GoFundMe page. After the funeral, I looked at it and it was two hundred and twenty thousand dollars, so I called up GoFundMe immediately and said, "Stop! Just close it now!"

I knew that I had to do something with this money.

So we immediately started the paperwork on the twenty-first—that's only nine days after Heather died—and started the Heather Heyer Foundation. I consider it my job now to help educate others about some of the things Heather was trying to educate me about and educate others about. I started doing some reflecting of my own on how race has impacted my life.

When Heather started first grade, we moved to Farmville, Virginia, which had not been desegregated until recently, way past the desegregation laws. She had a Black teacher who absolutely despised her. My son wasn't doing so well either. He had a big chip on his shoulder because his dad wasn't around, and I had various boyfriends who had not stayed either, so he was really hurting for a father figure. He ended up getting beaten up every day, picked at, his stuff stolen, knocked around. I realized: all the White kids in Farmville tended to go to Prince Edward Academy, a private segregated school;[**] they didn't go to the public schools back then.

When one of Heather's Black boyfriends lived with us for a period of time, and we

---

[*] On August 12, 2017, in Charlottesville, Virginia, Susan's daughter Heather Heyer was killed when a car plowed into a crowd of counterprotesters gathered to oppose a rally of White supremacists (described as one of the largest White supremacist events in recent U.S. history). Nineteen others were injured in the incident.

[**] White flight: After cities were racially integrated, many middle-class White people picked up their bags and moved to the suburbs. And while many believe that residential segregation has decreased, our cities and suburbs are in fact increasingly racially homogeneous today.

got followed in stores, *that's* when White privilege finally clicked for me, because I really didn't get the whole concept for a while. I had Black friends who were trying to explain it to me, and I just couldn't quite understand it. I had had to work hard too! I had been on welfare, my kids were from a single-parent home, and we struggled, so I had a hard time grasping White privilege. But it finally clicked in with me that day. I mean, I never got followed.

On Heather's Facebook page, which we left up, you can see how she dealt with people trying to contradict her. She asked some of the White supremacist girls, "Why are you here? Tell me how you feel about this?" That's what she was doing on the day she was killed. The girl just kept saying, "No comment." But I have to hope that that message somehow got into her heart and she at least went home thinking, "Well, why *am* I here?" I have to believe that Heather had an impact.

We had Heather's funeral five days after her death. And then that whole week I only slept ten hours. I cried the entire night, almost every night. I liken the grief to standing in the shallows of the ocean, and then the waves will wash over you from time to time. Sometimes it's a big wave and sometime it's a small wave, and when the waves come, you just let the tears roll, and know that you'll be okay when the wave goes away. I've seen so many people who have absolutely drowned in grief. Not me. I started wearing not all-black all the time. I actually bought a red shirt the other day—I mean, it's *vivid* red. I wore it, and, only for a minute, I felt kind of funny wearing it.

# Autumn/
## Pimikwusii/
## Blue Spruce
## Many Blue
## Flowers

**ESPAÑOLA, NEW MEXICO**

I really like mountains.

I've been powwow dancing since I could walk.

My favorite food is tamales.

I like to draw, paint, and sew.

*By the time* I was in seventh grade, my dad had already given me the rundown about the Pueblo Revolt, along with the Alcatraz* takeover—because my grandpa was part of that—and other really key things. So, I knew a good amount about our history. I was prepared for the constant erasure and denial I would experience for the rest of my life.

I remember my Hispano history teacher gave us this coloring page of a conquistador on a horse saying, "The mighty conquistadors are ready to take out the Indigenous pueblo *savages*," or something along those lines. And I was like, "Whaaaaaaaat." Thanks to my dad, I knew something wasn't right. I took that coloring page home and showed him, and my dad was *not* having it. He reported the teacher, and it got handled, but still . . . what really bothers me is that that teacher had been teaching for *so long*, and *so many* kids had gotten that coloring page.

U.S. history is taught in fifth, seventh, eighth, and eleventh grade classrooms throughout this country, and hundreds of students are fed dangerous lies like this. If we don't actively recognize and uplift the truths of Native history now, there might not be any people left with the knowledge to do so later.

Most pueblo kids didn't know their own history like I did; they didn't get to know how *awesome* our people are! But they *did* get that stupid coloring page.

I want other Native kids to know what I know. I want them to understand that we're the Seventh Generation,** the healing generation, so it's time for us all to pick up the slack and start helping out, start learning to communicate well, start living as how our ancestors would've wanted us to live. Let's respect the earth, and let's respect each other. Let's not take any fake crap from the history books, and let's start telling the truth.

* As of 2014, since it became a national park, more than 1.4 million people visit Alcatraz annually. If you look closely, you can spot some graffiti on the walls with messages like "INDIANS WELCOME" — residuals from the 1969 protest of 89 Native Americans who occupied the island for 19 months to reclaim their land before being removed by federal officials in 1971.

** The Indigenous phrase "Seven Generations" means that "each generation was responsible to teach, learn, and protect the three generations that had come before it, its own, and the next three," producing a less individualistic and more collectivistic culture.

# Ronnie M.

**KANSAS CITY, MISSOURI**

I love playing basketball and even though I'm short I can go to the hoop.

I have had the opportunity to meet James Brown.

My biggest role model is a pastor that I looked up to growing up, Huey P. Hervey.

*I was born* and raised in Wichita, Kansas, as a *beautiful* young man. My mom says I was the best-looking child in the family.

We were eight boys and four girls, and we had a beautiful life. We didn't have much, but we enjoyed it. We was raised to respect one another and to be obedient to the family. We was always told it doesn't make any difference who you are or how much money you had. You must love and understand everybody. The old folk used to talk about how, back in the day, my forefathers was tremendously done bad, less than three-fifths of a man. But through it all, they overcame, through the power of God, of loving one another, relying on one another. That strengthened us.

When I left Wichita—oh *baby*, I thought I knew everything then! I came here to Kansas City, I did a lot of factory work for Milbank Manufacturing Company, worked different odd jobs, worked as a busboy. Ooh, I could bus them dishes, honey, I was good. Making seventy-five cents, a dollar, one dollar twenty-five an hour, that was money, man, I thought that I was rich. I enjoyed it.

←----------------------------------------

The Three-fifths Compromise of 1787 counted every Black American as three-fifths of a person when determining state populations for choosing (all White) state representatives until the Fourteenth Amendment of 1868.

Growing up, I knew that segregation was real. But we was poor and didn't know we was poor, because everyone was taking care of one another. We had respect, and you don't see too much of that no more. If you got a whoopin' in the neighborhood, everyone in the neighborhood gave you a whoopin'. If I was somewhere I wasn't supposed to be, someone would say, "Aren't you Leona's boy? Well, boy, you better get your butt back home." He had the authority to give me a whoopin' and then we got another whoopin' back at the house.

Times have changed. Before, once children left the home, I didn't have to worry. Now, we have to be afraid, because when you put an influx of drugs in a neighborhood, you mess up the fabric of the neighborhood. Children are not being raised properly, with lack of teaching, lack of history, role models. We delivered the generation now who do whatever they wanna do. As we're growing, we're trying to do everything we can do to prevent crime that could tear down our community. You know, when I first came down here, it was so quiet they would say, "There ain't no crime over there, because nobody is over there!" Now, a lot of people would love to come down here because they love our music, but we have to show them that it's not that bad.

I'm currently the host of the American Jazz Museum and the Negro Leagues

Baseball Museum, and the guys who used to be here were educated, smart, and talented. They told stories. We're in the Blue Room, which used to be in the Street hotel. That's where your Blacks would come—your entertainers, your baseball players, people who had a lot of clout. They would always stay in the Blue Room, because at the time they couldn't go downtown, go past 27th Street. It would mean nothing for you to hang out and see a Count Basie and Duke Ellington, some of your baddest, baddest jazz artists, right where you're sitting! Oh man, the past is still all around us. Everything was alive. It's just so much culture. We was sharp, we stayed clean. We used to dress up and just go to the corner and just look at each other.

The most dangerous thing in the world is to have the mind-set of being better than another person. I am more proud of this younger generation saying, *Wait a minute, something is wrong.* I'm optimistic. It's better, I can see it. Through every storm, the sun is going to shine. I don't care how long it takes, but when the sun come out, you can see how people come together and respect and love one another. That, to me, is one of the best things in the world. And sometimes we have to go through trials to really see that. But it's going to be all right. Trust me, it's going to be all right.

I love to eat
gumbo z'herbes.

I like to read, I have
a lot of books.

I love to go
to dances.

Purple is
my favorite
color.

**Jackie**

**NEW ORLEANS, LOUISIANA**

*I am Creole* Black. It's controversial, I know people who don't like the word "Creole." But, being honest, here in New Orleans, it is *the land* of Creoles and Cajuns.* Though the Indians were already here, as we know. It's really their land.

I did my DNA test, and it came back with 30 percent West Africa, 1 percent Native America, 69 percent French and Spanish. If I lived in New York, I wouldn't be Black. But in Louisiana, if you have one drop** of Black blood, you are Black.

On the buses, there was a screen, and colored people had to sit behind it. I sat behind it because that's what we do as colored people. It didn't matter that I'm more White than Black, I had to sit behind the screen *or else.*

The Black people that were really Black in color, the really identifiable Blacks, had a harder time than I did. Even within the Creoles, we are prejudiced toward each other. We don't want our children to marry Black people, so those Black people were treated bad by both their own race *and* by White people. There were White-only bathrooms, yes, but if I really needed to go to the bathroom, and the closest one was a White one, I would use that one, no doubt! That's the advantage that I had, me with my light skin. My birth certificate also didn't label me as colored because I was born in a house, and my dad went to register my birth at the city hall, and since he didn't *look* Black, they didn't put "colored" on my birth certificate. It would've been different if I was born in the Black hospital.

A lot of people went to New York, or places like that, and crossed the colored line*** and just never looked back. But

* The word "Cajun" originates from the term "les Acadiens," used to describe French-speaking White colonists from Nova Scotia who settled in Louisiana between 1765–1785. "Creole" ancestry ranges, but many are the result of Black–White unions and have African, Caribbean, French, and Spanish heritage. Creoles were treated as Black people by racist Jim Crow laws, and Cajuns as Whites—even though they were similarly socially and economically stratified.

** Passed by state legislators in 1970, Louisiana law said that anyone having one thirty-second or more of "Negro blood" would be designated as Black. It was repealed in *1983*. Similarly, nationwide, the "answer to the question 'Who is Black?' has long been that a Black is any person with any known African Black ancestry."

*** "Crossing the color line," also known as "racial passing": when individuals knowingly or unknowingly have non-White lineage but present themselves as "White" because of their physical appearance, thus adopting some of the privileges of having a White social status.

now the younger generations have computers. They go digging. See, we were all at this barbeque at my friend Lloyd's house once. We knew that all their children went way up North, away from New Orleans, to Minnesota, I think. Lloyd gets a call one day, and a kid says, "I was searching the computer and I found you, who are you?" Lloyd's like, "Who are *you*? Where did you come from?" Turns out this kid is his grandson. Lloyd's son went and married a White woman and never told anyone he was Black! There's a lot of people like this, they have children and their children have children, and they all don't even know that they are Black. It's a lot of secrecy; it's hard living like that. I would never do it.

# Archibald

**ASHEVILLE, NORTH CAROLINA**

I joined the army, and then I sued the army while I was in it.

My mom and dad were pioneers in integrating a school in Baltimore.

My favorite place in the world is the Adirondacks.

## WASPiness is just

unbelievable in our family. I'm a Montgomery, and if I trace my family history, I can go back to Roger de Montgomery, born in the year *c.* 1030. I was told that he was the right-hand man when William the Conqueror came over in the Battle of Hastings. The Clothiers, the Packards, and the Montgomerys are all old Philadelphia families—Quaker and Episcopalian. My grandmother was a Clothier—it's very gauche, the Clothiers *made* their money rather than earned it— and she married a Packard, and thus became close friends with Grace Kelly. When I went on a bicycle trip with my friend, we got invited to Monaco and spent five days in the palace. When I got married, we went back to meet Princess Grace.

So, when we talk about the unearned privilege of people who pass things down from generation to generation, I understand that. Half of my cousins, they just come into thirty million dollars when they turn eighteen, and oh my God, what it's done to their lives!

I'm also sitting in this position of tremendous unearned privilege when, rightfully, people are questioning and challenging that. It's very easy to become defensive about it or feel guilty about it. But there is absolutely nothing I can do about my background.

We've gotten to this place where we're so culturally at odds that we can't talk to each other, where it's much easier to scream at each other and be angry. We have this terrible reaction and counterreaction, which causes fractures in ways that have me very, very worried. Young minds are wired for combat, they think, "These are my people, the victims, and those people are my oppressors, and so we're gonna smite them." We need to allow people to see where the bridges are. What happened at Yale, what happened at William and Mary, what happened at Evergreen, what happened at Middlebury, and at other colleges too, when somebody comes in and you hate their ideas, so it's okay to hit them in the face with a bottle? That's what Nazis do, that's what thugs do! And, you know, I wasn't using that as a racial slur, but boy, that's a word that White people can't use anymore, 'cause it is

←——————————————————————

In the past few years, students at college campuses like these have strongly protested against controversial, often far-right speakers. A 2017 Brookings study found that 39 percent of college students thought the First Amendment's freedom of speech clause protects hate speech (44 percent "no," 16 percent "I don't know"), and 19 percent believe it is acceptable to use violence to prevent the speaker from speaking (30 percent of males versus 10 percent of females; 20 percent of Democrats versus 22 percent of Republicans).

automatically assumed you're talking about a Black guy. I think of Nazi thugs when I think of thugs.

I don't have any answers at all, I'm just as confused as anyone else about how to go forward. I know that I need to be an ally and be quiet when others are talking about their stories, while acknowledging mine. But if people continue the anger and the vitriol and the bitterness and the violence, we just won't have any First Amendment at all on college campuses. Nobody will say anything because you'll get beat up or punched or punished for saying something, and boy, we don't wanna go that route. We've started down it already. I don't know, that can't be good, I don't think? Can you tell I'm confused?

Ashley

MONTGOMERY, ALABAMA

I was the first Black valedictorian in my high school.

My hometown is home to Bobby Lee Cook, who the television show Matlock was based on.

I was a competitive cheerleader.

*I'm originally from* Summerville, which is a small town in North Georgia. I went to an old high school—there since the 1960s, all-White before integration—and I graduated in 2004 as the first Black valedictorian. I was also the first person in my family to go to and graduate from college.

As a lawyer at the Equal Justice Initiative (EJI), it amazes me when people keep trying to wiggle out of something and say that it's not about race. I'd go as far as to say that just about everything is about race at some point. For instance, you are more likely to be sentenced to death if you are a Black person and your victim is White. If you are a White person and your victim is Black, you're more than likely not going to end up being sentenced to death.*

←—————————————————

\* EJI's main office is in Alabama, where each year nearly 65 percent of all murders involve Black victims, yet 73 percent of the people awaiting execution were convicted of crimes with White victims. Fewer than 5 percent of all murders involve Black defendants and White victims, but over 52 percent of Black people awaiting execution have been sentenced for killing someone White. These numbers vary across states and nationally, but still reflect an overall pattern of racial injustice in assignments of the death penalty.

When I go to work every day, I'm reminded of that because EJI's building is actually built on top of where the old slavery houses were located. A sign in the front of the building captions that, and all over, we've been getting historical markers to combat this narrative of the Confederate presence in Alabama. The purpose of the markers is to alert people that there is a very bloody and awful history being covered up by all the flags and the monuments. Like how, when you come in off of I-65 or I-85, as you get close to downtown, the first exit sign you are going to see is for the First White House of the Confederacy, up near the capitol. If you come in from I-65 South, there is a giant Confederate flag on the side of the interstate. It's just so huge.

The way my mama taught me growing up, you don't go onto anybody's yard that has the Confederate flag, because that is an indicator that they don't like Black people.** They don't mean me well.

←—————————————————

\** The Confederate battle flag was used by the Southern slave-owning states in the American Civil War. It was afterward adopted by the Ku Klux Klan, which was started by ex-Confederate soldiers in 1865. Some KKK members claim their costumes were designed to represent the ghosts of dead Confederate soldiers.

# Juanenna

**LITTLE ROCK, ARKANSAS**

I make and sell jewelry.

I like Spanish trap music.

I come from a very large family.

I drive for Uber on the weekends.

**Little Rock is** a good ol' boy city, and Arkansas is a good ol' boy state. That means: White male dominated, run, and operated. Old money controls everything, and all old money is probably rooted in something wrong. Matter of fact, from what I hear, this one family in Little Rock has the same family still working for them since slavery. If you don't know anybody that rich, you don't even know some White elite communities still exist. In those places, you can't even drive over without security running you.

In Northwest Arkansas, there's a lot of sundown towns—White communities that people of color shouldn't be in when the sun goes down. In a community called Sherrill, a Black family moved in years ago. They bought a trailer, set up cinder blocks, and went to work on Monday. When they came back, their house was gone. The people in the community had picked his house up and set it back up right outside of their town. And he was lucky, actually, to just have his house moved. My dad got a ticket there one time, and every time he even tried to talk to police about it, the ticket would go up. They would lie, say you were going to owe them forever, find a way to lock you up, and get away with it. So finally, my dad just saved and paid it all off at once. I met someone from there nothing like that, but I don't think he tells people where he's from.

When I was sixteen, our predominantly Black softball team played the state championship in Harrison, Arkansas. The KKK has its home there, and they banished Black people a long time ago, so it has a reputation to keep people of color away. We had to spend a night there in a hotel. I can't tell you how afraid we were. My dad was our coach, and I don't think he slept that night. I could tell that he was on edge and nervous, so it put me on alert too. We won the tournament the next day, and even though we were hungry and wanted to celebrate, we didn't waste any time loading up and leaving the town. We didn't want to stop anywhere. When I had two kids and drove through North Central Arkansas, I still started thinking at dusk, "What am I doing here? Am I crazy?" All you see is trees, it's isolated, and the fear just sets in. You could run, but you have people to look after. Even last year, when I had to get a tire on my way to Eureka Springs, I was not about to go that route, because if you're stranded there, you're in trouble.

This city and the state are just *beautiful*—some parts look like a storybook—but for non-Whites, there are just some places that you don't go.

---

The KKK "saw a boost in its membership in 2017. In fact more than half of today's Klans formed in the last three years." As of 2017, the KKK was still active in twenty-two states.

# Rhonda

**BRATTLEBORO, VERMONT**

I am trying to reduce, recycle, and reuse.

I do silversmithing and beadwork. I have been sewing lately.

I have been making koozies for mason jars.

I have one daughter named Nayana.

I have two different color eyes.

*I am Iñupiat* Athabaskan, which is an Alaskan Native. I mostly grew up in western Massachusetts, and went back home to Alaska in the summers to see my dad and my 80 million relatives. Growing up in western Massachusetts was very difficult. Of course, Massachusetts, we're talking Plymouth, Puritans, and the sort of myths that they champion hard to sell early on in kindergarten. It wasn't until I was probably eighteen or nineteen when I started to actually meet a lot more folks that were indigenous to this area. For me, it was an "aha" moment, like this is something that really has to change. We are teaching children early on that Native people are relegated to the past. There is nothing contemporary that is taught about Native people.

My husband is a half Korean and half American GI, so my daughter is a quarter Korean, a little bit more than a quarter Native, half-ish, a little bit less than half European descent. In third grade, she was told to read this book called *The Courage of Sarah Noble*. In the book all the Native people are identified as "savages" and "little brown mice," and they say that "the Indian will eat you." My daughter came home with spelling words that included "savage" and "squaw." It's been really challenging constantly having to speak with the administration. A lot of times I am having problems with the teachers that are twenty-five-year veterans.

Another year, my daughter's reading list had a book: *Touching Spirit Bear.* I read the book, and it was absolutely horrendous. I wrote a letter to the teacher and the principal. I also brought different reviews from the tribes the book is supposed to represent, like the American Indians in Children's Literature review, to their attention. I have to do this major research every time something comes up, otherwise I get shot down.

Sometimes, I'm like, "God, I need a break. I can't do two schools back-to-back." It is so taxing and time consuming to go in and explain to people why not having our own narrative is dangerous, and how it makes Native children feel. I mean, our schools reduce hundreds of Native cultures to a single image, and that's not who anybody is.

←────────────────────

What even is "an Indian"? The term was invented by English colonizers to homogenize hundreds of tribes with different economies, systems of government, languages, and religions.

# Konnor and Aaron

CLEVELAND, MISSISSIPPI

I'm an aspiring nurse.

I wanna be a physical therapist.

I like to draw.

I play the piano.

I'm a fan of love.

I'm pretty funny, if you ask around.

**Konnor:** There was Cleveland High and East Side High. East Side was known as an all-Black school, and Cleveland High was a mixture. We had like a fifty-year-long desegregation court order, so 2017 is the first year of the consolidation. Now all of us are at Cleveland Central High School.

**Aaron:** I went to Cleveland High. I just do my work and go home, pretty much. I don't really see a difference. We came together this year, yeah, but not like from one side of the track and the other side of the track.

**Konnor:** I see a difference. I went to East Side before they consolidated us. It's been an experience. It's been new. At first, I wasn't really too open-minded to it. I really wasn't optimistic about it at all, because I was used to what I was used to. I miss our traditions, like homecoming. We used to have a coronation the week of homecoming. We used to have a pep rally the day of homecoming. We didn't have that this year. This year there's also a larger population, which means larger class sizes, which means during classes you won't spend that one-on-one time with the teacher like you would last year. It's just making small adjustments like that. All the little things. They do matter. Also, you know, it hasn't really been a give-and-take. It's mostly been *give*, giving something up, for East Side students, and then they're mostly keeping the Cleveland High traditions. But there's no purpose dwelling on it, especially something that can't be changed.

**Aaron:** Here, in the Delta, you don't really see much mixing. Like White people usually shop downtown, Black people usually shop uptown. A lot of the Black people work in the restaurants, as servers. Walmart, that's honestly where everybody shops at. That's pretty much it.

**Konnor:** I have friends that are in interracial relationships. And like, me personally, that's not something I believe in. But there are interracial relationships, and I've heard things said like, "Boy, you gon' get lynched!" or something like that. Why don't I believe in interracial relationships? Because I think Black is beautiful. Personally, I'm not attracted to White women.

**Aaron:** I don't really have a problem with interracial relationships. Love is love. You love what you love.

←

**Desegregation does not equal integration. Segregation is the "separation of people on the basis of their race, or some other inappropriate characteristic. Desegregation is simply the ending of that practice"; it doesn't mean that integration, or "the conscious mixing of people on the basis of race," has been achieved.**

*Jo*

**WACO, TEXAS**

I love to talk to people.

I'm vegan and love to garden.

I'm a great cook and a great baker.

I'm very dedicated to social effort.

*I learned about* the lynching of a young Black man that happened in 1916 from Patricia Bernstein's book *The First Waco Horror*. It was the one-hundred-year anniversary recently, so I wanted to do something. People asked me, "What the hell are you doing bringing this up? This is in the past." "But," I tell them, "the past has a profound effect on today."

In 1916, there was the Fryer family, they were cotton farmers, and working for them was a young Black man who was "mentally retarded,"* named Jesse Washington. Jesse was seventeen years old. One day, the two Fryer children came home and found the mother dead in the doorway of the seed house. She had been bashed in the head with something heavy like a hammer, and immediately it was assumed that Jesse did it. Now it's very possible that Jesse killed her, but this was not the issue, what happened afterwards is. He had a so-called trial, and six so-called experienced defense attorneys who did nothing to defend him. Then May 15, 1916, at the courthouse in an existing courtroom, he was found guilty. The judge was in the middle of writing the verdict, but before he could finish, a mob in the courtroom grabbed Jesse and hauled him away. They dragged him about three blocks—all the time cutting and stabbing him—where they had him assemble a bunch of boxes under a tree. They wrapped a chain on his neck, covered him in coal oil, and hoisted him up from the street. They then lit the boxes below him on fire, and repeatedly pulled him into the fire and pulled him out. They tortured him like that for two hours. During this torture, they cut off parts of his body, some of which were taken as souvenirs. When he finally died, what remained of his body was tethered with a rope to a saddle on a horse a man paraded up and down the streets of downtown Waco.

To me, what's most horrendous about this is that ten to fifteen thousand men, women, and children, around half the population of Waco at the time, attended this. Kids were encouraged by their parents to watch. People came from far and wide with picnic lunches to watch this young boy be tortured for over two hours. After the lynching, there was one little article in

---

* The term "retarded," originally used as a medical term for people with intellectual disabilities (alongside "moron," "imbecile," "idiot," and "feeble-minded person"), has now become more frequently used as an offensive and hateful term.

the local paper, and, in my opinion, it basically became a forgotten thing.**

So, today, we formed a group. We had poetry groups, groups reading antilynching plays downtown in front of city hall where Jesse had been killed, and other various things. It culminated in a huge memorial service in one of the community centers downtown with only standing room left, and music. One of the things that we were looking for was an apology, and that word sent people flying. White men especially were just anti-apology. "I'm not apologizing for something I didn't do, blah, blah, blah."

Finally, at the memorial service in 2016, the hundredth anniversary, the mayor did somewhat apologize. He addressed the issue. He said that you have to own it. He expressed regret for it, and, you know, there was some healing in that room that day. To be honest, I'm not sure if I'm doing the right thing, but I find solace in knowing that I'm doing *something*. This horror still lingers over this town. If fifteen thousand people watched this seventeen-year-old boy get lynched in 1916, a hundred years later that sentiment must still be ingrained in their descendants, right?

←—————————————————————

** Black men were the most frequent lynching victims—it's estimated that 2,812 Black men were lynched between 1885 and 1915. However, "Mexicans, Jews, Native Americans, Black women, White progressives," and other non-WASP groups were sometimes also targeted.

# Lisa

**WILMINGTON, DELAWARE**

I'm into aliens.

I kind of has a quirky sense of humor.

I would like to travel outside the United States.

I think family is global.

*My mother's from* a very small town. There were specific rules as to how you were supposed to act in front of White people. We could only use the back door to enter the Big House. The Big House was plantation style. When I was growing up in the seventies, my grandfather was a sharecropper.* He had his own plot of land. He had a house and everything, but the people in the Big House were still in charge.

In the eighties, the man who owned the Big House died. My sisters and I went to pay respect to him, showed up at the front door with flowers, but we were told to go around the back. It's impacted my psychology a lot. I'm almost fifty, and I'm still trying to break out of it.

I live up North now, but, especially when I go down South, I get reminded of these things. When my daughter was twelve, we went down South again for my father's birthday—he moved back down there. We just went to have a good time at this restaurant, but it took us about half an hour to get a menu and water for the table. It took us about an hour and a half after that to get service. Meanwhile, all these tourists, not people of color, were getting water, breadsticks, all the stuff you're supposed to get. My sister and I just looked at each other. We knew what this was, but we didn't want to ruin it for everyone else. It's still like that down there.

Even up here, in Delaware, I see it. I stay in a hotel, and I've noticed several people so far who don't want to be on the elevator with me. I try to smile at them,** but it doesn't work. So, I wait for the next one. That's cool. I would rather you quietly get off than make it all nasty. It doesn't really

----

* In many ways, slavery evolved into sharecropping. Sharecropping—a form of economic exploitation in which "families rent small plots of land from a landowner in return for a portion of their crop to be given to the landowner at the end of each year"—was usually done by formerly enslaved people, working on former enslavers' plantations.

** Claude Steele, author of *Whistling Vivaldi: How Stereotypes Affect Us and What We Can Do*, describes the story that inspired his book's title: "an African-American graduate student . . . walking down the street dressed as a student [realized] that his mere presence was making Whites . . . avoid him or sort of cross the street to get away from him and so on. He realized from this kind of behavior that they were seeing him through the lens of a negative stereotype about African-Americans in that neighborhood, that perhaps as a young male, Black male, he might be violent. And it was making his whole experience of the situation tense and awkward. He learned how to whistle Vivaldi to deflect that stereotype."

need to be that way. Everyone has their preferences so if you don't want to be around me, that's fine. I don't care. Don't make it where it's very uncomfortable, don't piss me off. Don't disrespect my daughter. Just keep it classy, and let's not heat it up. If I do get pissed off, I just walk away.

How are you expected to take a stand for something if you literally can't stand?

# CHAPTER THREE

# OUR RICHNESS, RACE AND BEYOND

"*T*he average person cannot name one woman—other than Rosa Parks—who made a difference in the Civil Rights Movement. Can you?" he asked, leaning back in his red velvet chair.

We couldn't.

We were in the home of a local activist, our last stop on a long interviewing day trip to Montgomery, Alabama. Earlier that day we had visited the Rosa Parks Museum as well as the church where Dr. Martin Luther King, Jr., had been a pastor. Then, while wandering around downtown, we got a phone call. "All you know about the Civil Rights Movement is false," we were told. "Come to my mother's home, and I'll tell you the truth."

We canceled our plans for the rest of the day.

He was already waiting for us at the top of the stairs. It was a late fall afternoon, approaching dusk. The house behind him appeared well-kept, with walls made of sturdy brick and charming wooden white window frames and a blue "Historical Commission" post in front. But bars covered the windows and doors.

"Priya, this is *exactly* like the Garfield Halloween special," Winona whispered, attempting to lighten the mood. "Garfield and Odie wander into the house, they're attacked by the ghosts of the past, and then they have to run away. We did *not* work out enough for any of that."

Unimpressed, Priya did not respond.

The man's face betrayed no emotion. As we approached, up the sidewalk and two sets of stairs, he stood still. "Browder. Butler Browder," he said solemnly, extending his hand. He turned around to unlock the door, and we exchanged looks of uncertain curiosity.

Inside, the home seemed ordinary. In the living room, there were green couches with stretch marks and butt indents. To our right was a kitchen, with wooden shelves filled with nothing, white doilies on every surface, and, on the dinner table, a vase of bright, fresh flowers.

Butler pulled folding chairs into a circle and began his story immediately. "I am the son of Aurelia Eliscera Shines Browder," he said, inviting us to sit down. "She was one of the five women who led the Civil Rights Movement. Her name was on the case that desegregated the buses. We're in her home, which I grew up in . . . but most people don't know it's a historical site."

*What?! Five women?* In school, we had only learned about Martin Luther King, Jr., and Rosa Parks.

It felt like Butler read our thoughts. "My mom and her friends hired MLK to be their mouthpiece. They had to; people obviously wouldn't listen to a woman talking. And now, the women before Rosa Parks have all been downplayed and forgotten. Aurelia Browder. Mary Louise Smith Ware. Jo Ann Gibson Robinson— the *mother* of the Civil Rights Movement. Claudette Colvin. Susie McDonald. Do you know their names?"

Butler opened our minds to the fact that the Civil Rights Movement required a man to be effective. If a Black woman had taken charge, she would have been dismissed.

*Racial* identity was not the only identity that mattered.

Who we fully are is never exclusively about race. When the two of us think about our own identities, being Chinese American and Indian American always comes to mind first. We think about how, when we first joined a local anti-racist organization, every single person in the room was Black or White. The unspoken question was, "Why, as an Asian American, do you even care about race?" We think about how we feel closely acquainted with both oppression *and* privilege, how both White people and people of color we interview will end their storytelling with "you know what I mean?" as though we could somehow understand both their experiences. We think about how perhaps we wouldn't be so readily trusted if we were Black or Latinx or White.

But what if we were older, or fat, or trans? Would people still let us so willingly into their homes? In Rapid City, Lesleigh told us she was "a middle-class, White, queer, fat, Midwestern woman." While she now feels "ashamed to not have been focusing on race as an equal or greater contributing partner," she has been a fat activist for eighteen years because "everything about my physicality is fundamental to how people see me." We realized that each of our conversations, though centered around race, are shaped by *much* more than being "Asian American." If we were men, would our parents still have been so concerned about our safety? Would others have exclaimed, "I'm excited to educate such cute little girls!"? If we didn't grow up down the street from Princeton University, would we have been able to garner the resources to do this project? If we had any disabilities, or if we didn't speak English, how much harder would traveling have been?

Coined by Kimberlé Crenshaw in 1989—but developed heavily by Black feminist thinkers like Anna Julia Cooper and the Combahee River Collective, and experienced since the start of White supremacy, patriarchy, and capitalism—the term "intersectionality" refers to how societal structures not only reimagine who we are based on *all* of the overlapping parts of our identity, but also how this overlap produces *new* forms of domination in the process. We asked every person we met about how intersectionality has shaped their life. We asked them to consider not only race, but also factors like gender, sexuality, class, religion, ethnicity, nationality, ability, age, and physical appearance.

The focus of intersectionality is *not* to just make a checklist of all of our oppressed identities. It is not to battle those identities against one another in an "Oppression Olympics," and, crucially, not to use them as excuses to avoid race. (As Eduardo Bonilla-Silva said, "To go beyond race, we have to go through race.") Rather, our focus is a question: How can we work together to dismantle unjust systems at the root and liberate *everyone* in the process? The solutions, too, demand intersectionality: in New York, we grabbed coffee with an anti-ageism activist named Ashton, who showed us how, because aging is a shared and unifying human process, we can make our coalitions against *racism* all the more powerful by including people of all *ages*. The solutions demand we be allies to one another.

After our interview in Montgomery, Butler waved good-bye vigorously and smiled. "Your generation can do better. Pay attention. Don't let them downplay Black women again!"

Butler's right—we can do better. The average person cannot name one Black woman—other than Rosa Parks—who made a difference in the Civil Rights Movement. Can you? Today, we see not only Rosa Parks, but Marsha P. Johnson, an LGBTQ+ activist who provided food, clothing, and housing to transgender and non-gender-conforming youth in New York City, one of the first to ever do so. We see the Chicano Civil Rights Movement of the 1960s. We see Joan Baez, a multiracial folk singer who used her music for social change, refusing to play in any segregated venues. We see Aurelia Browder, Mary Louise Smith Ware, Jo Ann Gibson Robinson, Claudette Colvin, and Susie McDonald. As our understanding grows—of how race is connected to, shaped by, and stuck irrevocably to *all* other identities—we can finally begin to see one another's fullest selves: the richness of who we are.

# Lauren

PROVIDENCE, RHODE ISLAND

I am left-handed.

I have terrible night vision— the worst ever.

I am irrationally afraid of all kinds of birds, except for penguins— I think they are cute.

I gave a TED Talk.

*As a kid,* I thought very little about identity. I went to a very traditional Catholic school through eighth grade, and there was no discussion about identity. There was an assumption that I would perform well because my mom is Chinese. My mom always contacted my teacher to check on how I was doing, so she was stereotyped as a "tiger mom." But wouldn't *any* mom check on a daughter with a disability?

In high school, I took Mandarin and took a class trip to China. I was super excited. I had never been, and I always wanted to go. When I got there, I found out that, because of the one-child policy in China, if a family, especially in rural parts, had a kid with a disability, they usually sent you down a river. Literally down a river. They didn't want their one child to be disabled. I was heartbroken. My mom came from Hong Kong to the United States with this mentality, and then she had me.

I was born with cerebral palsy. It's a permanent disability. I have very limited ability to participate in normal, everyday things. I could never run around during recess. I could never go to summer camp.

People with disabilities are perceived of as "crippled"—a word used way too often— as not able to be independent, productive members of a community. At the same time, I had to fight the stereotype of being a girl and "fragile." I was never taught about

feminism. "Feminism" was a bad word; it meant being a man-hater. I was never ladylike enough for my family. When girls got into fights, they would immediately go on social media and write a cryptic, passive-aggressive Facebook status like, "Oh, good friends come and go." That's how girls were expected to be—fragile, catty, mean, weak—and I was not having any of it.

I never really realized that I had a *permanent* disability until I was ten or eleven. I had been doing tons of physical therapy, and I thought that if I just kept working at it, then one day, it would be gone. Once I made that distinction, I began to think about what *ability* really means. I began to see things around me that were ableist. For example, in our chemistry room, there was a poster that had braille at the top and bottom and read, "Don't forget to wear your goggles. You don't want to have to read braille!" So, what are you saying—that it's a punishment to be blind?

I'm originally from New York City, and there are hundreds and hundreds of subway stations across the five boroughs, but so few of them have elevators. People with disabilities are by far the largest minority in the world and the most underrepresented in everyday life. So the

←————————————————————

**Of the 472 subway stops in New York City, 80 percent are inaccessible to persons with disabilities as of 2017.**

fact that almost none of the subway stations in New York City are accessible to us is a problem.

How are you expected to take a stand for something if you literally can't stand? Think about the Women's March. As much as I wanted to go, I couldn't. There are people everywhere storming the streets—it just wouldn't be safe for me. I couldn't keep up with that crowd.

Part of the reason I am here today, though, is that we had a lot of socioeconomic privilege. I'm very fortunate, since I had so many medical problems, that my parents were successful, retired young, and were able to be full-time parents. But I didn't feel I actually got to exercise that privilege. For example, after-school activities would never accept me. That intersectionality between ability and privilege has always been a conflict.

Being comfortable talking to people with disabilities adds visibility. Because the more you don't talk about it, the more you don't ask, the more you use softer words like "handicapped," the more invisible our stories and experiences become. I don't mind when my friends ask, "Lauren, are you disabled?" I don't take offense to that, because it's true: I do have disabilities. Just don't be like, "Oh. What *happened*? What's *wrong*?" assuming that something *happened* to me, when in reality, I was born with it.

# Ahyoka "Niki"

TAHLEQUAH, OKLAHOMA

I was born in Oklahoma City.

My favorite film is _Boy Meets Girl_.

I am the youngest first-language Cherokee speaker that I know of, and I'm twenty-seven years old.

One of my favorite games to play is stickball, a traditional Cherokee game.

***I'm a Keetoowah*** Cherokee, full-blooded on my mother's side, though I'm light-skinned and light-eyed. At twenty-seven years old, I'm one of the youngest first-language Cherokee speakers, since we spoke only Cherokee at home. As a kid, I didn't know people spoke anything else!

I'm also president of my school's Catholic Student Organization, and a transgender person, a Two-Spirit* person living in rural—*really* rural—Oklahoma. I used to look very different. I was the popular, preppy-looking jock guy with a short haircut, I had tats, I was so skinny. But as a child, I just naturally came up as a girl. My family didn't put any kind of gender norms on me, because our language doesn't allow for it. We don't even have a word for "gender" in our language! If I say *he* is doing something or *she* is doing something, "doing" is the same word. All the words in our language are that way. In our traditional way of life, we believe that *I* don't tell *you* who *you* are, *you* tell me who *you* are, and that *is* who you are.

We lived way out in the woods, cooking on woodstoves and using an outhouse for the bathroom. My grandma told me, "When you get to school, you're going to be the only Cherokee there." I didn't know what she meant back then, because when I went to school, there were so many Cherokees.** When I got home and told her, she said, "No, you're the only one. To be Cherokee, to be who we are, is encompassed in an entire worldview that cannot be accessed without our language." The way I might describe something in Cherokee, if I were to describe it that way in English, it wouldn't make any sense. So, she was warning me that I'm going to be seen as different because I don't *think* like anyone else there. And that's exactly the experience I had.

My first day of school, they separated the children into two lines by boys and girls, and I didn't speak English, so I just looked around and followed what I saw. The girls went over there, so I went over there. This little boy comes up to me, tugging on me and telling me to go over to the other line. I didn't understand what was going on. I grew up in a huge family, so you kind of have to protect yourself, and eventually when he was pushing me around . . . I decked him and broke his nose. When I was sent home, I explained everything to my grandma. She had to sit

---

* A Two-Spirit person "identifies as having both a masculine and a feminine spirit, and is used by some Indigenous people to describe their sexual, gender and/or spiritual identity."

** Fewer than 12,000 people—much less than 1 percent of living Cherokees—speak the Cherokee language.

me down and explain why the world would never understand me.

The elders, like my grandma, understood me better. Middle-aged Cherokees now are completely unaccepting and unsupportive. They tell me that I'm going to hell, because they're the generation that went through the boarding schools, which robbed them of our traditional ways. My birth mother, who passed away a couple of months ago, went to boarding school and it totally messed her up.

I try talking to some of them—the middle-aged people, the people who hate me in my church, the students who whisper behind my back—but it's hard for me to talk about something as personal as my gender identity. It makes me feel like I'm saying to a stranger, "This is what kind of genitalia I have in my pants!"

It was especially difficult to talk with people within the church. Still today, if one of my friends asked me to be the godparent of their baby and stand there as their kid's baptized, I couldn't because the bishops said no. The church's catechism says that you're to approach homosexual people with respect, compassion, and sensitivity. All Catholics receive the same baptism; it's actual church doctrine that no Catholic is better than another one. But people do not always recognize that.

I identified as agnostic and atheist for a while, but I realized I wasn't going to church for others. I'm going there for the Eucharist and for owning my faith. I tell all LGBT people who are Catholic or Christian that leaving the church isn't going to help the church change. If they have to see you regularly, they'll have to see that they're making a mistake, and eventually they'll fix it. The church—and the world—moves very slowly, but it is moving. I always remember how, growing up in our ceremonial Cherokee way of life, there was a teaching we were told was given directly from God. It goes, Ꮻhi ᏰꙨ ᏕᏣꙒꙨᎠᎫ ᎢᏉꙨᎠᎫ. It means that we are all to live in such a way to teach that every living being on the earth is treated the same, included rather than left out.

That's how I reconcile being Native, and being Catholic, and being trans.

# Barry and Omar

**PROVIDENCE, RHODE ISLAND**

I like dancing.

I like music and I listen to it all.

My favorite food is rice with sauce on it.

I love my job, working with refugees.

I really want to run faster than my dad, of course.

I like learning about the mysteries of space.

I like learning about space.

*Omar:* Since I came to America ten years ago as a refugee from Gambia, I call myself a Black man, an African American, an African, a refugee, a Muslim, and an American. All these things have affected my life. For example, as a Black man driving in the streets of Providence, I'm always afraid of being pulled over. As an African man, I also have immigration challenges, as well as trouble with employment and language. As a Muslim man, I deal with surprise from people who don't understand why I'm not a man with a robe and a large beard, or a woman with a hijab—I dress like people in the mainstream! It's not a big deal; you don't have to shake, I'm a regular human. This is my son Barry. He and his brother are six and seven.

*Barry:* I like learning a lot, and reading, and going to school and waking up late. I like traveling and I've been to New York, Pennsylvania, Virginia, New Jersey—oh, yeah, and Gambia. We could make a sandhouse out of your foot with sand, or run after a rooster and grab it by the feet.

*Omar:* Unlike immigrating or traveling, I came here unprepared. In Gambia, I was a reporter, and I was tortured. It was chaos—I was only married for two months when we were separated, under very difficult circumstances. My life was hanging on the line and I did not know whether I would ever see her again. When we reunited three years later, I felt complete, my distress subsided, and for the first time I began to meaningfully look forward to the future. It was profoundly one of the most meaningful moments of my life.

Anyway, so I was forced to leave, and I ended up in Ghana. A year later, the U.S. government took me. I was just put on a plane. I had only heard the name "Rhode Island" the day before my arrival. I was being supported by case managers, and after nineteen days, I got a job putting in data at a bank. I learned basic cultural stuff like strong handshakes, timeliness, eye contact. In my culture we don't look at people in the eyes; we just look down.

I adjusted in America after extreme levels of trauma. Here, I started being called Black or African or African American rather than Gambian or a Fula. After a few months, I enrolled in night classes at a nearby college—now I'm in my third year of a doctorate after a bachelor's and two master's degrees. I teach part time and run a nonprofit called Refugee Dream Center, because the six months the federal government helps a refugee is practically impossible for most people. I also wrote a

An unprecedented number of over *65 million* people globally are displaced by war, conflict, or persecution, and studies in the past decade found that approximately 30 percent experienced post-traumatic stress disorder or depression.

book, mostly so my kids would grow up knowing my story.

*Barry:* He got chased north by the dictator when he was a reporter. All the way from Gambia to Senegal. For a couple miles.

*Omar:* In the refugee ward, we always talked about not *assimilating*, not abandoning your entire culture and taking a new one. Instead, we emphasize *integration*: strengthening your own cultural identity and embracing the new one. So at home we speak our native language, we pray five times a day when we're supposed to pray, and then on the weekends we go to the mosque.

*Barry:* We cannot eat bacon, sausage, pork, hot dogs, or pepperoni. And at home we speak Pulaar, but we call it Fula.

*Omar:* Yeah, our native tongue. We don't want them to lose that, or be less of who they are. You know, I named him "Barry" because at the bank, my first supervisor was an older woman who knew I was alone and embraced me like I was her son, stayed close to me, advocated for me. She introduced me to her family and her husband was like my dad; his name was Barry. Our second son, Samba, is named after my biological father in Africa. So the American dad and the African dad.

*Barry:* He lived in Sam-Mbollet.

*Omar:* That's the name of my village.

*Barry:* There's a sign, and if you go right past the sign, you're in a different country.

*Omar:* That was our first time going back, with the new government. It brought a sense of closure, because it was not by choice we left. It was very emotional. Very mixed—sad, but also free, and safe. I thought about all the activists and my friends in the media who had been killed . . . how I'm still here, and very lucky to be alive in this country.

# Hamza, Ayesha, and Saboor

PRINCETON, NEW JERSEY

can hold my breath for three minute... verified.

...ave bowed legs.

I yawn when I'm nervous.

I'm bad with directions.

I'm studying medicine.

I like photography and art.

I wear shorts even in the winter.

I broke my elbow on a tightrope.

**Saboor:** Culture plays a big role in my life. Islam is my culture. I love when my family prays together. It gives me a sense that we will always be together.

Most of my classmates are Christian, and that makes me different, because when they go to church I have to say I go to mosque. And they're like, "What is the mosque?"

At field day, when other kids score, most of them make a cross across their chest, but I make the *dua* on the field, which is when you kinda bend your arms outward to worship.

**Hamza:** Do people know you're Pakistani, or do they just know you as a Muslim?[*]

**Saboor:** People know I'm Pakistani because whenever I forget my lunch, most of the lunches at school are made of meat. And I'm like, I can't eat that because I'm Pakistani *and* Muslim, and I eat meat called "*halal.*"

**Hamza:** I asked Saboor that because I've always felt more Muslim than Pakistani. I think the most Pakistani thing about me is that I'm Islamic, and that I follow Islam in my own personal way. Like, I consider myself a feminist. I don't harbor homophobic views.

---------------------------→

* In 2017, hate crimes targeting Muslim Americans rose by 15 percent.

**Ayesha:** For me, Islam is meant to be a culture and a way of life. If anything skews its message, it's cultural representation. There's a history of masculine dominance, women are oppressed. It is pretty much the case for a majority of countries.

Islam has a human component. It's specifically stated that you follow the Qur'an *and* Sunnah, or the teachings of the prophet Muhammad. Because God recognized that just words aren't enough to completely understand how to live a life.

Some Muslims are culturally aware but religiously lacking. They forget that the Sunnah is just as important. It's what you interpret day to day, because the world is ever-changing. The Qur'an was written so long ago, so it's hard to relate to something like that. Our prophet's last sermon, where he says, "All mankind is from Adam and Eve. An Arab has no superiority over a non-Arab, nor does a non-Arab have any superiority over an Arab; a White has no superiority over a Black, nor does a Black have any superiority over a White; [none have superiority over another] except by piety and good action," stressed a legacy he wanted to leave behind. I think the Pakistani culture, set forth by entitled and empowered men, takes away from that. They cite the Qur'an without context and use it for their purpose, keeping uneducated people in the dark. This happens in America too. I mean, Pakistan even had a woman for prime minister, something the U.S. hasn't accomplished yet.

*Hamza:* Yeah, I agree that the problem isn't a problem with Islam itself, but with America's perception of the Muslim. Like, in Saudi Arabia, they didn't allow women to drive. But what people have to understand is that it's not like in the Qur'an they said women couldn't ride camels! What also adds to the confusion about us is the geographic ambiguity—how Americans understand the Middle Eastern versus someone of *desi* origin who's Muslim. We're constantly clumped together. We constantly have to explain ourselves. That singular conception of Muslims from all across the world is where I feel more boxed in, rather than within Islam itself.

*Ayesha:* I like to read up on world news, like, for example, how Palestinian people are being treated—but every time I talk about it, people shake it off, like it's not their issue, not important. If I talked about a shooting that happened in a U.S. state, though, which I think is equally as important, then people care. Terrorist attacks are 100 percent accepted to speak out about if it occurs in Western countries, but if those same terrorist attacks occur in Pakistan and the Middle East, it's their fault.

** As of April 19, 2018, "At least 9,600 Palestinians and 1,251 Israelis have been killed by someone from the other side since 2000."

*Hamza:* There's definitely a lot of apathy toward issues outside of the Western world. I was having a conversation with an academic, and after giving me his explanation of the conflict between Israel and Palestine,** he called it an unfixable problem. But just imagine if the social issues we care about in America, like sexual harassment or environmental justice or guns or race, were all labeled as "unfixable problems." That would be such a disservice.

*Ayesha:* My grandparents have gone through the separation of Pakistan, and the mass murder that happened there, so it makes it more relevant for me. I don't blame people for not knowing about global issues, but I do blame them for not caring, or not caring to know. Why don't people feel the same about all human lives?

*Hamza:* I don't really feel like I have a choice to be apathetic. I don't perceive myself as just American, because I have the hyphenated identity of being both Pakistani American and Muslim American—that being said, I don't just care about what I'm hyphenated next to. I don't just care about Pakistani issues or American or Muslim issues. My ideal world would be one where people say, "I'm Human American" or "I'm Human French."

# Shermaine

**WASHINGTON, D.C.**

I have an extreme fear of heights.

I play flag football.

I was born for the stage.

*As a kid* growing up in D.C., I made the connection between hard work and academic achievement, and how these things can change your socioeconomic status. I told myself: "If I work hard enough, I will achieve my dreams." Well, I later realized my mind-set was toxic. There are institutionalized barriers for women and people of color so that, no matter how hard you work, the finish line always moves further and further away from you.

After doing over a year at Phillips Academy, Andover, I had an issue with my gallbladder and had to be discharged from school. I thought, "I'll never get into a good college now, because I have to go to a D.C. public school." So I dropped out and got a job as an inventory specialist at CVS. One day, someone reminded me that if I don't have any initials behind my name, especially because of how I look, I'm disposable.

I didn't have the resources to *know* to go back to school . . . except for this one White AP English teacher. When I stopped showing up to school, he would literally call my house and drive through my neighborhood to see where I was. He convinced me to finish school, maybe even go to college. I did, because of him. This teacher later went to all my college theater performances, my master's graduation ceremony—everything. He's been a constant advocate in my life, basically a surrogate pop since my dad died.

In college, I felt underprepared, because the only AP course I had in my high school was English, whereas my peers from wealthier school systems had taken several APs. I had to stay up four hours more to study, and teach myself how to use Excel and PowerPoint, whereas others had already been given the material. I also had imposter syndrome—how could I aspire to be a lecturer or researcher, if I didn't see anyone who looks like me doing it?

I wanted to become a scientist. My dad had hypertension and diabetes, but didn't get the right advice from his physician, so he died much earlier than he had to. I realized that there are biases in the medical system at work, too. For example, African Americans have the highest death rate and shortest survival rate for most cancers. It's an important public health crisis that I wanted to tackle, so I went to get a master's in cancer biology, prevention, and control at Georgetown.

After that, I went to get a PhD. I was intoxicated with the American dream. I figured I could keep working hard and get what I earned. Well, my White advisor had different plans for me. I had to say hi to him every morning. He needed to know where I was at all times, and he didn't allow me to leave until *way* past my hours. Meanwhile, there was another grad student in my lab—a White male—who could stay there for however long, without any supervision. When there were issues in the lab, my advisor would publicly explode on me, screaming, cursing, and saying, "I don't know who you think you are, but if you want to play this game I guarantee I'll win." One day, I slept in the lab just to get him data—not necessarily safe in the middle of night, in Detroit. I *gave* and *gave* and *gave* because I believed that if I worked harder, he would appreciate it one day. But it was never enough, I guess.

I felt stuck because my advisor would be the person to write my job letters of recommendation. He had a lot of power over my future. It was hard to find allies when he lied about me to his faculty friends. When my project was done, he became even more hostile and told everyone I wasn't ready to go. I was free labor.

To fight it, I told my dean, and he told me to cc him on every correspondence with my advisor. But he still warned me that my advisor's position meant that he could do anything to me. It made me become disillusioned with my American dream. I realized that both people and historical forces can put all your hard work to waste. Your destiny is kind of predetermined based on who you are. They hand PhDs to some people, but others have to give up a kidney to get a degree.•

I got through it partly because I would call my AP English teacher and just bawl my eyes out every day. I never really trusted White people before him, but he taught me that not every White person's out to get me like my advisor.

Most importantly, he taught me how to love my White husband. The world just makes our different skin colors very hard to forget. On our *first date*, someone yelled out of their car, "What are you doing with that Black whore?••" A part of me just kinda died. I felt degraded and embarrassed in front of this guy I liked. I felt like I had brought it upon myself.

At a school thing for my son, there was a security checkpoint to sign in. I was two steps behind Paul. Paul walks straight past the security guard and into the school, but the guard stops *me* and tells me I need to sign in. It's just those little things that kinda eat away at your day.

I was pregnant while writing the dissertation, and juggling that with a

---

•  A study that looked at students enrolled, from 1992 through 2012, at over twenty research universities found that 36 percent of Black and Latino PhD students in STEM ended up leaving their programs, and only 44 percent earned a doctorate degree within the normal seven years' time line.

••  Among Black-White marriages in the year 2000, 73 percent had a Black *husband* and a White *wife*.

crazy advisor was a lot. I wanted to quit, but I didn't. It would've sent the wrong message to my mixed-race son, that his White dad can be a successful lawyer, but your mom, who's Black, isn't successful. I don't want him to think that Black people can't hack it.

Now, I'm working at the National Science Foundation to advance the participation of women in science.••• I want to let women know that it's not you but the system that needs to be changed. As a country, if we're serious about diversifying STEM [science, technology, engineering, and math], increasing innovation, and keeping America competitive, then we need to start addressing some of these barriers that impede the participation and success of people like me.

---

••• **The National Science Foundation found in 2013 that Black females are 10.7 percent of female bachelor's degree recipients and 13 percent of female master's degrees recipients . . . but less than 1 percent for doctoral degrees or jobs.**

# Butler

**MONTGOMERY, ALABAMA**

I work with the young to try to give them perspective on the Civil Rights Movement.

I like to cook ribs, chicken, and steak.

I like to hunt.

In my free time, I fish.

WORLD'S MOST COURAGEOUS WOMEN

BROWDER vs. GAYLE 1956
Ended Plessy vs Ferguson
Separate but Equal Doctrine of 1896

*Rosa Parks was* the plan. She was the one who was *supposed* to be the plaintiff in the lawsuit, but when it came time to actually file that lawsuit, they found out that Parks couldn't be the plaintiff. She had already been found guilty before at the city court, so filing anything to do with the buses or segregation would mean it would immediately go *back* again to city court. Anybody with any sense wouldn't want that. The only hope they had was to go to federal court. So they had to look for someone else. On May 11, 1956, four women testified in court, not to what happened to Rosa Parks, but to what happened to them *prior* to Rosa Parks. These four women weren't trying to become figures in the community. They were just doing their part to make life better.

First, they found a young lady who was fifteen years old, named Claudette Colvin. She had been arrested and found guilty for sitting in the *Black* section and not giving up her seat to a White customer. Next, they found a teenage girl, Mary Louise Smith Ware, who had also been arrested when sitting in the rear of the bus, not near the White section either. Then there was a lady named Susie McDonald—we called her "Mama Sue." Mama Sue was very light-skinned, so much so that they thought she was White. She was seated in the rear of the bus and the bus driver asked her to get up and come to the front, to the White

section. She refused, saying that she was Black, and that she was seated where she was supposed to be.* Finally, there was my mother, Aurelia Browder, who was arrested by a bus driver and detained in 1948.

When Claudette had been arrested in March 1955, she went to the NAACP and told them. She tried to get them to help, and they did. They had her believing that she was going to be the lead plaintiff in a case they would file. But E. D. Nixon, head of Montgomery's NAACP chapter, did not feel that a dark-skinned girl like Claudette should be plaintiff. He wanted somebody light-skinned because he wanted to appeal to the White judges who would hear the case. He thought the light-skinned person would have a better shot at winning.

How did my mother get involved? Well, the month after Claudette was arrested, my mother had a *second* incident on the bus in April 1955. She too went to E. D. Nixon, asking them to do something, asking if *she* could do something, but E. D. Nixon told her that she was too outspoken, not docile enough, to be the lead plaintiff in the case

---------------------------------->

* **You hear that Rosa Parks was arrested for sitting in the White section on the bus. That's not true. When Rosa Parks was arrested, she was really arrested for sitting in the area for Black people, closest to the White section, and refusing to get up when the White section overflowed.**

that they were planning. He said that they wanted someone who was mild-mannered and all that.

But E. D. Nixon didn't get his way. My mother ended up being lead plaintiff. If you examine the stories of the four women who testified, the only person who was unimpeachable as a plaintiff was my mother. Unlike the others, her claim could immediately go to the federal district court. So, because they had no other choice, they ended up having to make Aurelia Browder the lead plaintiff of *Browder v. Gayle*—the case that overturned *Plessy v. Ferguson* and desegregated the buses.

When President Clinton gave Rosa Parks the Presidential Medal of Freedom in 1996, she said, "All I did was not give up my seat on the bus." Clinton remarked, "Oh, how modest." In fact, she was telling the truth.

Our society was driven by men and what men say, but those men were afraid to challenge the segregation laws. They were afraid that they would be killed. They were afraid that they would lose their jobs. These women didn't care.••

My mother, Aurelia Browder, was the strongest figure, male or otherwise, I had in my life. I remember once, I answered a call and a man was on the phone, using profanities and saying violent things. I was seven, so I gave the phone to my mother. She explained to the man that her bedroom was located in front of the house, and that her children were in the back of the house. "If you've got a problem, you've got it with me, not with my children," she said. Another time, my sister answered the phone. They threatened to bomb the house. My mother said, "Bomb it. I've got insurance. We are not going anywhere."

I remember all of it. During that time, this house had a wood porch. Every morning, I had to get up and clean up that porch of the rice, flour, rotten tomatoes, and eggs that people would throw. One time, there was real dynamite, but the fuse was out of it. Other times, it was broomsticks cut up to look like dynamite. It was the Ku Klux Klan, White Citizens' Council, or city officials.

My aunt once said to my mother, "Those White people are going to kill you." My mother told her something in the vein that if she can't stand for something, having lived would have been for nothing.

←

•• Butler added, "The mother of the Civil Rights Movement was not Rosa Parks, but a woman named Jo Ann Robinson. The night Rosa was arrested, in 1955, Jo Ann Robinson printed out 35,000 handbills calling for a boycott of the Montgomery bus system. Jo Ann Robinson was, in fact, intimidated and harassed on a bus in 1949, six years before Parks. She and other supporters passed out these fliers on Friday, calling for a boycott of the buses that Monday. Jo Ann Robinson was the *spark*."

I learned from my mama my principles. I became an advocate for discrimination cases and a mediator. I involved myself the same way my mother involved herself in the on-goings of the Civil Rights Movement. Had it not been for her standing as she did, I don't think I would have had the backbone. I mean, I don't have the backbone that women have. I am very much a man, but I have to take my hat off to the women of that period. I fear that young people, because they don't know their history, won't realize or recognize racism as racism, or other injustices, when they are confronted with them.

# Deb

**SALT LAKE CITY, UTAH**

I recently discovered through my heritage DNA that I am from ten ethnicities, even though I was raised 100 percent Latina.

I hate flying things, like bugs and moths.

I think I'm a cool mom.

CT
★ ★
ERS!

UT

JUSTICE 4 PATRICK HARMON

*I was in* a very toxic relationship with my daughter's father. He hurt me, right here in this apartment, and I defended myself. He called the police on me. He's a very White-looking Mexican, and all he had to do was say, "She has a mental illness," and they treated me *totally differently.* They were aggressive. They grabbed and handcuffed me, they took me out there and publicly humiliated me. Do I feel like I would have been treated differently if I looked White? Maybe. I don't know. But I do know that the second they heard the words "mental illness," the officers didn't know how to handle it. And I felt like I didn't get the patient treatment that I've seen mentally ill White women get.

It's very hard to deal with mental illness. It has made me prone to get into situations I don't want. It's a chemical imbalance I have struggled with since I was seventeen. And I hadn't gotten in trouble since the beginning—but suddenly, after twenty years, I find myself with domestic violence charges. They so easily believed the man. They didn't give me a chance, but treated me like I was going to be violent. I'm not a violent person. I'm a mentally ill person.

People are not bipolar; they have or live with bipolar disorder. This one lady was clearly having an episode in the back of a police car, and the officer pounded on the trunk, saying, "Hey, crazy! Stop!" I said, "That's the problem. You guys are perpetuating stigma when you use the word 'crazy' to describe somebody in mental distress. And then if you take them to jail rather than the hospital, or throw them back into their abusive environment and then rearrest them . . . you're traumatizing them further."

I take it personally when people say casually, "Oh, she's so bipolar." It's not a casual thing. People are suffering in silence. I grew up in a family that didn't want to talk about it, so I didn't get treatment . . . until I moved to Utah.

If I didn't have friends here to help me, it would be really hard. This is a low-income building. I do what I can to take care of my daughter. Some days, I can't handle it. I wake up and I'm cranky. I took this book out from the library—the only children's book on it they have—that explains bipolar to little kids. I read it to her, and I hope she understands. She's the reason I get up in the mornings. Probably my biggest fear is that she will inherit my mental illness.

←———————————————————————————

In the United States, there are approximately 7.9 million people with a severe mental illness (SMI)—leading to one in ten calls for police service, and occupying over one in five American prison and jail beds. Half of people with SMI are untreated, and they are sixteen times more likely to be killed during a police encounter.

# Deja

**PHILADELPHIA, PENNSYLVANIA**

The beach and anywhere with my family is my happy place.

New Orleans is my favorite city.

I like to fish.

*The majority of* people think trans women[*] are out there doing sex work because they want to. When I rode along with some vice cops from the Philadelphia Police Department, I was in the car and they were basically saying that it's a *party* for the trans girls to be out there selling themselves. When we got down to the group of cisgender girls, the cop said that they were there because they had to be.

In reality, the culture for trans people is that you really can't go to school. You really can't work. When society, government, churches, and schools tell you that you should not exist . . . what else can you do? For me, it was nightlife. You all get together at night, you go party, you make your money from sex work, and that's how you survive. As soon as a trans girl comes out, she sees all the other trans girls doing sex work, so she jumps right in and gets stuck there. That's what happened to me—I had two older sisters who did really well in school, one even excelled in sports, and the culture was, you're going to grow up, you're going to go to college. That got sidelined for me.

When I moved from the Delaware suburbs to Philadelphia, it was not only the first time that I saw another trans person—because I didn't even know they existed—but also when I noticed that, in the trans community, the Black girls all hung one place, the Latino girls all hung one place, and the White girls all hung separately somewhere else.

I realized that race matters, even among trans women. I am mixed. I am Latino and White. Actually, Mexican, Serbian, German, and Irish. My last name is Alvarez, and I'm very proud of it. In the sex work industry, there were not many women of my complexion—women of color and mixed-race women—so you kind of played off of that to make your money. But meanwhile, I feel like I've had to work way harder[**] than White trans women to get opportunities outside the sex industry. For my first job in Philadelphia, I was paid to pass out condoms for ten hours a week. They told me, "You, trans woman, can't do anything but this." I didn't listen to them. I was working sixty hours a week, even though I was still paid for ten. I wanted to show that I could do more and was worth more. People discount my hard work by

←

[*]  **Cisgender people identify with the gender identity they were given at birth. Transgender is an "encompassing term of many gender identities of those who do not identify or exclusively identify with their sex assigned at birth."**

[**]  **According to the 2015 National Transgender Discrimination Survey, "Black and Black Multiracial NTDS respondents had the highest rate of sex trade participation overall (39.9%), followed by those who identified as Hispanic or Latino/a (33.2%). Those who identified as 'White only' had the lowest rate of participation at 6.3%."**

saying, "Oh, she only gets these opportunities because she looks White." Okay, I might be White-appearing, but when I fill out an application and send in my résumé, my last name is still Alvarez.

Trans women are only seen as victims—not as skilled, articulate, smart, driven women. We are seen as sex workers who have been traumatized by the world. On social media, men will say to me, "Oh, you're very attractive. I see you're trans and you don't do sex work. Why do all the trans women do sex work?" Well, first of all, I have done sex work. I never hide that from anybody. Second, let me ask you a question. When you approach these trans women, are you approaching them because you want to have sex with them? Do you ask to hang out with them at their house, instead of "Hey, do you want to grab a coffee with me?" If you continue to treat people as though they are only one thing, how do you expect them to respond?

*You know what*, maybe this isn't all we can do. I realized we too are keeping ourselves in that box that society put us in. We are allowing our oppressors to control us. They are saying, "Oh, they're all prostitutes," but at the same time, when we talk about equality, they shoot us down. We started branching out a little, realizing that we are capable of more. Talking to each other from other cities, other states, realizing that there is a large network of trans people across the United States. While many of us may have to do sex work right now to survive . . . what we can also do right now is set ourselves up for a better future.

# Keah

**LOCKPORT, NEW YORK**

I love cheesecake.

I can't write without music in the background.

I love popular culture.

I like to eat pepperoni out of the bag.

*I've always been* aware of my Blackness first. I learned about that very quickly. My family is full of Black people who are proud to be who they are. For me, being Black was always something that was beautiful, even before anything else was. I am also a Black woman with a disability. Much of the way that I navigate the world is indistinguishable from my Blackness and my womanhood and my disability.

I was at Walmart by myself—I was twelve, I think—at the TV section. This woman came up to me, complete stranger, and she was like, "I don't know what it is that you have, sweetie, but I am praying for you." And I'm twelve years old, looking for an Avril Lavigne CD or something, and I'm just like, "What?" and she just walked away after giving me a thumbs up.

Throughout my life, people have this weird delusion that they need to try and cheer me up about my disability. The world has an issue with me. It made me uncomfortable so much in my life, until I was maybe twenty-four. I'm twenty-six now, so my journey to self-love as a whole is very new. I was a person who didn't love herself for years and years and years, because I thought that was what I was supposed to feel about myself. It took effort to change that.

One day in 2016, right after Christmas, I woke up and was like, "I'm tired of tearing myself down. Tired of being me." I look in the mirror, and I look so gross. I have messy hair, and nighttime breath, all the stuff, but I look in the mirror, and I say, "*Wow,* look at you. You look *great.*" I got up every morning after that morning and I said four things that I liked about myself in the mirror every day. I would keep saying it until I believed it.

Social media changed the game. Before the Internet, I didn't know anybody else with a disability. I didn't hang out with other kids with disabilities. I didn't want to. I wanted to blend in so badly. But, with the Internet, I've met people who have disabilities and who love themselves. I learned to love them before I learned how to love myself.

Today, with the Internet, my voice travels out there. It gives me power, because I'm not inhibited physically.

←

Around 650 million people, or approximately 10 percent of the world's population, live with a disability. This makes them the "world's largest minority."

# Tracye

**WASHINGTON, D.C.**

Beyoncé is my favorite artist (and favorite everything else).

My favorite thing to wear is nothing.

My favorite decade is the nineties.

My favorite soul food is anything deep fried.

"*When did you* realize you were Black?" People think the answer should be obvious: since day one. But it's kind of like asking, "When did you realize you're poor?" Growing up, you don't realize you're poor until someone tells you that you're poor. I didn't realize I was Black until I had Black experiences, like being eleven years old and getting pulled over by the police because they thought I was a twenty-one-year-old that just robbed a store. Or constantly being reminded in my head of the things my mother told me: keep your hands out of your pockets, say "yes sir, no sir," no sudden movements—you know, "the Black talk."

I felt like I was being reminded *over* and *over* again that I exist at this intersection of Black and poor. Let me clarify: I'm only cash-poor, I'm *beyond* rich in personality! But being at the intersection of being Black, cash-poor, homeless, unemployed, all these different things, I'm reminded *every single day*. I'm reminded when I have to hop the gate at the Metro just to go somewhere and risk not only a $350 fine, but also being put in handcuffs or shot.

I grew up in Iowa. People always say, "I didn't know Black people lived in Iowa," and I have to remind them of the Great Black Migration. They're like "Oh yeah," and I'm like, "Oh yeah, that history was erased. You're growing up in public school." Right now, we're sitting across from the Rotunda of the National Archives, where the Declaration of "Independence" is being kept. It does not represent any of us at this table—that's cute.

I also grew up in foster care from age twelve to eighteen. I lived with this White family that made green bean casserole. Have you ever had green bean casserole? That shit's real. In eighth grade, I was placed in this residential treatment center called Broomwood with minors who had committed crimes. Why? Because they couldn't find me a foster home. I was criminalized because of where I was—Waverly, Iowa. I was still called a "Broomie" even after I was no longer there.

In sophomore year, I went to this high school where fifth through twelfth grades were all in the same building. These were farm kids of, like, rural Iowa hunters. It was not uncommon for people to have shotguns in the back of their pickup trucks that they drove to school. I was the only Black kid. A group started called the Anti-Tracye Club. That's cool, I guess. I was honored they put so much energy into hating me. Like, thanks, bitch. I remember

⟶

Between 1916 and 1970, over 6 million Southern Black Americans moved to northern and western cities, in part to attempt to escape the social and economic oppression of the post-slavery South.

being called a nigger every single day. I remember being threatened one day by somebody saying, "I'm gonna fucking shoot you, nigger. I'm gonna go in my truck and grab a gun and shoot you right now." I just cried my eyes out because I was terrified. There was no security. He could've just shot me. And no one would understand, like, "Oh, he didn't mean it, don't play the race card." Oh, small-town Iowa. I lived with that fear.

I could keep going, but okay, let's talk about my experience with the police. Fuck the police. Next. I'm kidding, it's hard. It's hard and complicated. Because, like, "fuck the police," but when I was rallying in Charlottesville on July 8, 2017, all the officers that were confronting us were Black officers. The rally was over the same statue people were protesting later on August 11 and 12. We were getting ready to leave, just as the KKK members were all escorted out of the city by the police, but the police were escalating their tactics. They brought out riot gear and lined up in formation. I saw a Black woman being handcuffed and brutalized and I and others linked arms to intervene. I just remember seeing this fight between two Black officers, talking about me, another Black person. They pulled off my bandanna and tried to pepper spray me directly in the face; they dragged me on the sidewalk to put me in flex cuffs. I got kicked. Once again, while the White

officers sat back and almost kind of chuckled, like, "Look, even other Black people don't care about your Black life either." So then we got to that point: all skin-folk ain't kinfolk. People are like, "But I'm a Black officer," but you're the face of the state and you're part of my oppression right now.

Does one "join" the movement, or does one simply get absorbed into it? I feel like, you don't join. You just find out. I'm Black in America. My ancestors didn't march, and run, and flee for me to sit idly by and just watch. Only recently, it's been like everything I'm feeling is validated. We say there's room for everyone in the movement, you just have to find out where you fit in with your strengths and weaknesses. Like, I'm really good at direct actions, turning up in the streets. My weak point is being strategic. So I'm learning to be more detailed-oriented and work toward a goal. Others are good at talking with people, and I'm a little bit more rowdy, a little bit more radical. And sometimes that's more needed than the more academic activists. We can both exist at the same time, because Blackness is just as complex. I appreciate that.

I was reminded of the intersection I live in again, this year, being Black and queer. I was at the Capital Pride parade and people were aggressive when I pointed out that not everyone holding a banner was a person of color, or nonbinary, or gender-nonconforming, or trans, or *all* these other things that should be celebrated at Capital Pride too—I realized at that moment that I was first Black, then gay. I couldn't truly be gay when marriage equality happened because I still had to fight just to live as a Black man. So I'm always reminded of the intersection that I exist in. Always.

Anything else I want to add? Free all my niggas. Abolish the police state. Abolish prisons. I was interviewed by some Chinese TV news, and he was like, "What?" I was like, "Free all my niggas." He was like, "What??" I was like, "Free. All. My. Niggas." He was like, "Okay." They did not run that part of that interview.

# Vaughn

**RAPID CITY, SOUTH DAKOTA**

I do a lot of motivational speaking to youth recovery groups.

I love taking vocal lessons.

My favorite job was as a wildland firefighter.

I grew up breakdancing.

*A lot of* people mistake Lakota culture for *poverty* culture. I didn't understand the difference until I was about twenty-three.

Poverty culture is when you accept entry-level positions and fast food and all that. You don't ever think you can do something beyond that. You sell yourself short. You accept it all rather than think you can transform it. A lot of people are really lost. They begin to adopt poverty culture into Lakota culture, and they think being impoverished is just who we are. It never was—that was from colonization.

Our Lakota values were what eventually propelled me to fulfill my potential and be all that I was born to be. In Lakota culture, you have the virtues of respect, wisdom, generosity, compassion, courage, and humility. There's just a lot there. I grew up with it at home, but as a teenager I began to identify with poverty culture and hip hop culture. I remember watching *106 & Park* on TV and seeing people struggling in the background of these music videos. I identified with the struggle. They glamorized it in a sense for me, and I began to adopt a lot of those traits into my own life.

I grew up on Pine Ridge Reservation, around an hour away from here. These reservations are the most impoverished counties in South Dakota. That's challenging—we're dealing with the consequences of legislation that is hundreds of years old, that confined Native Americans to reservations that prevented us from our buffalo hunting traditions, that terminated our faith and practices and assimilated us to mainstream society.

We have a creek that runs through here, which we used to call the *"Mni Luzahan"*— creek with fast or swiftly moving water— and so they called it Rapid Creek, and now we have Rapid City. What we call the Black Hills was translated from our *Paha Sapa*. The history of Rapid City is imprinted with Native Americans. But history must be taught by people who can graciously teach it, not by people still affected by and projecting the trauma. My brother-in-law does not trust law enforcement whatsoever, and I'm like, well, why? He hasn't had bad experiences with them as an adult, but he says it's the criticisms nationally that make him distrustful. He won't engage with law enforcement, won't help them be better, because of the distrust. You're imprisoned by your distrust, you're imprisoned by this fear; they imprison you from creating better solutions for our children. That's the consequence of not teaching these things within school systems . . . people learn it down the road and they become hurt by it.

I realize that being emotional about these issues does not allow me to create effective solutions to change. People are justified in being upset—I mean, on just about every street corner, we have a U.S. president here, and you know the policies they designed. But I think as a community leader, I don't have the luxury of being upset. It creates a dialogue of opposition. Sometimes it's necessary, but I think our current leadership in Rapid City is really opening the doors to growth. At this community forum with the mayor, around two hundred majority Native American people presented all these grievances, some from over two hundred years ago about the Black Hills being taken illegally. I stood up and said if we feel that there is discrimination in our city and police department, then we need to change the organizational culture of the police department. We can do that through diversity: let's get Native American police officers on the force. It shifted the venting session to talking about solutions.

I'm now chair of our community advisory committee, and we've done a lot of work in the last two years: we advocated for body-worn cameras, which were just implemented in January, we do a lot of community engagement, we've made recommendations to policy in police regulation, we're doing diversity initiatives.

We're also working to redefine jails. Basically, we want to stop incarcerating people who we're mad at but who are no actual public safety risk—people with driver's license, petty offenses, public intoxication. You can't incarcerate addiction out of someone. We also want to stop letting economic status keep people incarcerated. Our initiative is to reduce our Native American jail population* by 20 percent by 2020. As of 2018, within one year, we've already accomplished 10 percent of that. And we have a program called Young Adult Diversion. If you're eighteen to twenty-five, those are the times that your brain is not fully developed, and bad decisions can go on to haunt these young people for the rest of their lives. If they complete our program, then we dismiss the crime. No employer is able to find it. Before, we had community service. I've done it when I was younger, and that was excruciating. I didn't feel like it changed me; I just didn't enjoy it. We call it "community enhancement." An example: this young lady wanted to get connected to her culture through a jingle dress dance, so we gave her the resources and connections to design her own dance and start competing. They dismissed her charge, and she does it now all the time at powwow.

We weren't just warriors: we were historians, diplomats, hunters,

---------------------------------------→

• **Native Americans are incarcerated at a rate 38 percent higher than the national average, according to the Bureau of Justice Statistics. Native Americans are more likely to be killed by police than any other racial group, according to the Center on Juvenile and Criminal Justice. In South Dakota, the state with the fourth highest percentage of Native American residents, Native Americans compose nearly 60 percent of the federal caseload, but only 8.5 percent of the total population.**

storytellers, and very strong police officers. We had police practices from the 1600s, 1700s, probably even before that. They are very much the best practices today. One of them is restorative justice, but our traditional police officers called it the *kichita*. If a crime occurred, the *kichita* would bring the victim and the perpetrator together; they would talk about what just happened, how that crime has compromised the trust of this band of a hundred, two hundred, three hundred people, and how maybe restoration would be made. We had to act with unity. We, Americans, just recently started talking about that in the last ten or twenty years, but this has been a traditional Indigenous practice for centuries.

We can learn so much from Lakota culture, rather than the poverty culture created through legislation. One last example of how legislation impacts us today: if you were Native and didn't send your children to boarding school,** then they withheld your rations. You were stripped of identity. You couldn't speak your language, you were given a Christian name. Having long hair is very important to Lakota people, for both men and women, but if you were a male, you were stripped of your hair. Many children experienced abuse. We are the products of that, and it disrupts our ability to parent. So growing up, I didn't hear "I love you" or "I'm proud of you" or any positive reinforcement, because for generations, we didn't receive that in boarding schools. We received a lot of punishment. Now, when my son comes home, he sometimes says, "I love you; you're awesome." I love it. It's some of the first times I've ever heard it.

---

** In the late 1870s, the U.S. government's approach to addressing "the Indian problem" shifted from genocide to complete racial assimilation. Reservation boarding schools were created and run by both the government and religious institutions, often stripping children away from their families and cultures.

# CHAPTER FOUR

# OUR BEST FRIENDS ARE STILL STRANGERS

We found two strangers sitting on a park bench underneath a canopy of ash trees.

It was a picturesque scene. Sunlight sneaked through the trees and dappled their faces, a slight breeze rustled the girl's dark hair, and someone strummed a guitar nearby. Walking up to them, we noticed that the guy's arm was draped over the girl's shoulder. Their names, we learned later, were Jean Luke and Susannah. They were a couple.

There were three of us interviewing that day: Yasna, our Japanese-Afro-Caribbean-American friend, had taken the Greyhound bus with us down the three hours of winding highway between Seattle and Portland. As we introduced ourselves, Jean Luke raised his eyebrows in suspicion. He was a scrawny White guy with spiky hair and a lingering smirk. Etched on his black T-shirt was a cartoon Japanese schoolgirl wearing a tiny skirt, surrounded by the words "KILL LA KILL" in glaring red.

He folded back the tinfoil that held his burrito together and took a bite. "Yeah, whatever, I'll answer your questions," he said. He motioned his head at Susannah. "But my girlfriend here doesn't speak good English." He proceeded to explain, black beans and yellow corn churning in his mouth, how Portland is the least racist place in America, that he's color-blind—"Look! My girlfriend's Japanese!"—and that we should really, really try the food cart down the street because "this burrito is insane."

Earlier that day, we had stopped by the Oregon Historical Society, climbed our way to the research floor, and dug through piles of crackly, stiff newspaper clippings that glowed yellow from age. The librarian had dropped them with a *thud* on our table, remarking, "Took me a while to find these race ones! Hardly anyone asks for them!"

As we read, the headlines spun in our heads to the sound of eerie silence. We learned that, as of 2011, landlords and leasing agents discriminated against Black and Latino renters 64 percent of the time. In 2014, Black and Native American students in area schools were suspended four to five times more than White students. By the 1920s, Oregon had developed the highest per capita Ku Klux Klan membership in the country. And today, Portland is the Whitest city of its size in the United States.

"There's no racism here," Jean Luke had said to us with a shrug. "That's all I've got to say."

We turned to Susannah, but she avoided eye contact.

All throughout the country, we kept seeing huge misunderstandings in relationships where race *wasn't* talked about. In Washington State, an old man confessed, his eyes glassy with regret, that he never told his children about the Japanese-American internment camp he was in. "I was ashamed," he said. In North Carolina, a Black woman told us that for thirty-five years, she and her husband never discussed being an interracial couple, so she felt like "he never knew her or her Blackness." They divorced. In Oklahoma, a Nicaraguan-American man told us how his wife is "a White Southern girl" who, when they met, "had no idea that Nicaragua was a country and thought Mexican was a language." They stayed together. "Why?" we asked. "We *talked* about it," he responded simply.

In Nebraska, an African-American woman named Shelley (whose full story is in this chapter) e-mailed us after we interviewed her and her White adoptive father, saying, "Words cannot describe the positive, cathartic experience you provided me this week. I talk about [race] all of the time but rarely have I talked about it *with* my dad. The door is open now to talk [amid political differences]."

We examined our own closest relationships. In our memories of everyday conversations with friends, we remember things like—"My boss is an idiot." "Wait, what happened to that cute guy in your math class?" "Oh my gosh, your beach photos look sooo amazing." Looking back, we realized that for many, the norm is to share only *ego stories*: stories that orbit around the superficial, and skim past any deeper understandings of who we are.

Within minutes of meeting our interviewees, we tried something different: we asked for their *soul stories*, intimate stories about their identities. We didn't go on autopilot—eyes glazing over, fighting an itch to check our phones, nodding our heads in empty agreement because we weren't truly listening. Instead, we became radical listeners. We tuned out of our own internal dialogue, and actually *listened*. As a result, people opened up to us.

We ended up feeling closer to these strangers—a Japanese-American man in Washington, an African-American woman in North Carolina, a Nicaraguan-American man in Oklahoma—than we did to most of our best friends. Some of our interviewees have become our most beloved advisors, and one even FaceTimed us from a hospital room, "only, like, ten minutes to go!" before the birth of his son. Many of them e-mail us out of the blue, just wanting to say hi. We were shocked that so many people trusted *us* with their deeply personal stories about race—because, to them, *we* were the strangers! We decided, if *they* could open up to *us*, there's no excuse to keep avoiding conversations about race with our own friends.

Every single one of us is born with an identity that we had no part in crafting, and when forming relationships, we can't glide past the soul stories that develop as a result, or claim to be "color-blind." If we do, we miss out on understanding one another's fullest selves. We deprive ourselves of richer relationships, and set ourselves up for unnecessary conflict.

Let us clarify: we're not encouraging you to grab your nearest friend of color and force them to talk about race. Not everyone will be as open to sharing their stories with you as the people we met were with us. We are challenging you to look within yourself and decipher how race, culture, and other parts of your identity have changed *your* worldview. Then, we hope this chapter prompts you to look truthfully at your closest relationships and ask yourself: "Do I *truly* understand the people around me? Can I do better?"

After we interviewed Jean Luke, Susannah opened up. Her brown eyes shimmered with tears. She described, hesitantly, then faster and faster in Japanese (through Yasna, who's fluent) how "this place will always see me as an outsider." She looked sadly at Jean Luke, who was brushing bits of burrito off his T-shirt. He didn't understand the language. "I feel so alone," she whispered.

---

→

If you're interested in learning more about how the two of us (Winona and Priya) did better, check out our second TED Talk, given during the spring 2018 TED Residency. We examine our own journey to develop racial and cultural intimacy with each other through sharing our soul stories.

# Burton and Shelley

**OMAHA, NEBRASKA**

I lost $1 million in three months, and I have no regrets.

I used to climb trees for a living.

I know President Obama.

I have gone skydiving.

I ran a business called Positive Pants.

I won the STEM Innovators Award.

I've run five marathons.

*Shelley:* My childhood life felt like it was crumbling around me at all times. My mom is from Rolling Fork, Mississippi, so her accent is thick and slow and very prominent. I remember my teacher said, "How many syllables are in the word p-i-l-l?" I raised my hand so quickly and said that "pi-ill" had two syllables, because that's just the way my mother said it. I was promptly told that I was wrong and placed into special education for a speech disorder.

My mom had a history of mental illness. I was the oldest of four at the house. We saw a lot. There were police officers called to our house for any number of reasons: domestic violence, my mom had a mental breakdown, or whatever. I wondered: Are the police officers talking to the teachers? Do they know that all hell is breaking loose at my house? I mean, I never told my teachers, "I didn't do my homework because my mom was arrested." There

------------------------------------------→

In some cases, Black children are underrepresented in special education when compared with White children of a similar class, behavior, and academic achievement. A *New York Times* article states, "They are far more likely to be exposed to the gestational, environmental and economic risk factors that often result in disabilities. Yet Black children are less likely to be told they have disabilities, and to be treated for them, than otherwise similar White children."

were certain things that I just wasn't going to say, but in my imagination, these adults would care enough to figure it out. They didn't.

My younger sister (closest in age to me) and I ended up going to live with Jo and Burton Holland. We had known these people all of our lives—we saw them casually at Bible study, at their day care sometimes. They were probably the first White couple we ever interacted with—and they suddenly stepped up to take us in. My two youngest siblings ended up going into foster care. They were moved from bad foster home to bad foster home, and they started becoming more engaged in high-risk social behavior.

*Burton:* When our family is together, I can see via people's eyes what they're thinking. They can tell me whatever they want to with their mouth, but they can't hide what's in their heart. Their eyes show it. Half of our kids are Black and half are White. When our White daughters carry Shelley's son, I see the same thing in other people that I saw in the sixties with my grandfather. He didn't believe Black people were bad, he just thought, "We don't cross races. We just don't do that."

I grew up with my grandfather. He didn't speak to his oldest son for eighteen years because he married a lady from the North, and the Civil War thing was still part of his life—the Blacks weren't the issue, it was

Northerners, states' rights stuff, he said. When we called our family and said we were adopting, they were like, "That's great!" We said, "Well, there's one thing. It's a Black family." It got real quiet. Later, they said, "Well, there's going to be a lot of problems with that"—but the first time one of my kids sat in my grandfather's lap for two hours, it was no longer about race. It was about his grandson. And once it became that, everything changed. People say one thing, but sometimes their heart could say something else.

My kids will be ranting and raving about something they saw on social media or something that's happening in the world, like Black Lives Matter. They'll be going on and on about how "White people just need to change." I'm like, "Mom and Dad too? Grandpa and Grandma too?" They're like, "No, no. They're different." But why are we different?

*Shelley:* It's similar with my White friends. Because I very much focus on issues of racial inequity, police brutality, and so many other things in my work, some have told me, "You don't love White people." I'm like, "If I didn't love you, I wouldn't call you out on these issues. But because I love you, I believe in us, I believe that there are things you don't see, and I believe that you could even be different or better, I will absolutely call stuff out."

# Rosa

**TULSA, OKLAHOMA**

I'm kind of a fashionista—
my outfits normally have a theme.

I'm part of a feminist
Internet group that
raises money for
struggling women.

My favorite color is purple.

I love cold weather.

*I moved to* Broken Arrow, Oklahoma, at four years old because my mom was escaping an abusive relationship and poverty in Mexico. But two years later, my mom found another boyfriend. He was an alcoholic, and sexually abused me up until freshman year of high school. I still have post-traumatic stress disorder and borderline personality disorder today from that trauma. He got a Driving Under the Influence (DUI) offense and was deported.

Even then, I didn't really realize what growing up undocumented meant. It only clicked when I saw my friends getting part-time jobs. I told my mom, "Hey, I want to get a job at this grocery store," and she said, "Well, you can't. You weren't born here." And I was like, "Huh?"

I started seeing all my friends driving, getting jobs, and applying for Free Application for Federal Student Aid (FAFSA) so they could go to college—stuff that I couldn't do. I didn't know where my life was going.

After 2012, when Obama passed Deferred Action for Childhood Arrivals (DACA), I saw the opportunity to be able to do everything that everybody else was doing. It opened that door for me. I could finally be normal!

Around that time, I also became more aware of my sexuality. It was hard because undocumented people who happen to be gay or trans or bisexual have two closets to come out of. I wasn't as hesitant to come out about being pansexual queer; I was actually more hesitant to come out as being undocumented.

With my friends, I used my sexuality to deflect attention from my undocumented-ness. I thought that people would think they knew everything about me once I talked about my sexuality, because it's such a personal topic, so maybe they wouldn't ask any more questions.

Still, talking about sexuality is all very taboo. When I came out to my very traditional Catholic mom—shortly after my brother came out as gay—she called us both sinners going to hell. She said we weren't her children anymore, and wouldn't take us to school. Later, she just pretended it was all fine.

People with this two-closet experience need a lot of representation because they are more fearful, and that's why I've become more vocal about who I am. I've noticed some men think, "Nah, she doesn't know any better," only because I am a young twenty-one-year-old small female. We have to be strong. I want people to see me in the community, at a rally, on TV, and say, "I identify with that. I'm queer, I'm undocumented, and if she can go out and be this powerful and represent our community, then I can too."

←

**At least 267,000 LGBT adult undocumented immigrants live in the United States. Of all 904,000 total LGBT adult immigrants, 30 percent are undocumented.**

# TJ and Cecil

**DELAND, FLORIDA**

I can write and snap with both hands.

I have the same zodiac sign as Beyoncé.

For cultural reasons, I used to kiss people I just met and I had to realize like, yo, this kissing thing is not a thing everywhere else.

I'm an avid SpongeBob enthusiast.

I've been skydiving and bungee jumping in New Zealand.

I speak Cantonese fluently.

**Cecil:** In sex ed class in middle school, this lady nonchalantly mentioned that sometimes boys like boys and girls like girls. I had this mind-blowing moment because nobody ever said those words to me before. That was me!

I remember bringing home my first girlfriend to have dim sum with my parents. I thought it was pleasant, but later my father was mad at me for embarrassing my family by being so affectionate with my girlfriend in such a public place. I was really angry at the time, but now I realize he wasn't really mad at me for being gay. He was embarrassed because he had friends in that restaurant who asked him later, "Is your daughter gay?" and he and my mom both didn't know what to say. Fifteen years later, I can say that my parents had a coming out as well. They decided to take it out on me, but really they didn't know how to come out. I can relate to that, I didn't know how to come out either!

I've kinda always not followed tradition. People don't expect a Chinese five-foot-eight outspoken individual like me. I don't fit the mold. My advice? Be patient with yourself and those around you. Have grace and compassion. If I didn't, I wouldn't have given my parents a second chance, and they wouldn't be in my life today.

**TJ:** I decided I was just not going to be anything—I didn't date anyone, I just focused on school and attended church four days a week. I knew I preferred being with women, and I knew that I didn't identify as a woman. Back home there's a whole stack of dresses and skirts that my mom bought for me, and that I never wore, all with the tags still on them.

I came out as a trans man in junior year. I questioned if I'm a good person because of my understanding of the Bible. My uncle was like, "You grew up in the church, I don't understand why *now* you go to college and all of a sudden you're LGBT? Where did that come from?" The women in my family were like, "Did we not raise you right?"

Eventually I stopped questioning, because I understood that your sex and your gender are two different things. To this day, though, three of my uncles and an aunt still refer to me by my birth name, and I have to prepare myself every holiday season because I know that I'm going to get Bible verses thrown at me. Since I work for a diversity and inclusion office, my uncle thinks I "made gay professional." For my mom, it's been more of a safety thing—she didn't want to turn on the news and see me as a headline.

My advice? Be able to talk about your emotions. Don't just be vocal on global issues, or just for others . . . but be able to articulate your own challenges. Also, don't rely on television to answer your biggest questions in life. I relied on Nickelodeon and *Degrassi* characters for way too long, and that never worked.

---

Sex: what the doctor who delivered you assigned you, based on physical characteristics.
Gender: how you experience or present yourself.

# William

**BOSTON, MASSACHUSETTS**

I'm good at entertaining little kids.

I like to hear stories from people, and I like to tell stories.

I like playing games, I love Scrabble.

I'm a nickname giver.

*When I was* a little kid, a White guy would come by once a week or so and collect a quarter for life insurance. He would always do funny things for us: make faces, do a magic trick. I used to say to my grandma that he seems like a nice White man, and she would snap, "You have to watch him, you always watch White people, or else they'll do you in." That mind-set's embedded in her—after all, she *did* have a reason to think that, with what White people had done to her and her mother and father.

There are two conditions that I think permeate the development of people, particularly White people and Black people, in this country: superiority and suspicion. To this day, there's often a lingering feeling of superiority among White folk. It's just almost grown into them, reinforced and retold. On the other hand, people of color are told to be suspicious of all White people. These things have a psychological hold, and it's so damaging to the human spirit.

One way to divest oneself of those is *through association.*

When we begin to explore the American story, we find these close, loving, cross-racial friendships. We can't be ignorant of that part of our history. We can be *energized* by this history, and emulate this legacy that most people don't know about. Did you know? Black people *and* White people started the NAACP.

In reality, our history includes *all of us.* Nothing was done in a vacuum. When we teach about slavery and abolitionism, we teach little kids about Harriet Tubman, but not Thomas Garrett.* Garrett was Harriet Tubman's good friend, a White man who collaborated with her! Over the course of years, Garrett estimated that he housed 2,700 runaway slaves in his house. Another example: The city of San Francisco tried to discriminate against Chinese Americans, because about 89 percent of the laundry workers were of Chinese descent. But then, a Chinese man named Yick Wo pressed the case and in 1886 won in the U.S. Supreme Court! He had three attorneys helping him, one of whom was D. L. Smoot— interestingly, an ex–Confederate artillery captain from the Civil War. Can you believe that friendship? Oh, and one of my favorites, Xernona Clayton, a Black woman, got the *Grand Dragon* of the Ku Klux Klan to leave the Klan. Oh, and there was also a tremendous relationship between Teedyuscung, King of the Delawares, and this White guy named Charles Thomson, who was the Secretary

---

• **This made us wonder: What is the balance of lifting up people like Garrett without overshadowing, or undermining, the already sparse representation and celebration of non-White heroes (like Harriet Tubman) in history classes?**

of the Continental Congress. Thomson was actually adopted into the Delaware Nation because of this friendship.

We need racial amity.** You've got to get to know people. You have to constantly weed your own garden, find your own prejudices—and for me, for my grandma, that was against White people for a while. But, today, my wife is White, and I work all the time to create more and more diverse friendships. A lot of what I do with my beliefs shapes my Bahá'i faith because of the principle of the unity and the Oneness of the human family. I also find strength in knowing that before me, for as long as this country's been alive, there have been a sprinkle of *positive* cross-racial friendships that made some race impact. That, to me, is pretty fabulous and hopeful. That's the only way we're going to get anything done in this country: working together.

** **William is the founding executive director of the National Center for Race Amity. Their belief is that "Race relations in America will not substantially improve unless the public discourse on race moves beyond the blame-grievance-rejection framework to one that recognizes and celebrates our ability to overcome racial prejudice through association, amity, and collaboration."**

# Sandra

**WASHINGTON, D.C.**

My mother, sister, and I all have the same haircut.

I am deeply Buddhist, and for my vacations, I like to go on silent meditation retreats.

I tend to think in terms of military terms and fighting terms.

I've lived in the mountains of West Virginia for five years.

*I'm Korean American.* My family came here back in the seventies, so I carry an intense amount of very Korean traits, and a lot of American traits, and a lot of traits that have nothing to do with either culture—and both cultures don't like those traits.

When I'm with my Korean family, I have an understanding of how to move with them. I know what I need to do in order for them to feel like I care about them. I ask about food—I ask if they've eaten, I offer them food—it's all very food-based. So with my partner, who's not Korean, he's had to really grasp the fact that I'm so food-centric, and he's just not. Culturally, I always keep him in my consciousness, so if I go get a glass of water for myself, I automatically am also going to get him a glass of water . . . even if he doesn't actually want it.

I hold quite a bit of intergenerational trauma around food and hunger, actually, so if you tell me I can't *feed* you, it's like you're telling me I can't *hug* you. As recent as my grandparents' and parents' generations, there were a lot of hunger and poverty issues in my family. This is why we don't usually ask how you are, we ask how you've eaten, because they kind of have the same meaning for us.

Making and sharing food is one of the most fundamental ways of showing love in my culture. One time, we were talking about my partner not wanting us to have an expectation of considering each other when we were making meals. It had triggered me because I felt like, "You don't care if I've eaten," which in my intergenerational trauma body says, "You don't care if I die." I completely admit that was not at all what he was saying—he always cooks for me when I'm at his place. It was a disproportionate reaction, but I understood that it was a layered response. It's not just this lifetime of things happening to me, it's this intergenerational trauma, it's the collective experience. There's a lot that feeds into it.

Living with my partner, who doesn't share my Korean roots, I've realized that we all—all of us in America—don't actually know how to be in community together, how to communicate, how to love each other. My question to you is: How can we have more shared understandings of how to provide care for each other, when we come from a place where we don't even have a shared culture?

←————————————————

Intergenerational trauma is "the cumulative emotional and psychological wounding, across generations, emanating from massive group trauma exposure." An example Sandra shares: "If I wanted to work with Japanese folks who colonized Korea during my grandparents' and great-grandparents' time, I have a visceral reaction against it. I need to do more healing work in order to have space for that."

# John and Lydia

**LAKEVILLE, MINNESOTA**

When I was growing up, I wanted to be a priest.

I love to camp in the wilderness.

I want to be a journalist when I'm older.

I really like being five feet tall.

I never had fettuccine alfredo until I met my wife.

I'm on a speech team.

**John:** Law enforcement is one of those jobs where I could be sitting here having a conversation in a coffee shop, and four minutes later I got a hysterical guy trying to fight people with a gun that I'm talking to. That's the stuff that people don't see. Cops work really, really hard.

**Lydia:** I do worry about my dad being safe. There's been a lot of times when my mom and I are just sitting at dinner and we haven't heard from him and he's not home from work and we can't help but wonder . . .

**John:** Police work is at times also very ugly work. You're applying force, you're doing it in public, and people don't understand. You need to have volumes and volumes and volumes of statutes in your head and ready at a moment's notice.

And, yes, we all have biases. It's not just race, it's culture: what you put on your body, how you color your hair, what you wear, how you act. More than once I've looked at people and gone, "Oh boy . . ." But then you start talking to the person, and then you go, "Wow, you're an impressive person!" But that's not the first impression I had.*

There are very visible, public cases like Philando Castile and Jamar Clark that affect the perception of police. But it's a small fraction of what's happening, and for some reason it gets a bunch of press.

**Lydia:** It's hard because, yes, it can be frustrating that the media doesn't portray the good things that police officers do, but I also think that it should be expected that the media shows the ugly—or else who would? Being a person of color** and being a daughter of a police officer, I can see both sides, and I wish that they could both come together.

* Research finds that police officers, and people more generally, tend to associate African Americans with threat. This is just one example of implicit bias, which refers to "the attitudes or stereotypes that affect our understanding, actions, and decisions in an unconscious manner." Implicit biases are pervasive, generally favor our own in-group, do not necessarily align with our declared beliefs, and can reinforce explicit biases. They are developed from an early age through persistent implicit and explicit messaging—for example, from the media we watch or role models we learn to admire—and they can be gradually unlearned with deliberate effort. Interestingly, the presence of implicit bias when tested will vary with internal stressors like lack of sleep (less sleep equals the appearance of more bias).

** Lydia told us that even though her parents will tell her, "You're beautiful no matter what," others will say, "Oh, you're a different kind of pretty." She said, "I literally had a guy tell me he didn't like me because I was brown." When she's with her parents, people put on the "doing-the-math look," and Lydia will respond, "Biology taught you right, White plus White does not equal brown."

*John:* I've traveled to Haiti, Kenya, Ethiopia, to teach police officers and—coming from a small, White, rural town in Minnesota—that helped me understand race much more. Adopting two Colombian kids and living there for a bit also helped. Lydia and my son, Mitch, grew up in Lakeville, a White suburb, a lot of it is, they're White—

*Lydia:* What, Dad? I'm not!•••

*John:* Okay, not really. It's the heritage that's the most important part. I love to watch Lydia be very proud of her Colombian heritage. I look at my heritage and I go, "I'm a mutt," because there isn't any one heritage that I can celebrate and go, "this is me."

←——————————————————————————————————

••• Lydia told us individually: "I'm a closet leftist. I feel like my parents know; they're just in denial. I'm extremely outspoken about equal rights."

I've realized that we all—all of us in America—don't actually know how to be in community together, how to communicate, how to love each other. My question to you is: How can we have more shared understandings of how to provide care for each other, when we come from a place where we don't even have a shared culture?

# Tyler W.

**LAPWAI, IDAHO**

I listen to a lot of different genres, like Billie Holiday, Louis Armstrong.

I've been to Costa Rica, Paris, and Israel.

I'm in the army and thinking of going to college.

My favorite food is _pho._

*Even though I'm* doing well, I've even applied to be a tribal police officer, I'm afraid for myself. A lot of youth get stuck. On other reservations, I've seen four to ten suicides* a day.

On this reservation, it's hard to break away from certain people. They'll guilt-trip you, like, "Come on, you don't want to drink? You're too cool to smoke weed?" And you know, just alcohol and weed can be a blessing, I guess, because there are also harder drugs out there, like heroin and meth.

The only people I have here are my grandma and my grandpa. I'm the oldest out of my siblings and never had my mom or my father. If my grandparents didn't take me in, we would've been out on the street. Every day I try to help as much as I can—I've heard stories about the elder who lives down the street, how her house is infested with mice, mice droppings on the couch, on the bed, on the tables, everywhere, and her grandchildren don't help out with anything. They just care about the materialistic things. The drugs, the alcohol.

I'd rather talk about the positive things, though. I was always told to not focus on myself, but to think about what's going to be left for these little guys. My sister here, she wants to pick up our traditional healing dance. My brother, this one right here, he's leading youth projects on the reservation. And my other sister, she's in a place where she's getting help. I watch her son, Juan, every so often. Juan is three; his teachers say that he's really excelling, that he's a good role model for his classmates. Together, we celebrate our culture. Thanksgiving's coming up, and while most people say, "Columbus discovered America," we say, "No, we discovered him, floating lost at sea."

What I want other kids to think about is how when we're in the cradleboard, we learn to watch the world, and once we get old enough, *then* we start touching things. We need to observe and learn oral teachings from our grandparents or parents or uncles and aunties about what to touch, and what not to. That's why, with all the alcohol, substances, and abuse**—I strive away from all that, even if it makes me different from my friends or family.

* Native American youth are 3.5 times more likely to die by suicide than any other ethnic group.

** Eight percent of Native American eighth graders report regular use of marijuana, compared with 1.3 percent of other eighth graders. Native youth abuse heroin and prescription drugs two to three times more than the national average. And Native Americans are the most likely ethnic group (16.4 percent) to report drinking before fifteen years old.

# Laureen and Cara

**WASHINGTON, D.C.**

**LAUREEN:** I was called a Halfrican in Kenya because I wasn't Kenyan but I wasn't White. • I am definitely afraid of sharks. • I once saw somebody come back to life. • I am the more OCD one in the relationship.

**CARA:** I'm a writer. • I like gold mannequins. • I really like driving. • I took a train all the way from Arkansas to San Francisco. • I dabble in art.

*Laureen:* I didn't find out I was adopted until I was fifteen. My parents had just gotten divorced, and I was snooping around on my dad's computer. I found a document on there, and after I confronted him, he told me. That's when this story folded out.

My dad, Larry, is White. In 1986, he moved to the Philippines to work on the naval bases there. Many naval men would date the local women from clubs near Subic Bay. He started to date a Filipina woman named Amy, twenty years younger than him.

When they went down to visit her family, he saw a little girl with *kwashiorkor*, or a pot belly. She was the daughter of Amy's sister, Brenda. Larry turned to Brenda and said, "Let me take that little girl with me, and take care of her for you."

At first, Brenda said, "No, that's my baby," and he said all right. But later, as they were leaving, Brenda ran out with her little girl and said okay. Brenda ended up going missing, while Amy and Larry started raising the girl. Her name was Laureen.

I was raised as Lauren. We moved to this tiny town called Zinc, Arkansas, where I didn't see anyone within miles who looked like me. We'd get stuff in the mail with Ku Klux Klan information all the time. It was my dad's country and his culture. It was the very heart of White America. It was devastatingly poor, isolated, and racist.

I was constantly uncomfortable. I got called the n-word. I got called a White n-word. I got called races and ethnicities that weren't Filipino. Part of it was lack of knowledge. Part of it was to be hateful. They would use those words to spit at you.

The only time I was around other people of color was when these older White dudes, who had acquired younger Filipina wives, would come together monthly and play poker. It was very disgusting to be around this sexualization of Asian women.

Amy was unhappy and eventually left. A few years later, my dad got a mail-order bride from China to live with us for a few months. She spoke hardly any English, couldn't drive, and was just subservient. I felt very bad for her. I felt like that relationship wasn't so different from what Amy and Larry had.

Originally, I assumed Cara was straight. She had never identified as straight, but she was very feminine. That's how I understood gender at that time—presenting myself as female meant wearing a cardigan with a flowery top. I had always spoken her sexuality for her.

Cara was one of a few people who knew about my adoption story, and she asked me

if I wanted to be called Laureen. I said, "I don't know. I guess I'm not opposed to it." And so she began calling me Laureen.

In graduate school, we had to write our names down and tell a story about it. I thought, "I don't have any stories." I wrote down Lauren on this paper. Then, I added a small, extra "e" on it. I was very scared to do it, because I had never really delved into that identity. I learned through it that self-reflection is such a key part in the pedagogy of the oppressed, and one of the vehicles that will lead you to liberation. I think we all reclaim culture differently. For me, part of that was reclaiming my name.

I don't remember the last time I talked to my dad. I came out to him by e-mail in 2011. He said he doesn't tolerate that, but I would always be his daughter. Before our wedding, I texted, "You are more than welcome to attend, but I also understand if you don't." I never heard from him. He never said anything about it.

I've been given a lot of shit about being adopted. Many times, he would guilt me by talking about how he saved me. That really fucked me up. My dad has actively participated in seventy-five years of White supremacy and patriarchy—in how he hates people, how he said, "Let me have that, that's mine" in the Philippines, how he treats women, and how he has treated me. A friend told me once, "Your history with your dad is such a direct correlation with the history of the Philippines with the U.S.: the abuse created from being taken over."

He's still out in Arkansas in the middle of nowhere. He is on to his fifth or sixth girlfriend, or something like that. I have tried to still have a relationship, but therapy helped me realize I didn't have to put myself through trauma every time we talk on the phone. That is not worth my joy. I haven't really spoken to Amy in years either. Brenda isn't alive, and I have never met my birth dad.

For me, family has always evolved. My history has definitely left me with a lot of abandonment issues, and I've always seen family in the friends I can build community with. I want my children to know that they may look like either one or neither one of us . . . but at the root, family will always be the people who want to go through everything with you. That, to me, is much stronger than the diaspora* or supremacy or that which divides people, even within blood families.

*Cara:* My predominantly White family is very polite and kind and sweet. They're Southern, and they open the door for people.

They do all the right things, they don't hurt anybody. But they also don't challenge the status quo, and that's the problem.

I have a responsibility to make sure my partner is safe, and to teach those White people in my life that their narrative is damaging. It is not necessarily about acknowledging privilege. That's become such a popular thing to say. Really, you are saying nothing at all. I am well aware of White privilege. *We know.* What are you doing about it? What self-reflection have you actually done?

I try to take the time to recognize that I got to this position in my life in a very different way than my wife did. I have always seen myself as an individual and not as part of the greater White race.** I have never had to justify my existence. I have never had to assimilate to stay alive, emotionally or physically. I did not have to work as hard. I admire Laureen's journey in identity, and I think that if that journey were given to a White person, they would have crumbled. I am pushing my White peers and family members to see that.

---

* The term *diaspora,* originally referring specifically to the Jewish diaspora, has since radically shifted in meaning and now often (rightly or wrongly) refers to any group or population living away from their homeland, regardless of whether they have been forced to move. In one article on the "diaspora" of the term *diaspora,* the author "proposes to treat diaspora not as a bounded entity but as an idiom, stance and claim."

** Cara called this the "core of Whiteness." Unlike most people of color, who describe an "aha" moment of realizing they are, for example, Black or Asian or Hispanic, many White people can go their whole lives not truly recognizing that they are White. They have the luxury of living as an individual.

# CHAPTER FIVE

# THE WORDS WE USE MATTER

*I*t's 1938, and 70 million people are tuned into the match. Joe Louis's muscles ripple as his fist makes impact with Max Schmeling's body. *Boom*. You catch the glisten of his boxing glove before it strikes Schmeling's face again. *Boom*. "Louis measures him—right to the body! A left to the jaw," the commentator says, his pitch high, his words spitting out as fast as the punches. "Aaaand Schmeling is down! Five, six, seven, eight . . . The fight is over!"

Adjacent to Detroit's Hart Plaza, we were looking at an 8,000-pound, 24-foot-long monument of Joe Louis's fist. It was the meeting point for our tour.

"This," our tour guide, Kathy, shouted, gesturing behind her at *The Fist*, "was built in Venice, California. The monument's known as *The Fist*, and it belongs to our very own boxer, Joe Louis. It symbolizes to many people how Detroit is the *Comeback City*. You see, this city's getting much safer and cleaner than it ever was before. Our city's spirit is *strong,* just like Mr. Louis here!"

Priya raised her hand, squinting from the sun. "Why *Comeback* City?"

"Well"—Kathy's face scrunched up from distaste—"the city used to be very, very dangerous and—"

"Oh, well, after all, it was majority *Black,* right?" a visor-wearing tourist in the group said matter-of-factly.

Our eyes widened.

The group was silent.

"No, no, not like *that*," the tourist, Susan, stammered. She nervously adjusted her visor. "I'm *color-blind,* for Christ's sake!"

It was important to us to explain to Susan that being *color-blind* was nothing to be proud of—after all, if you can't see race, you can't see racism either. Instead, we cited Mellody Hobson, and suggested she become *color-brave.* Or, as critical race theory calls for, we recommended "race-conscious" decision making. As we spoke, her eyes wandered and her body language seemed to say, *"Oh, boo hoo, stop being so picky about words!"*

Later in the tour, while crossing the street, Winona ran up to Kathy, notebook and pen in hand. "Hey, Kathy, I have a question about gentrification in the city . . ."

"Huh? Gentri-what? What is that?"

We were appalled. We explained what gentrification was and how it impacts communities of color.

After the tour, we interviewed a student named Kasim at Wayne State University, who again showcased our point: "People here always say, 'Comeback City this and Comeback City that.' It just feels like a punch in the gut because it's code for gentrification. I was kicked out of my home. They upped the rent ridiculously on my family, like by four times the original rent, and I was homeless for a little bit. It's clear that all the Black people are getting kicked out, and all the White millennials are moving in. The city's getting safer, yes, but at what cost?"

The ignorance around "color-blind" and "gentrification" in Detroit was not an anomaly, and we quickly became exhausted. We didn't have the bandwidth, authority, or proper education ourselves to share with *everyone* what to never say, or what terms to know. Across the nation, we felt a gap between those with the "right" language to talk about race, and those without. We wondered how much this gap got in the way of productive conversations about race.

The point of this chapter is not to provide you with a list of the "right" and "wrong" words, but to simply bring your consciousness *into* your words. The words we use matter. Words can show malice or ignorance. Words can make manifest dangerous ideologies and actions. Words—*your* words—hold tremendous power.

Traveling throughout the country, we noticed that because of generational differences and socioeconomic factors, the meaning of words is often contextual. At least five times, we were called "Oriental" by elderly folks. The term was once more commonly used, but now simply made us feel "exotic"—another Othering word we heard often. Another example: Martin Luther King, Jr., had said that he wanted a "color-blind society," but since then the phrase has transformed into a misleading veil, shielding people who want to avoid talking about race altogether. So, to many people today, saying that you're color-blind, or that we live in a "post-racial" society, is like declaring, "Hey! I don't care about racism!"

Nevertheless, in Arkansas, we met an African-American civil rights activist who told us, "I just wish the world was a bit more color-blind, you know?" He was not actively racist, he just didn't have the same contextual vocabulary that we learned for talking about race. What we consider to be the "right" words is always evolving.

Whom we had less and less patience for, however, were the people who misused words, not because of socioeconomic or generational differences, but because they didn't *care*. Susan, the visor-wearing tourist, didn't believe that her words had impact, and ignored the complaints of people on the receiving end of them. "People are too sensitive," she had said, rolling her eyes.

Don't be that person. Recognize that the words you use matter. If a doctor walked up to a patient with a tumor and called it a bruise, wouldn't that drastically change the patient's treatment and likelihood of survival? Similarly, you must understand the weight of your words when diagnosing the racism in our nation. Ask yourself, "What's the history behind this phrase? Why do different words have different impact depending on the race of the person saying them? How might this word minimize or invalidate another's experience?"

Later, we realized that Kathy was silent about *The Fist*'s more—as she said— "controversial meanings." We learned that in the 1938 Louis versus Schmeling boxing match, Schmeling was supported by the Nazi regime. He was Hitler's poster boy, a glowing example of Hitler's theory of Aryan physical supremacy. And who was Louis? A Black man representing America. His right-hand knockout makes Schmeling, and the racism he represented, land with a *thud* on the ring floor.

To several of the Detroit locals we interviewed, Louis's monument doesn't symbolize the "Comeback City," which has become code for the rampant gentrification and displacement of Black families. Instead, Louis's 8,000-pound, 24-foot-long bronze fist also symbolizes a "tireless fight for justice." Furthermore, *The Fist* speaks to Detroit's rich, flawed, and resilient racial history—how Michigan Avenue is built upon the Indigenous people's Great Sauk Trail, how Martin Luther King, Jr.'s "I Have a Dream" speech boomed through this city first, how Detroit was a major hub for the Underground Railroad.

Standing in *The Fist*'s shadow, amid many ignorant remarks, we were reminded of something: intent should match impact. After all, whether you mean to or not, the words you use, and your silence, can both pack a mighty mean punch.

# Mahala

**RAPID CITY, SOUTH DAKOTA**

*I cannot cook at all but I love to eat.*

I have three kids, two stepsons and one biological son: Dylan, Garrett, and Jibri.

I love poetry.

Our oldest son is married to Swati, who is Newar from Nepal, and so we've been there twice.

*My mom is* mostly Irish, Scottish, English, and German, and my dad is African American. My grandparents didn't speak to my mom for a couple years when she married my father. But when I was born, and I came out extremely light with freckles and a red afro, then they decided they would have contact with us again because I didn't have dark skin. I've experienced a lot of struggle and loss, but I also feel extremely blessed to have the life that I have. I love being biracial, love having a mom who is an out lesbian. To grow up with those intersectional identities has made me compassionate and loving and a seeker of justice. I'm glad that there's starting to be more and more and more of us.

The first time I knew that I was different was when I was in fourth grade, and I was dating this boy. I was so excited, my first boyfriend, and I went up to him one day at lunch. He was with a bunch of other White boys, and he turned around and looked at me and said, "You cannot sit by me." I said, "What?" And he said, "You didn't tell me you were Black, and I don't date dirty Black girls."

When I have my hair in cornrows, White people will always come up to me and rub my hair and say, "I wanna do that too! Where can I do that?" Because they think I'm White. For a long time, I would explain that, no, I'm half-Black, this is what my hair can do, but now I refuse.

Recently, a woman came up to me and grabbed my hair and said, "Is this real?" I looked at her, and she had really big breasts, and I said, "Oh my God, are your breasts real?" She was horrified, but I think I got my point across. White people say really awful and horrendous things to me, thinking I'm White too, and I always have to speak up. It hurts, and I end up saying awful things like, "Are your boobs real?" as a response.

My son is African American and much darker than I am. In my case, I would either get yelled at in the Black community for trying to be too Black, because I'm so White, or for denying that I'm Black and saying that I was trying to pass for White. In fact, I don't call myself a Black woman. I call myself a biracial person, because my lived experience is different from people who are darker than me, and out of respect for that and honor for that, I don't feel like I can claim the identity of a Black woman. But my son, his experience is completely different. He is a Black male whether he likes it or not.

The first time my son was called a nigger was in preschool. I got called down because the teacher said he put his hands around a little girl's neck. When I talked with my son about it, he said the girl told him he couldn't play with her because he was a nigger. He didn't know what that meant, but he knew he couldn't play, so he got really upset.

When he was in elementary school, he was told by a kid that he was really lucky that he could roll around in the dirt and nobody could tell if he was clean or dirty. When he was sixteen, I stopped at a gas station, gave him my credit card, and asked him to go in and grab something because I wasn't feeling well. My son was wearing a dress shirt and bow tie, because he is very, very stylish, and when he goes in to pay, the White person at the counter looks at him and says, "If that credit card is stolen, we have your license plate on camera, and you'll be arrested." It doesn't matter if he wears a hoodie or a dress shirt, he's still considered a thief.

My son used to work at a shoe store in the mall, and there was a Lakota kid who came in and stole some shoes. My son's White boss said, "I get so frustrated with these prairie niggers" to my son. My son, who had been called nigger several times by then, was like, "Wow, to insult a Native person, they have to compare them to a Black person."

Mahala added that her relationship with local Native Americans in South Dakota "is complicated." She said, "There's friction here between Black people and Native people because Black Buffalo Soldiers were brought here in the 1860s to annihilate the Native population. Sometimes, I feel like we're being pitted against each other and the real problem is being ignored."

# Hunter

**OXFORD, MISSISSIPPI**

I love the University of Alabama.

I've made a couple of documentaries.

I'm from good ol' Tennessee.

Each of my grandparents have around ten siblings.

*My grandpa once* held a KKK meeting. He worked at a convenience store in town, and I remember he thought an African-American male in town was causing some trouble at the store. So, he invited some KKK members to his house to discuss. My mom told me she *literally* saw men in hoods come out of the woods.

From an early age, I was really conscious of how my parents and family members in general would talk about people who were not White. The n-word was used a lot—even with casual things like watching a football game. In high school, race really wasn't talked about that much outside of U.S. history and slavery. Even then, slavery was taught like most Southern schools teaching about the Civil War—as if it wasn't about slavery or human rights or all of those things. They would make exceptions and excuses.

I would hear these negative words used *about* African Americans, but there weren't many African Americans around. In college, I started working in a nearby lower-income elementary school, and that was one of the first experiences I had working with people of color. I got really interested in race and educational opportunity, because I realized that the schools that I went to . . . well, I realized that schools in general were shaped by a community's problems—you know, the problems within a community affect its schools. I realized that the schools I went to benefited from

the wealth that was moving into the area, but these schools filled with children of color were being abandoned. I taught in the east central part of Mississippi, and I noticed certain towns I taught at, West Point and Macon and Starkville, were all, like, 60 percent African American and 40 percent White. But the schools were like 82 percent black. A lot of the White families send their kids to the private schools—and go to great lengths to do that—just to stay out of the public schools.

I went into it trying to be very humble. I didn't go in there thinking I knew the answers, I tried to just listen and observe, you know? I just felt really grateful to be involved in the community, to have the opportunity to teach. Education for me has been something that I've formed my identity through. I was the first person in my family to graduate from a major four-

---

"Segregation academies" began popping up following the *Brown v. Board of Education* decision in 1954. White parents founded these Southern private schools after the Supreme Court ruled that segregated public schools were unconstitutional, just so that their White kids wouldn't have to attend public schools with Black kids. In 1976, the court ruled these private schools unconstitutional. They have been called "freedom of choice" schools, and the "school choice" debate continues.

year institution, and I'm the first person to get a master's degree. So, the difference between me and, say, my grandfather is something I think about a lot.

I tell my story, but I often think about how important it is to give voice to people who may not have the advantages of telling their story like I do. In a discussion, I wouldn't want to be the first person to talk, even if I could say the same thing, and even though unfortunately I would be more readily listened to than a person of color. Sometimes for a White person, the best words to use are not any at all, *at first*. On the other hand, in social movements, White people need to speak up and be invested. In the movement against the Vietnam War, a *lot* of White people spoke up, because it involved them. Imagine if they were as equally invested in the Black Lives Matter movement, or educational equity. That would have a huge impact.

# Treniya

ATLANTA, GEORGIA

My favorite food are potatoes in any form.

I know every dance routine to every Beyoncé song.

Sometimes, I like animals more than humans.

I want to be Michelle Obama 2.0.

*I am an* African-American woman, and I love it, I love it, I love it. I wouldn't want to be any other race. When I was younger, I might've been like, "Oh my God, I'm a Black girl, I have dark skin, my hair is curly and it's nappy, and all these pretty White girls, oh my goodness," but now I'm older and just like, "You know, I'm bomb." I couldn't imagine being any other color. I love being Black. I just love everything—culture-wise, how we walk, talk, dress, joke—I just love it. I'm so proud. It's a good feeling, to know that my ancestors, my grandpa and my grandma fought for us. But sometimes we take it for granted today. We use the n-word so loosely, and they fought for it to stop. Black men today talk bad about Black women. Back then, Black men were fighting for Black women, and now they are fighting Black women. Rappers, in music, it's just disgusting the way they talk about women. There's this rapper named Kodak Black, who made a line like, "Where them yellow bones, I don't want no Black bitch."

My godmother told me to address myself as T. Bronaugh,* not Niya or Treniya. I had to make a whole new e-mail. She's a Black woman doing very well in D.C., and she

———————————————————————→

* In a 2017 study, researchers found that "White applicants receive 36 percent more callbacks than equally qualified African Americans" while "[W]hite applicants receive on average 24 percent more callbacks than Latinos."

knew that there would be stereotypes. When my sisters were naming their babies, the first thing in consideration was, "Can they get a job with this name?"

My sister was going through Facebook, and typed in my last name. All these people came up, these Black people, and we were like, "Cool! Cousins, cousins, cousins." But there was also this White guy with our last name. My sister messaged him asking, "Are you our cousin?" I was thinking, "No, that's impossible." He was like, "I don't want you to get offended, but my great-grandfather down the line owned slaves." He looked through his family history archives, and found out his great-grandfather owned a slave name that was our great-great-great-great-grandmother—Mary, or something. So, our last name was actually *his*.

I don't want this White man's last name! A lot of African Americans have a lot of White, Westernized, British, English last names. But Africans, Haitians, Jamaicans—they come to America and you can tell because they have ethnic last names. I listen to people who know where they're from, know how people from their culture act, and I feel pain. I'll never get to know that because that was robbed from me when my ancestors were stolen and brought here to America. All these Black people know they're Jamaican, Trinidadian, Nigerian, but when people ask me where I'm from, I'm like, "I'm from Pittsburgh." It sucks, kinda.

I'm not just a granddaughter of a slave, I

refuse to be like that, to carry that with me. A lot of people carry that with them, but you gotta think past that. We come from something, we were something before we became slaves. I tell myself I come from a queen from a tribe somewhere. Before, when I thought of Africa, I thought of what they taught in school. You think of the skinny, skinny Black children crying and hungry.** That's what I thought, but actually Africa is one of the richest continents resource-wise. It's just gorgeous, the tribes, it's just beautiful. I'm in the process of learning more, but Africa isn't just starving, and struggling, and needing. I'm more than that.

---

** Treniya added, "What bothers me is that classic image of the White savior, like a White girl taking a 'volunteer trip' during the summer, and who helps those 'hungry Black kids' without ever realizing her ancestors *made* those kids hungry and rampaged that country and sold their ancestors into slavery."

# Jasmine and Karli

BALTIMORE, MARYLAND

My grandfather, father, and cousin are all named Tony.

I am an artist.

I do this thing called "sun sneezing." When I walk into bright light, it makes me sneeze.

I have been to El Salvador to see a volcano.

I am vegetarian.

I am diabetic.

I like to use watercolors.

*Jasmine:* People perceive me as a "light-skinned Black girl." For a long time, I thought I was "Native American," so when people categorized me as a light-skinned Black person, I felt offended. It was like they weren't addressing all of me.

Later, I found out that I am actually *not* Native American. On my grandfather's birth certificate, it says that he's Native American, but he took a DNA test, and he's actually 0.2 percent Native American. Turns out, a distant relative of ours was wanted by the police, so he forged his birth certificate to say that he's Native—that way he could hide on reservations from law enforcement.*

So, yeah, I am *not* Native American at all—that still feels weird to say. It was really hard to take in because I had tried so hard as a child and as a teenager to figure out how to be more connected to the Native American side of me. I had bulldozed past all the Whitewashing of Native history and clung to that part of my heritage, so it became a core part of my identity. I had immersed myself in my Native culture—or what I *thought* was my culture—and I was just starting to feel proud. Then, all of a sudden, I woke up one day and was told that what I thought I was my whole life is a lie. Like, guess what, Jasmine, you're just Black.

It really showed me that race is a concept that's completely in our heads. It doesn't exist. Sometimes I feel like, because I am so connected to Native culture, does that make me Native still? Regardless of my DNA? I don't think so. Because what I once imagined as a beautiful, strong Native American ancestor was, in reality, a White guy who was this con artist. So, I don't know, I really don't know . . .

*Karli:* Growing up, my grandad always said that *his* grandad was a "wild man," so everyone assumed that he was Native American. They'd joke, "Oh, Karli, put Native American on your college applications. You have that 0.1 percent Navajo that everyone wants." It made me feel like White people in America see these different backgrounds, we see that people have heritages, and really cool cultures, and we feel like we're missing out.

I did not end up putting Native American on college applications. That suggestion annoyed me so much. It annoyed me because it goes back to the idea of affirmative action,** and that I don't

---

* In 1978, the Supreme Court case *Oliphant v. Suquamish* stripped tribes of the right to arrest and prosecute non-Indians who commit crimes on Indian land.

** Affirmative action is "designed to address the historical inequities that have devastated communities for generations." As of 2018, White students are four times more likely than Black students to be enrolled in top-scoring schools.

need or deserve affirmative action. I mean, at school, *I* don't count as representation of Indigenous people. I would be taking that spot away from someone else. I know for a lot of White people the idea of affirmative action is like something being taken away from *us*, but it's not.

Not long ago, Jasmine and I were both trying to get this scholarship for an Outward Bound trip. Only one person from our school could get it, but we were fine with that. I went in for the interview, my mom took me, and apparently while I was in the interview, they were talking to her and the other parents about how they really want to encourage more minorities into the program. That's something I agree with, because I feel like outdoorsy things are very stereotypically White, and non-White people should join as many traditionally White spaces as they possibly can. In the end, Jasmine got it. I didn't. My mom said things like, "Don't worry, Karli, it was just because she's Black, it's just because she's mixed." I hated hearing that because this is my best friend, and I know my mom loves Jasmine as well, but hearing all these excuses made me feel so uncomfortable. To me, the excuses are really just a way for White people to make themselves feel better, to have someone else to blame if they don't get something. I mean, I already have access to things like hiking, so it makes sense to me that, because Jasmine doesn't, she gets offered that opportunity.

*Growing up with* Black parents in Detroit, race was as innate as breathing, but gender was more intellectual. I lived with a lot of male cousins. They played sports, and I played sports. They treated us all the same. So, my gender came to my consciousness later on, when I began recognizing how people saw me as I grew, and how that didn't feel congruent with how I felt.

It started out as sexuality. I knew that everybody said that I'm a girl, so I must be a girl. Therefore, I came out as lesbian. But I also knew it was something else that I didn't want to share. I went all through high school without dating anybody, and people didn't question me. My gender would come up often—like people would ask why I'm dressing neutrally or like a boy—but I just lumped it, like many people do, into my sexuality.*

I'm aware that my gender is still not easily recognizable, and calling someone who looks like me "ma'am" is perfectly fine. I chose not to take the physical course of

action to modify my body, because I am a singer. When you take the sex hormones, your voice is irreparable, and I love my voice. So I just modify my appearance to reflect "being male."

Still, I have to be careful about how I respond. Getting "she-bombed"** all the time feels like a racial microaggression, and I have to get affirmation all the time. I understand why people get gender reassigned, because they want the way they feel and the way they look to match.

I have friends who are like, "call me *they*." It was annoying because I had to change the sentence structure in my head *before* I said the sentence. Now, I'm feeling like "they" is pretty dope. "They" has always been around, even when I was not cognizant of the gender piece and it was just the sexuality piece. I was like, "Oh

---

** *Getting she-bombed* means when people use the wrong gender pronouns, such as "she/her/hers" for AJ. To avoid this, ask people what their preferred pronouns are. Self-identifying males typically take the pronouns "he/him/his," and self-identifying females take "she/her/hers." Gender-neutral or genderqueer pronouns are "they/them/their." Some may take any and all pronouns, or ones unmentioned here. Genderqueer "people see gender not as binary with men or women, but as a spectrum that ranges from masculinity to femininity."

---

* Gender identity is an internal knowledge of being male, female, or another gender, while sexual orientation is determined by the gender you are attracted to, regardless of whether or not you are transgender. A transgender woman was labeled as a male at birth; if she is exclusively attracted to women, she is a lesbian transgender woman.

yeah, I'm dating someone. They are so cool," when I didn't want to come out to somebody. For people who are trans, it is not always this or that, male or female. It's this other thing. I like that "they" managed to incorporate that duality.

You can't control what people think. You can't control how they see the world. You can't control whether they see you as you want to be seen, but you are who you are. The biggest thing that I would say is, trust yourself. Trust who you are and always remember it. I still protect those pure aspects of that little boy growing up before he was told to be a girl.

# Amanda

NEW YORK CITY, NEW YORK

My favorite part of the brain is the hippocampus because of how the neurons look in the inside.

I've torn my ACL twice— skiing and then dancing.

I repeat a Thai phrase in my head to calm me down on plane rides: Namo tasa ba ga wah toh ah ra ha toh sam ma sam put ta sa.

*When I was* thirteen or fourteen, I was walking in the mall and a White man walked by me and grabbed my ass. It was the first time I thought about the fetishization of Asian women.* It was just painful. From a sexual perspective, you're submissive, but in the workforce you're the threatening kind of smart—but not smart enough to lead** because, hey, aren't you an immigrant? Do you even speak English? Asian women are often viewed with these paradoxical lenses. You're submissive but also intellectually intimidating. It's a stereotype that I benefit from and suffer

from, it's a double-edged sword. For example, my Black friends in tech don't have the same privilege of walking into a room and not having to prove themselves because people already assume they're competent.

I was raised Thai and Indonesian. I always found these cultures so beautiful and colorful. Growing up, I learned Thai dance, I learned Indonesian dance. My parents don't speak each other's languages. My mom speaks Chinese and Indonesian and my dad speaks Thai, so they only speak to each other in English. I'm recently connecting more with my Chinese side.

I get the "where are you from"*** question a bunch. It happens in the most random of places, in an elevator, in a subway car. Like a constant reminder, "You don't belong here! You don't belong here!" On one hand, it might be a curiosity, which, yay, people should be curious, but it's especially upsetting when, right off the bat, you're asked it, and people already have an assumption in their head. I always wonder, why do I owe this information to you? I'm more than happy to talk about where I'm

---

* Asians as a group are perceived as more feminine than Whites. Historically, Asian men, particularly Chinese Americans, were seen as "threatening" and competed with groups like Irish Americans for jobs. Around World War I, when women also started taking factory jobs, Chinese men, discriminated against elsewhere, were left with the "feminine" work like running laundromats. Black people, on the other hand, are often equated with masculinity. One historical reason: slave labor included "masculine" roles, like agriculture.

** Bamboo Ceiling: In a 2015 study on five big tech firms in Silicon Valley, Asian Americans were 27 percent of the workforce, but held only 19 percent of management and 14 percent of executive positions. Meanwhile, Whites represented "62% of professionals and 80% of executives in these firms."

*** Some of our ideas on other phrasings to consider instead of "Where are you from?": "What is your cultural background? Where is home for you? What is your family like? How does your race or culture impact you? What are some important parts of your identity?"

from and my culture , I love that, but it's just rude for people to ask about it *straight away.*

My last name is seventeen letters long. I actually appreciate any *genuine* questions because it's an opportunity for me to share a little bit about Thai culture. What I really find annoying and offensive is when people don't try. For example, I was at a prestigious science event a couple of months ago, and they were reading people's names on stage. When they got to mine, they said Amanda "Ping-blah-blah-blah." You should never do that. You should never laugh or erase my name like that. You should ask how to say it, make it clear that, hey, I might mess this up, but I'm going to try. I make a point to ask how to pronounce people's names. It shows that I care.

Since I was very, very little, since the minute I learned how to spell my last name, I was always very proud of it. But I realized other people are sometimes embarrassed for me. Even from an institutional standpoint, it doesn't fit in the Scantron form. You're getting all the messages from *the government,* that it's too long, that it's not right.

# Aleksa and John M.

**GREENVILLE, SOUTH CAROLINA**

My favorite color is pink.

I'm Peruvian.

I'm the son of two immigrants.

I play the piano.

If I had to go to one country, I'd go to Italy.

I'm a violin performance studies major.

My favorite snack is Lay's Classic Potato Chips.

**John:** Most people know me as "the Peruvian guy." It's given me an identity, and a chance to embrace my culture. It feels specific, like I'm Peruvian, not just some Hispanic guy.* Maybe 10 percent of my school is Hispanic—but not many people are Peruvian.

**Aleksa:** Growing up, race was important, but it's hit me more now, in sixth grade, because now there are groups. In our school, you have the African Americans, you have the White people, then you have the Hispanics. In elementary school, you looked at everybody the same. But now, people are like, "Okay, you're Hispanic, you need to hang out with the Hispanics."

I'm not exactly sure why the change happened, but maybe it relates to the media. In class, you're forced to watch the news, and we learn that Hispanics are "illegal" bad people** who bring drugs over here. Everybody has to give their opinion of what's going on, and a lot of people can be really rude. Somebody once was like, "It's good that they're building the wall," and the teacher was just quiet about it. I felt like he should have said something to defend the Hispanic people in the room, but he said in the beginning of the year that he's not allowed to state his opinion.***

**John:** Our parents are immigrants, though, and when they came here in the nineties, they didn't bring any drugs or anything like that. Most of the people who come are nice people, just trying to make a new life for themselves and get away from

---

* Race and ethnicity are different. Think of race as a homogenizing social category that takes many vastly different ethnicities—Peruvian, Chilean, Spanish, Mexican, etc.—and turns them all into "Hispanic."

** "Illegal immigrant" or "illegal aliens" are loaded terms that have been called out for their dehumanizing and marginalizing connotations toward people living in the United States without documentation. One way to think about it, from a 2012 article in *Time*: "In what other contexts do we call someone illegal? If someone is driving a car at 14, we say 'underage driver,' not 'illegal driver.' If someone is driving under the influence, we call them a 'drunk driver,' not an 'illegal driver.' Put another way: How would you feel if you—or your family members or friends—were referred to as illegal?"

*** This is a murky area. Teachers are held accountable to the institutions they are part of, and so the First Amendment right to freedom of speech does not necessarily protect them in the classroom. However, our high school teacher explained it to us this way: "There is a difference between free speech and hate speech. And between truth and lies. When something is hate speech, or a lie, or an incomplete understanding of the truth, it cannot be tolerated and I will speak out."

whatever problems they had in their home country. It doesn't seem to matter, because people will still not treat us well.

Once, I went to get my driving permit in a rich and White part of Greenville. I brought two of the three necessary documents, but I had forgotten the Social Security papers or birth certificate or something like that, so they didn't let me take the test. But as we were leaving, I watched this White girl, who just had her school ID, being allowed to take the test.

Another time, at my high school, the day after the 2016 presidential election, there were rows of pickup trucks at the end of the parking lot, all with Confederate flags on them. My friend, who's African American, and I were walking in the parking lot to my car, and one of the pickup trucks swerved right in front of us, purposefully. We moved quickly to the left, and he drove around us, over the curb, and got back on the road. Then, we heard him say, "Damn, they didn't get hit." And then he drove off.

**Lita**

**MILWAUKEE, WISCONSIN**

My favorite food is tacos.

I'm a business marketing major.

My Starbucks order is an iced latte with almond milk.

I'm from Minneapolis, Minnesota.

*Things here are* definitely brushed off quickly. My friend is from Pakistan, and it's an inside joke to call him a "towel head" and to wish him "Happy 9/11." It's all brushed off as funny. The attitude here is that racist things are jokes, and it's almost crazy to be offended by something like that.

A lot of people that aren't Black use the n-word, and people get super confused if I say, "Hey, you can't say that, you're White." Those same people think racism doesn't exist. I've sat in a room where everyone was White except for that Pakistani kid, and they discussed whether it was okay for them to say the n-word—their conclusion was that it's fine, because they've said it around their Black friends and their Black friends haven't been mad. Black girls at my school have told me that they hate going to college here because they feel like they can't get into parties. And it's true, there are legit "no Black girl" parties.

Once, we were going into a bar, and this Black guy comes in wearing a sweat suit, jogger outfit. They didn't let him in because it was seen as too casual—but girls with leggings would have been let in. A lot of establishments will say "no street clothes,"

which I feel like is code for keeping people they consider "ghetto" or "not White" out.

Currently, I'm dating a Sikh, Indian-American male named Jay. Before dating him, I was unaware about so many things in his culture—like arranged marriages. I could never meet his parents because it's against their religion to date, and that's not even talking about the fact that I'm White.

I noticed Jay will be excited even if a White person is nice to him, and it's crazy that that's so ingrained in his brain. We were at the beach with his Indian-American friends, and they ended up playing volleyball with this White group. After they shook hands and the White people left, they were like "*Wow*, the White people talked to us!" Maybe it's because more often White people will ignore them, or be afraid of them, or be distant because of their accents.

I would say that if you see racism, you have the right to speak up. It's hard sometimes if there's a Black person in the room, and they don't say anything, but do it regardless . . . if you think something is wrong, explain why it's wrong because sometimes people don't know.

---

Who can use the n-word? Ta-Nehisi Coates says, "The rules of its use are clear: Black people can use it, having reclaimed it and given it new meaning. White people cannot. It's simply impossible to separate from its history as a disgusting racial slur and a vestige of centuries of enslavement and mistreatment."

# Brontë

I stayed on the DeLand Chick-fil-A property for twenty-four hours during its grand opening and won free Chick-fil-A for a year.

I have citizenship in the United States and Antigua and Barbuda.

All of my pets have been named after food; I have a tiny turtle named Hamburger, and a larger one named Turtle-ini.

*You never realize* how brown you are until you see people on Snapchat taking shots with their grandma at Thanksgiving. Meanwhile, I accidentally said "crap" in front of my mom and was *terrified*. To explain: I'm a first-generation American; both of my parents were born in Antigua, a small island in the Caribbean. And, to be honest, I've always *felt* first-gen American. Like, I never introduce myself as just "American," I feel naked without the "first-gen."

In fourth grade, someone said, "You talk White." I never understood what that meant. I enunciate, I speak correctly, so does that mean I talk White? I remember someone called me an "Oreo,"\* and I also didn't get that one—I was like, "I'm not a cookie, that's stupid."

I guess what adds to people calling me "White," is that I'm a theater major. *Aaaand* my name's Brontë, so I was literally named after a super White author lady (my mom's a huge fan). But I bring my Blackness to theater by doing plays that aren't traditionally done, plays that *require* diverse casts—plays that protest.\*\* In my productions, you sit down and see so many different types of people with so many different body sizes, faces, and colors. So, yes, I might have a "White name," I might "talk White," whatever, but I'm not trying to hide *anything* about who I am, my Blackness or "immigrant-ness."

I remember, when I started private military school in sixth grade, they would always try to drill into my head that *"You need to be super patriotic, kid,"* but I just didn't care that much. Yes, I love the fact that I'm able to live in this country, and have the rights of American citizens, but I don't want to give back to the culture in that way. I don't really care about giving back to the country that hasn't really helped me with my character.

In college, I finally found my people. I'm around people who are different. Those are the people that I've been able to have conversations with about what makes us so different, and how we can use those differences to our collective advantage.

---

\* Since Oreos are two dark chocolate cookies stuck together by a white cream filling, the term has been used since at least the 1960s as a racial slur to label a Black person who might be Black on the outside, but supposedly "acts White" on the inside.

\*\* As of the 2014–2015 season, White actors held 70 percent of Broadway roles in New York City, making them the only Broadway theater professionals who overrepresent their racial population size in the New York City and tristate area.

**FARGO, NORTH DAKOTA**

I like to read and research.

I graduated from Minnesota State University Moorhead in 2008.

I wrote a book called My Journey to America.

I'm running for mayor of Moorhead.

MY JOURNEY TO AMERICA

A KURDISH AMERICAN STORY

NEWZAD BRIFKI

*I'm very honored* to be Kurdish. I'm really committed to my cultural background, but I'm also sad because the Kurds are one of the biggest ethnic groups in the world—estimated around 30 million people—without their own country. It seems like nobody cares if they have a country or not.

I was raised as a Muslim but my religion is God. I left the Kurdistan region of Iraq* in 1988 when I was three, and we went to Mardin, Turkey, to stay in a refugee camp for four years. We were surrounded by Turkish soldiers. There was a lack of hygiene and food, and it was hard to stay warm in the winter because of the snow. I was a child, and I remember one day these teens went out for food or something. They had an argument with a villager, and when Turkish soldiers found out, they chased the kids back to camp. While they ran, the Turkish soldiers shot at them. There was gunfire all over. At that time, I was standing outside my brother's café next to this bearded man. He was squatting, eating seeds. I just saw him drop to the ground with blood everywhere. He was killed right in front of me.

We came to the United States in 1992. My mom was a widow, and our neighborhood was really welcoming. My cousins, aunts, uncle, and sister are still in the Kurdistan region of Iraq. Not Iraq only—you *have* to say "Kurdistan region of" because we don't consider ourselves Iraqi. We just don't have a choice. This language reflects what you think about the whole conflict. People there always have to worry about attacks by ISIS or other terrorist groups, attacks by Iraq, bombs being dropped by Turkey. It's a crazy place to live.

So I'm very happy and honored to be part of this country.** I'm also working to educate the greater community about who the Kurds are. Many of our history books have been written by our oppressors, and our real history has been through music, storytelling, and songs, using instruments like the *saz*. I want people to know Kurds have been a huge part of this country's history too: working on farm fields, boosting the economy, and fighting in our wars.

---

* Kurdistan was divided into four regions after World War I: a region in southeastern Turkey, northwestern Iran, northern Iraq, and northern Syria. Newzad expressed frustration at the violence of Kurdish history, including the secret British–French Sykes-Picot agreement in 1916, which divided Middle Eastern countries under European occupation and "left us out" with no independent Kurdish state (even though the Kurds are their own ethnic group).

** Estimates say approximately 40,000 Kurds live in the United States; the largest Kurdish population is in Nashville, Tennessee.

# CHAPTER SIX

# WE NEED TO STOP FIGHTING AMONG OURSELVES

*W*e were not prepared to interview a dozen full-blooded Keetoowah Cherokees all at once. When we arrived at a dark green building in Tahlequah, Oklahoma, we thought we were about to interview a man named Robert Whitekiller about his last name. Instead, we were met with an entire cafeteria table of eleven or twelve elders from the United Keetoowah Band of Cherokee Indians, waiting expectantly as we trooped in with one dangling clip-on microphone, our camera battery flashing low.

At the time, we were staying in Tulsa with a young White couple named Sam and Haley. Our first evening together, they had bought us two burritos each, and we had munched slowly while Sam recounted his parents' alarming reaction to his transition from female to male. The following two days, we would listen to members of Muslim, African-American, and Latinx (pronounced Lat-EEN-ex) communities continue talking about many other kinds of divisions within their communities—within races, ethnicities, and families. We noted that Tulsa, like everywhere, was already divided *between* races, and we wondered why people so frequently fought *within* races too. Where did these divides come from?

As we hesitantly approached the cafeteria table, Robert patted us on the back and introduced everyone as members of the Elder Council. A man in a bright orange polo waved an arm, proudly declaring, "*Everyone* at this table is a full-blooded Indian."

"What's the significance of being full-blooded?" Priya asked.

"Psh," one elder scoffed. "It's a negative thing, the mixing. Full-blooded people have our pride. We are one people, you know. One hundred percent Keetoowah Cherokee. One blood."

We held our breath. *Was he against interracial marriages?* Haven't people of color fought for centuries for them? Many of the members pulled out their wallets, extracting small, laminated identification cards. We reached out to take the card from one man, but he held on to it tightly and with deliberate care. We leaned in, admiring a colorful, circular symbol in the top-left corner; to the right, TRIBAL ENROLLMENT was highlighted in bright blue, and underneath, BLOOD QUANTUM: *8/8* was printed in black. "This says our blood," another said. "We Keetoowahs have a blood quantum. A quarter. Any less, and you're not Keetoowah."

Robert sighed. "We Keetoowahs were the first Natives here. That's a big deal. Ten years before the Trail of Tears we moved out here—"

"—Yeah, so this land was all Indian land," another elder interrupted. "But now we're a landless tribe; this complex where Keetoowah is, is only seventy-six acres. Meanwhile, there's another larger Cherokee group given more money and power, and *they* don't even look Cherokee, don't talk Cherokee, they White as can be."

The group vigorously nodded and murmured, expressing common outrage with the other Cherokees. Winona, hoping to bring the group back into focus, asked Robert to continue what he was going to say. "Oh yes," Robert said, shaking his head. "Now, each generation gets smaller and smaller. All of our girls and boys marry the Caucasians and people of different tribes. There are very few full-bloods. Even Indians are evolving, and nothing stays the same. I wish it would, but it don't. We're trying to keep our language going so that we can be a tribe."

Soon, others chimed in about the other Cherokees "evolving" too fast, and the room again descended into chaos.

We felt uneasy. Here it was again: the *intra*-racial conflict! When Robert and the Elder Council spoke about "living in the White man's world," we heard almost a resigned apathy; when they spoke about the more powerful Cherokees with less Indian blood, they seemed *furious.*

In Española, New Mexico, we had also talked about blood quantums with a group called Tewa Women United—a multicultural and multiracial Native women's organization formed on a shared language, Tewa. This women's organization focuses on addressing violence against "girls, women, and Mother Earth" through cultural strengths. The director, Corrine (who had also driven us back to Santa Fe that day), did not believe in blood quantums. She told us, "Blood quantums are a big political issue among Native Americans. For example, there are interracial kids who may be the most in-tune spiritually, who are eager to learn, yet they don't get thoughtful attention because of the color of their skin."

She then explained something that's always stuck in our minds. "White supremacy . . . is the foundation of all of this. You see brown people harming brown people, and it doesn't make sense. . . . We're doing it to ourselves, *why?!* We have to understand that hurt people, hurt people. People escaping religious persecution are more likely to implement the same kind of religious violence in their communities. Here, did you know that the government implemented the blood quantums? Now we're implementing them on ourselves, breaking us down by breed, by blood. How do you unlearn this stuff?"

*The government implemented the blood quantums.* We remembered Corrine's words, and an understanding began to click. After all, Robert had told us that the "government of the White man" would be able to *take away* tribal land as the tribe's population decreased. And sure enough, with generations of blood mixing, a large population became "White as can be," unable to enroll in a tribe because they didn't meet the blood quantum. The U.S.

government eventually acquired more and more of their land. *That* was why the Keetoowahs prided themselves on being full-blooded: it preserved their people, their culture, their language, their land.

We're not looking to make a statement on blood quantums—an issue with *much* more complexity—but through many conversations like this one, we came to understand exactly what Corrine had told us: *White supremacy is the foundation of all of this.* The whole issue of blood quantums was widely implemented by the U.S. government in the Indian Reorganization Act of 1934 to limit *Native citizenship.* It widely ignored traditional Indigenous practices, which never defined belonging to a tribe by blood quantum, and it necessitated Natives to adapt to "the White man's world." This White invention continues to divide Natives today.

We're all fighting the same fight—to dismantle White supremacy—and we must recognize that the logic of White empire also takes the form of global colorism, caste systems, and other sites of intraracial conflict, too. Many of these are a part of the trap that Whiteness has created.

# Mareo

**TULSA, OKLAHOMA**

I am compassionate.

I am handsome.

Women are beautiful—but that's not about me.

I knew Terence Crutcher well.

*There is a* lot of division within Afro-American people. In our community, color division between lighter- and darker-skinned Blacks has been taught from the slave plantations. The light-skinned slaves, who could've also been related to the slave master or another White owner, worked in the house and got more leeway. When you hear the term "house nigga," a Black person is seen as more *White*, closer to White privilege. There's a lot of hate and division among the community when it comes to being Black—and it's a cycle we have to break. We have to become whole within our race, if we want to really sit down with any other race.

Willie Lynch[*] is known as the one who wrote the process of how to make a slave. Slave masters lived by his manuscript. His core idea: *keep them divided.* They can't bring power to themselves if they can't come together. Generations and generations pass, and we're still dealing with it.

I broke free from it. As Tulsa's Black Lives Matter president, I need to enlighten others to love each other and not kick each other when down. That's the crawfish (or crabs) in the bucket syndrome: You can put them in a bucket, and when one tries to climb up, they'll all band together and claw him down. If they let him out, he could help the rest come out of the bucket too. We have the same crawfish-in-a-bucket mentality in the Afro-American community here in Tulsa: *We don't want you to make it, because we're not.*

Tulsa wasn't always this way. Greenwood was the Black Wall Street, and there were thirty-five blocks of Black businesses. They were just starting to do business with countries. It would've been like New York; people already came from different countries to shop and eat! I remember the stories my grandmother told me: it had everything, stores, motel, doctor's office, dentist. They owned everything, and it was awesome. We're so far from that now. In 1921, planes dropped bombs on the Black community. *Bombs.* It was a race massacre[**] that still affects us today.

My life kind of took a turn when I came

---

[*] The "Willie Lynch Syndrome" allegedly comes from a British slave owner named William Lynch, who gave a speech in Virginia in 1712 called "The Making of a Slave." Some say that the term "lynching" comes from his last name.

[**] The Tulsa Race Riot of 1921 is an important event in Tulsa history. Black Wall Street, formerly the wealthiest Black neighborhood in the country, was looted and burned by White rioters. Historians believe as many as three hundred people were killed and, according to reports, eight thousand left homeless.

back to Tulsa from Bristow, Oklahoma. I got involved in gangs.

It used to be a saying around here: *You come on vacation, you leave with probation.* Prisons heavily contribute to our state's income.••• Prisons—not cattle, beans, or oil. We're known for that. Being Black can land you in prison. Partial sentences, the same crime that a White guy committed, you get more time for because you're Black.

The criminal justice system•••• is so messed up. Here in Oklahoma, the majority of White people deal with powdered cocaine. And Black people like cocaine in rocks, crack. People would get more time in prison for crack cocaine than powdered cocaine. Police brutality is real: I was called nigger, and slapped, and punched, and all kinds of different stuff by police officers. It's bad. Now that we have cell phones and technology, it's being captured—but it's *always* been going on. Race relations means holding people accountable, no matter what the title.

I was in prison, I was on my way to getting out in three months, and I was in a transition house. Then I was sent back to a minimum yard. When I got there, I was angry and hurt. I would cuss people out, spew hate at everyone. My life became a wreck. A lot of people in gangs are really just stuck, trapped.

I was a trustee, and I went to the death row unit to feed the death row inmates. When I got there, it was so quiet. Real quiet. No talking. That could've been me. I thought it was God. He showed me that so I could see and be grateful. I started going to Bible classes and the chapel almost every day in prison. God changed me from the inside, then changed the way I looked, talked, walked, looked at other people. My bitterness and unforgivingness and hate went away. I haven't drank alcohol or smoked weed or cigarettes in years. I came out a whole different person.

It's been nine years. Every day of the week I'm doing something that has to do with God. I got my degree, and now I'm a reverend, an ordained minister. This is how I've done it. So anyone else can do it too.

I remember my mom would throw up the Black fist to me, have me throw back

---

••• As of May 2018, Oklahoma has voted to increase funding to pay private prisons for housing inmates. Tulsa's newspaper reported in 2014 that private prisons have given, since 2004, more than $400,000 to political candidates.

•••• Nationally, 2.2 million U.S. citizens are locked up in prisons today. That population reflects 25 percent of the world's prison population, while only 5 percent of the world's people live in the United States. Black and Latinx Americans—only around 25 percent of our population—make up 59 percent of our prisons; the odds are 50/50 that young Black males living in urban areas end up in jail.

the Black fist. I learned about Malcolm X through her, and I can see why he wasn't in the textbooks. He was more, "Hey, if you shoot me, I'll shoot you back!" Martin Luther King, Jr., was like, "You slap me, I'll turn the other cheek for you to slap me again. Next, you can hit the back of my head." When I became a reverend, I began to see both Malcolm and Martin. I have each one of them in me. I see the way to effective activism is not to lash out in anger. You sit down, get a real understanding, and try to compromise.

I've been speaking on Afro-Americans and gang rivals coming together. I'm so passionate for Blacks to stop killing each other. Whether it's the Underground Railroad, or Malcolm X, Martin Luther King, Jr., or the Black Panthers, it took people uniting to make change. See, Martin was the leader, but without being united, Martin was just a person. We have to stand as a united front for Black rights, not only Black people, but White people, Asian, Hispanic, Indian people . . . If we all say we want change, it will happen.

# April

**PHILADELPHIA, PENNSYLVANIA**

I love to protest.

I love my art.

I love being around people.

I love to bike—I want to ride my bike down the Schuylkill River Trail.

**Growing up, my** family was extremely racist. We would literally move if people of color moved into our neighborhood; that's how bad my father was. Racial slurs were common language.

My father started to turn on me, too, because I was very feminine and he thought I was gay. My family tried everything they could to fix that—I was taken out of school, away from my seven brothers, and put into an all-boys school—which only made everything worse. Back then there was no such thing as "transgender." I started being treated how my father and brothers were treating people of color. I represented, except for color, everything my family hated.

I found that when I was a White male, I was just respected. I got jobs easily. Whatever I had to say mattered. When I transitioned and became a woman, it just hit me out of the blue that I no longer had this privilege. I felt like a second-class citizen—that's how women are treated* in this country. To me, being trans is actually a step below that. And it's weird now that I've been disabled for three years, all people see is my disability. Nobody sees that I'm transgender anymore. I'm just treated like a disabled White woman.

I did not come out to my family. They came to the hospital after I survived an attempted murder, a trans hate crime,** actually—I was shot twice and stabbed seven times. That's why I'm disabled today. I'll probably die because of it. I was flown to a trauma center over in New Jersey, and none of my family at that point knew I was trans, wearing a dress and all. They found out then and disowned me. Not a single one of my brothers has spoken to me since. Not a word.

My father just passed away this week. One of my nieces told me via Messenger, because none of my family members told me what happened. I was not allowed to visit him or anything. I looked up the obituary, and I was actually in it by my old name, my male name. I called the funeral home, and they changed it, but it created so much havoc. My family actually got the funeral home to reverse it—they were all very staunch conservative Republicans who didn't even know I existed, so when I

---

* The Shriver Report found that if women were paid at the same rate as men, the poverty rate for women would be reduced by half. And in 2012, the U.S. economy would have produced $447.6 billion more in income—2.9 percent of GDP.

** In 2017, the Human Rights Campaign reported at least twenty-eight deaths of transgender people due to fatal violence, the most ever recorded. This violence disproportionately impacts trans women of color.

changed my name in that obituary, people were all, "Who's April?"

I just wish that my family would accept me, as I am.

My son Tommy accepted me. Tommy and I were really close. He would come visit me and bring his friends. When he died in August 2014, I wasn't told. My family held a funeral, cremated him, and I found out after. I heard a lot of his friends were asking, "Where's April? Tommy would have wanted April here." All of this solely because I'm transgender, and nobody wanted me around. That was really, really rough for a long time. It was a punishment thing, I guess. It's taken me four years to find out where his ashes were and where he was buried. I just found this out. Being disabled makes it hard to get places, but I'll get over there.

Because of my disability, I learned that disabled people are treated terribly.••• It feels like if this administration had their way, they would take away our independence and they would put us all in nursing homes. I was in a nursing home for nine months and let me tell you what, that was a disgusting, horrible, cruel, decivilized place, and you're stuck there!

I was really, really invested in the trans community while I was able-bodied—on the board of directors of organizations and all that. When I became disabled, in the beginning a lot of friends came to see me. Then, after a couple of months, people began pulling back. They had trans events at different locations where I couldn't get in because of my disability. I'm the only disabled trans woman around here, and it became a huge education how different it was. So, I'm not involved now at all in the trans community. I think it's because I represent what could happen to them, a reminder in a way.

I believe everybody should be able to speak out, no matter who you are. People of color are often saying that if you're White— you don't get it, be quiet, you just listen. My

••• Some statistics to consider: Persons with disabilities experience an increased risk of becoming victims of violent crime, and women with disabilities specifically experience a high rate of sexual assault and domestic violence. For instance, studies show that women who experience forms of developmental disabilities are four to ten times more likely to experience a sexual assault than other American women.

Seventy percent of unemployed Americans with disabilities cite workplace discrimination and a lack of adequate transportation as major factors preventing them from working; 12.5 percent of persons with disabilities in America have a bachelor's degree (the national average is 30.3 percent), and a study in California found that 22 percent have experienced difficulty accessing health care facilities.

friends will basically tell me to just shut up. How am I supposed to take that? You're telling me to not have a right to say anything about what I have been through because I am White. I understand you want to be heard, but I have experiences too, you're excluding others' voices. This keeps polarizing everyone else against each other.

# Danelle

**SANDERS, ARIZONA**

I really love cows.

I enjoy watching sunsets.

I did discus in high school when I was on the track team.

My favorite food is mac and cheese.

*I'm a multiracial* person within my tribe, the Diné people. When I was growing up, many people would try to delegitimize who I was. I'm African American and Native American, but for a long time I didn't even know that I was African American. I also recently learned that I am Mexican. But, in my eyes, I was just Navajo. I felt it was the one thing I knew for sure. But it was hard to say so, even though I lived on the reservation my whole life, because people would say, "You don't *look* like a Navajo."

I was raised by my biological aunt and uncle on the Navajo Nation in Arizona near the New Mexico state line. People from the reservation assumed because of my hair and skin color that I must be some amount of Black. Some of my family and classmates would ask to compare our skin tones and then say, "Whoa, you're darker than me," as though it were a bad thing. Microaggressions like those would get to me. By asking all these pointed questions, they made me feel like I wasn't one whole race. Like if I was only half of something, then it just wasn't good enough. I felt like I didn't have a place where I fit. I felt ostracized and different from everyone else.

This past spring, I contacted my biological mom and said, "Yo, you need to tell me about my biological father." She wouldn't tell me anything before. That day, she finally told me that my dad was African American, and also part Mexican. It confirmed, for me, my multiracial identity, and the speculations I've had my whole life. Now that I am in college, I get to talk more about race and the struggles I had with it growing up.

There were some classmates I grew up with who were only part Navajo too—but they didn't visibly look different. Now, it's comforting to hear other people say, "I've been through the same thing." It's made me realize that just because you look different, doesn't mean it's a bad thing. The melanin in your body is just as beautiful as the curls in your hair. I've come to realize that being Black is a beautiful thing. Speaking Navajo, and understanding it, makes me proud. It was hard to get to this point because people were always telling me different things. You just have to look in the mirror and be like, "You're beautiful, you're wonderful, you have a purpose in this world."

---

Samuel in New Jersey told us, "People usually identify me by my Taiwanese side, ignoring that I'm half-Jewish. It feels like multiracial people are frequently identified by whatever part of them is of less value, or more oppressed. My friend who's Black and Japanese, for example, is usually just called Black."

# Jason

**LOS ANGELES, CALIFORNIA**

*My initial career goal was to be a sports journalist.*

*My favorite thing is finding really good vegan ice cream.*

*I think that Los Angeles is actually beautiful (mountains and hikes).*

*I grew up* here in Santa Monica, right in Los Angeles. It has a proud history of being progressive and racially diverse, and in some ways it is, and it was also a very sheltered place to grow up. I had a lot of diverse friends growing up, but I didn't have a lot of conversations about racism or race. I think I first understood race as something that impacts people with the tape of four White police officers beating Rodney King in 1991 within an inch of his life.

In 1948, my grandmother moved to Mexico City from Eastern Europe after surviving the Holocaust, and my mom later immigrated to the United States and met my dad. To me, I'm clear that my heritage is really about the story of Whiteness as it stems from Europe. I remember in high school I started listening to a lot of hip hop—Mos Def, the Roots, Common . . . I was, like, really fascinated by Black culture, and I felt like Whiteness was boring and bland. I think I was participating in some sort of escapism by doing that—part of it was knowing and trying to escape this shameful history connected to Whiteness. Going to a summer camp for 150 young people to have intense, painfully honest dialogue about race for seven days was later a pivotal moment in my life.

My grandma is still alive—she's ninety-seven years old, and she's amazing but her memory is going. She can't remember anything from like ten minutes ago, but she's got long-term memories that are razor sharp, so she tells me stories from the concentration camps, all the anti-Jewish sentiment* before the Holocaust. She was not considered White; she was a racialized Other in all the same ways in which people of color in this country have been racialized through pseudoscience. Those experiences are connected through genocide.

The difference is that my grandparents could start their lives again in a new country. They already had three brothers in Mexico City with lumberyards and textile factories and other capitalist ventures, and they were part of a European, capitalist exchange where they brought European capital into a developing state like Mexico after years of colonization. Then, many Jews have been able to assimilate—there's an open door for having White skin—so I don't think people interact with me like I'm Jewish, but rather like I'm White. If they learn that I'm Jewish, there's still typically a sense of respect because I think that much of

* Anti-Jewish sentiment is also widespread in the United States. Just one historical example: in 1913, a manager of a factory, a Jewish man named Leo Frank, was falsely accused by the factory aide (who was later found guilty) of killing a worker named Mary Phagan in a pencil factory. Although the governor called out a lack of evidence, a mob dragged Frank from prison and lynched him. In 2017, the Anti-Defamation League reported the number of anti-Semitic incidents was nearly 57 percent higher than 2016: 1,986 incidents ranging from physical assaults to vandalism to bomb threats.

Jewish oppression has been acknowledged. There are many genocide groups that haven't been acknowledged. This is a funky way of saying this, but it's a privileged experience of genocide,** because people understand what happened to my people, you know? That's an important psychological piece of trauma.

In my family, I'm living the safest existence as a Jewish person. Meanwhile, my family's history of oppression teaches me how important it was that so many Germans and Hungarians and non-Jewish Europeans stood by and watched—so if Jews say "never again" to the Holocaust, I say "never again" to anybody. It's not just responsibility; the larger lesson in history is that, if I think that I'm safe allowing other people to be treated and exploited in violent ways, it's an illusion. I'm ultimately unsafe, that's the kind of stuff that undercuts democracy and eventually gives rise to the falling apart of social fabrics.

One thing I don't think we make enough space to talk about today is Palestine and Israel. My grandmother came really close to moving to Israel, and I experienced in my family this tacit, unquestioned allegiance to Israel. Like, this underlying belief that

$$\longrightarrow$$

** Pakistan's Bengali genocide? Belgium's Congolese genocide? Germany's Herero and Nama genocide? All of these genocides—*all* related to European colonization—are much less well known than the Holocaust.

Jewish people deserve a homeland in a land that has historically been incredibly diverse, and which has never just been about Jewish people. I have a really hard time with the nation-state. There is a White privileging and power that is held, especially by Ashkenazi Jews of European descent in Israel. I think it is worth talking about, but the hard part for a lot of Jewish people is that there is a historical, collective sense of trauma and a need to have our own state to be safe. I have empathy for that, but I don't necessarily agree that that makes us safer; I think in a lot of ways, the hardline approach of policies in Israel around settlements, encroaching land, and taking rights away from Palestinians actually increases anti-Semitism in the world. One of the most frustrating things for me is that if I'm willing to criticize Israel or raise questions about it, I feel like there are a lot of Jews who feel like I'm being anti-Semitic or have internalized self-hatred, and for me, Jewish identity is something different than allegiance to a nation-state. I'm even nervous to talk about it, because working at this large nonprofit that educates students about hate, we do a lot of work around the Holocaust, and we also have a lot of Jewish funders—so there's a lot of silence around not touching that subject, you know? And I fear sometimes, like some of my colleagues that I love and trust, what would they think if they knew how I really felt on those issues?

# Renee

**SANTA FE, NEW MEXICO**

I loved Frida Kahlo before it was a thing.

I was very shy when I was little; I'm now pretty outgoing.

The smell of rain in New Mexico smells completely different from anywhere else. I love it.

I love to dance and wish I had pursued it more while growing up.

**_Machismo*_ dominates politics.** In New Mexico, although it is great that we have many people of color in office—who wouldn't call themselves people of color, but Hispanic—today, the majority of people in office are men. But it is shifting. There was not a Chicana** representing the city she grew up in, and that is why I ultimately decided to take a risk and run. I'm trying to shake up the machismo in here.

I cannot deny that my roots are in Mexico, because we're _so_ close to the border. But I also knew I had Spanish blood from my mom, and some Indigenous from my dad. Literally, New Mexico history is a part of me. I'm a true mestizo***—in truth, we _all_ are down here.

The privilege I have of a college education

has given me a greater worldview. People categorize themselves and others by saying they're Hispanic or Hispaniola compared to Latinos or immigrants. They do not see how they are connected, only the differences. I'm also privileged because I can fight for my rights, all our rights, I have the power to do this whole politics thing. My dad couldn't. He was a migrant worker in Texas, and he went through such hate and such backbreaking labor, but he _still_ remained upbeat, he _still_ smiled through the sweat. He was from Texas, yeah, but people saw his skin and treated him like an undocumented immigrant. He would get overlooked as Hispanic for jobs where he was probably the most qualified. My grandpa would always say, "Hey, we didn't cross the border, the border crossed us!"

People complain that I make too big of a deal about things, but inequality really does trickle down to the decisions we make about things—even things like funding and budgets. Guess which parts of town don't have sidewalks?

Here, the people with Spanish ancestry are number one, then the Mexicans, then the Indigenous at the very, very bottom. There is also a diverse affluent group in Santa Fe, so to me class is more of a dividing factor that does not get acknowledged enough. However, I think people of color do tend to be the most marginalized, also through color, based on

---

\* **Strong or aggressive masculine pride.**

\*\* **Most popularly defined as a Mexican-American female raised in the United States. "Chicana" was coined by Mexican-American women during the Chicano movement, and "Chicana feminism" has come to represent a challenge to their traditional "household" role.**

\*\*\* **A person of mixed background, especially both White European and Indigenous ancestry. One-third of Hispanic people living in the U.S. in 2014 said they identified as "mestizo," "mulatto," or another mixed-race combination, terms tied to Latin America's colonial history.**

the experiences I have gone through for having darker skin versus what my sister has gone through for having lighter skin.

In this office, there are only two women out of my nine colleagues, including the mayor. It is frustrating to explain the fact that I will often say something, and then my male counterpart would say the same thing. I will call people out, not so that I can put them down, but so they can acknowledge what just happened. I have found women who are bold and strong and passionate are seen very differently than a male with the same characteristics. Still, I am here because, even though we are very diverse, there is a lot of frustration from unaddressed racial and class divisions in our city.

# Howard and Delores

**RAPID CITY, SOUTH DAKOTA**

I strive for compassion.

I have a good sense of humor.

I am open-minded.

I am supportive.

I am human.

I support the gay rights movement.

I support the women's rights movement.

I support African Americans.

I LOVE BEING BLACK

Fall is my favorite season.

Fuchsia is my favorite color.

*Howard:* When I was eighteen, I was thinking all the time about the oneness of mankind, and overcoming prejudice by hanging out with others different from me. So I was talking with this White woman—I wasn't hitting on her, I thought I was just explaining the teachings—and I said, "Let's go have coffee!" She said, "I can't be seen in public with you." I asked her, "What are you trying to say?" She said that if you're with a Black man, and you're a White woman, people assume you must come from a bad family or be a prostitute.

*Delores:* But that was in the seventies.

*Howard:* No, no, it's still here. That woman is now with a White man.

*Delores:* So it's a tough thing, to be interracial. We're brave, and we're supporting each other.

*Howard:* Whites need to come out of their comfort zones and mingle with Black people. They prefer Natives over us, and Natives were trained to prefer Whites over Blacks. A lot of people don't have the courage to associate with Black people.

*Delores:* Young people are more idealistic—

*Howard:* But most of them fall in the dictates of society. The young Indian man prefers a young White woman over a Black woman. It's still like that. Colorism* is a big thing. The more you look White, the more experiences you're removed from. We live in a culture that is completely dominated by White people, and in my life, color is a problem every day. Every day I walk out the door, my color represents something to the world that is distasteful. I've been beat up by cops, bricks have been thrown, my mom was beat up and raped by a White man in Georgia, our women are using skin whiteners that can cause cancer.

*Delores:* At the same time, there's a lot of young people supporting the movement. Why do you think the group that I'm a part of wants to change things? I'm seventy-five, I grew up on a reservation, and I remember the first time I went to the local White school. This White boy purposefully threw up on me. My friend told the monitor in Indian what happened, and the monitor didn't know what she was saying. I played hooky from

———————————————→

* Colorism refers to a global skin color stratification in which White is associated with beauty and Black with ugliness. Parents will often hope that their children of color have lighter skin, which would "make their lives easier."

school because it was so racist. Boys didn't want to hold my hand; they wouldn't want to dance with me. We're trying now to talk about race and make things better.

**Howard:** Well, your group let me know that they can't change any of this. So I don't go no more. They don't want to hear the Black man . . .

**Delores:** You were real candid and they were afraid of the anger, that's all.

**Howard:** In this area there are more Natives, and I understand and support that. The point is: when the Europeans brought Africans here, there was a unity between many of the tribes and the Africans. They saw that we were both mistreated people. Europeans were able to convince Natives that hanging out with Black people won't do you any good, and their best interest was to be our enemies. They used us to fight them, and they used them to hunt down slaves. So there's some bad blood there,** so to speak. We need to wring that out and unite as oppressed people. We both have learned to look at each other through the lenses of White people. We've been divided and conquered. We're not smart enough, sometimes, to realize that neither one of us is treated well in this country. Why are we at each other's throats? Why are we enemies?

**Delores:** And with Standing Rock, a lot of intelligent people like Jesse Jackson support Natives and their struggle. And we ask how we can help Black Lives Matter protests. A lot of African Americans, you know, think we worship the devil. We have to educate each other!

---

** Many Indigenous communities have histories of slave holding—and the well-to-do members of some tribes, like the Cherokee, also owned enslaved Africans.

# Ronny D.

HONOLULU, HAWAI'I

One of my favorite quotes is, "Every difficult road leads to a beautiful destination."

My favorite color is blue because when I daydream I look up at the blue sky.

My role model is Martin Luther King, Jr.

I have every movie in The Fast and the Furious franchise.

*During childhood, people* don't really pay attention to their race. Most people didn't care about what race was until we reached that point in middle school where we started becoming fully aware of what we are and what everybody else is. I remember in middle school, I became fully aware of what everybody's race was because at that time, our teacher was telling us what everybody else was.

I'm half Marshallese, and half Pohnpei. My people are part of Micronesia, but since my parents thought us Marshallese are very independent from Micronesia, they would say, "Micronesian people are bad." Everybody in my family would also hate Chuukese people, and I was just like, "Why?" But I just had to go with it. In middle school, I never had a Chuuk friend, and then in high school, I started seeing Chuukese people and would just get into fights and call them cockroaches. I was just hating Chuukese people.

The Baha'i faith gave me a new perspective in life. It was as simple as others saying, "Whoa, that person's bad," and I would go to that person and find that that person ain't actually bad. He or she is just probably going through some things. I still see goodness in their hearts. Last year, I swear, I even started becoming friends with them. Even though there are some things like black magic that I don't like about my culture, I'm now really proud of it.

Where I currently live, there's a lot of Hawaiians and not many Marshallese people. They're racist toward us Marshallese because they think we're the same as Chuukese people. Now they call *us* cockroaches.

---

Ethnic group indigenous to the Chuuk islands in Micronesia.

# Lisa E.

**CHICAGO, ILLINOIS**

I've been told I'm too sarcastic for my own good.

My students are terrified of my eyebrows.

I am a singer and an actor.

I can fall asleep anywhere.

*I'm the daughter* of a Holocaust survivor. Even though being Jewish is still considered White, I'm still an *Other* to a lot of people in this country. I remember being at soccer camp, and constantly being yelled at about my horns, about my nose, about my tail. I had never heard that stuff before. Like, "Do your horns* pop the ball? Do you trip on your tail?"

I work in Chicago public schools. I want my students to have a voice, and have a place where they can learn about their agency, as well as the structures that are in place. I want them to learn that it is all a social construct that has been put in place so that people in power keep their power. But there were times when I asked, "Why is it that my inner city, Title 1, free-and-reduced-lunch kids are the only ones that have to learn about social justice? Why are they the only ones that seem to be learning about it?"

A lot of people ask me, "Can't you just relax and have fun?" But the truth is, not always. I have a friend who told me I ruined Disney for the Gender Studies kids because we totally rip it to shreds. My parents took us to Disney World, and it was my worst

nightmare. My daughter Bella, who was seven at the time, didn't want to be a princess. They call all the girls "princesses," and she was like, "Um, you can call me 'warrior,' thanks." And I was like, "I love my feminist."

She was the first one to point out that Jasmine is only in the Morocco section of Disney World, and Mulan is only in China. Those are the only places where those two princesses exist. They are nowhere else in the theme park. And Bella was like, "What the hell." She was like, "That, *and* you go to the *Star Wars* ride and they have no Rey stuff? What is this?"

And I was like, "I know. I know you're angry." But she was like, "That's not right, Mom. Mulan is *better* than a princess. She's basically a queen, and she saved everything, and they're keeping her in China? Everyone knows Mulan's from China, but she doesn't need to just be there, and all the White princesses elsewhere." So, it doesn't mean we can't enjoy pieces of things, but it means I have to teach my kids to look critically at stuff.

To avoid burnout, I have them turn it on and turn it off. It's really hard, especially when you realize there are people who can't turn it off. It's a privilege to turn stuff off, just like it's a privilege to "not be political." I also realize that *all women are not the same.* Our feminism cannot be divided by being White and exclusionary. I mean, look at Black Feminist Theory! I use

---

\* This stereotype comes from a misreading of the Latin verb *karan*, "sent forth beams" in the Hebrew Bible, which is used to describe Moses. Instead, the phrase was interpreted as *karen*, or "grew horns."

the Audre Lorde** quote all the time: I'm afraid that my children are going to become part of the patriarchy, she's afraid that her children are going to get shot.

The more people I can bring in, who can speak for themselves instead of me speaking for them, the better. I don't want to speak for people, or have the voice of authority. I make a really important point of making sure that my students have their own voice, and bring their own stories in.

To deal with the almost endless complexity of the topic, I make the space for it to be messy, for people to mess up, and to apologize. To be honest, I use myself a lot. I explain to students that I put myself out there for them, because if I'm gonna ask them to struggle to make these distinctions, and to make connections, and talk about stuff, I have to be willing to do it too. I talk about my struggles as a mom, I talk about my struggles as a White person, I talk about my struggles as a Jew, my struggles as a woman. Sometimes, I don't have emotional space for my six- and my eight-year-old when I get home. You lay yourself bare, and you ask your students to, too.

No matter where you are, your students definitely have some kind of weight—from things like race, gender, sexuality, class— on them. It's just up to you whether or not you're tuning into it and helping them understand, deconstruct, and alleviate that weight off of them.

←——————————————————————————————

** The exact quote by Audre Lorde, a Black feminist author, is: "Some problems we share as women, some we do not. You fear your children will grow up to join the patriarchy and testify against you; we fear our children will be dragged from a car and shot down in the street, and you will turn your backs on the reasons they are dying."

# Patience, Lee'Najah, and Tarlice

**BROOKLYN CENTER, MINNESOTA**

**PATIENCE:** I can dance. • I can sing. • I can cook. • My name is Patience—it took three days to give birth to me. I've been stubborn since birth.

**TARLICE:** I know how to dance. • I know how to sing, I like to sing old-school songs. • I'm from the north side of Minneapolis. • I love being an African American.

**LEE'NAJAH:** I'm Black. • I can try to cook. • I can't sing . . . but I can dance. • I can speak a whole bunch of different languages: English, sarcasm, street, food.

*Tarlice:* What I don't like about my neighborhood is that the shootings are really close to my house. Down the street or right in front. It makes it hard to focus on school, because I can't go to sleep. One time I almost thought somebody broke into our house. I grew up on the northern side of Minneapolis, where a lot of police are, and early in the morning at one or two o'clock I hear sirens. I talk to my mom about the police, and how on the news Trayvon Martin and Philando Castile were shot for no reason. The police make me feel fear, mostly.

*Lee'Najah:* Yeah, fear. One time I was on the bus, getting dropped off with my friends, and I saw the police cuff a man on the ground just because he was walking. We saw him just walking down the street peacefully.

*Tarlice:* We talk about race at school in our Social Justice club. When something racist happens, we can see how each other is feeling. We're raising money for the school—

*Lee'Najah:* And we want to raise enough money to go to Birmingham, Alabama, to visit places Martin Luther King, Jr., went. He represents peace and love. I wish people would know that racism is not cool. It's not funny. It doesn't make you popular. You shouldn't do it.

*Tarlice:* People in school do it to be cool.

*Lee'Najah:* Just to earn clout. African-American kids and White kids.

*Patience:* The boys are like, "Oh, African girls stink."

*Lee'Najah:* Just because some people didn't grow up around much money, doesn't mean all African girls stink.

*Patience:* On the bus, this woman made a racist song about Asian people, and now everybody sings it on the bus. It goes—

*All:* "Ching chong ching ching chong meow meow meow meow."

*Lee'Najah:* She was talking about this YouTuber named "RiceGum" and said that he eats cats and dogs.

*Patience:* Just 'cause he's Asian.•

*Lee'Najah:* Me, I try to be friends with everybody. I'm a very friendly person . . . when I want to be. [All laugh.] Y'all laugh like I'm not a friendly person. Treating people different because of the color of their skin is wrong. Because I've

←——————————————————

• **While young African-American students mock and stereotype Asian Americans, anti-Blackness is also pervasive in the Asian-American community. Dana and Joanne, two Korean-American students we interviewed in Ann Arbor, were excited about the growing activism within the Asian-American sorority community. Dana added, "I learned especially about A-pride activism, and realized it isn't perfect. We tend to piggyback off of the movements of other people of color, but only picking and choosing what furthers ourselves. We need to be able to recognize the anti-Blackness, and actually show that we are for solidarity."**

experienced it—me being Black—and it feels hurtful. Like one of my teachers called me a nigger and told me that all we do is get in trouble. He said that we should have never came here. My response was that my people didn't ask to come here, we were brought here. And then I got sent out of the class for saying that. He was a minority—he was Mexican—and it hurt to get racially profiled by someone else who also receives a lot of racial profiling.

*Patience:* Some teachers are more supportive. My advisory teacher, Ms. Bri, was really supportive of my friends and I who came out as bisexual. A lot of Black people have something against gay and bisexual people, so I could never tell my mom, dad, or my siblings. My dad is the true definition of homophobic. My brothers know, but they don't really talk to me about it. My mom took my phone one day and found out I was talking to this one girl. I told her I was bisexual. She said, "Nah, there ain't so such thing,** you're gay, you're nasty, and you're going to hell." And then, the next day I asked her for deodorant, and she was like, "You just keep it, I don't share stuff with gay girls."

I got kinda lucky because she forgot eventually, but I cried for two days straight. I cried right before I got on the bus. My eyes got really puffy, so everyone asked what was wrong. I wouldn't tell nobody. Sometimes my friends can help— one friend was like, "Girl, what you telling me for, I'm gay! We in this together." She was making me laugh, making me feel better about the situation. If my teachers and parents were more supportive, though, everything would be so much easier.

---

** The myth: Bisexuality does not exist. Bisexual people are just confused, sitting on a fence between straightness and gayness. The reality: This is wrong. In fact, today more people may identity as bisexual than as gay or lesbian. Because of "bi-invisibility" or "bi-negativity" from both heterosexual and gay/lesbian communities, research has found that bisexual people are significantly less out to family and friends. They are also more likely to experience disparities in poverty, employment, violence, and health.

# Robert

**SUQUAMISH, WASHINGTON**

I have a ten-year-old son, so I like to play basketball with him, go out with him, and teach him anything I can.

I love to explore. Even as a kid, if I saw a trail, I had to go down it and see what was on that trail.

I am a direct descendant of Chief Kitsap, and that's who they named Kitsap County after.

*In school, after* they asked us where we all were from, this one kid looked at me and goes, "You're not Indian, you're White." When I told my mom, she was like, "Well, you *are* mostly White." It was a culture shock, because I had mostly grown up around my dad's Suquamish family and culture. That became the norm: I'm just the White guy. It was kinda funny, because growing up I'd also say things like, *"Screw White people!"* And here I was, lookin' all White.

The whole stereotype is: To be an Indian, you gotta *look* like an Indian.* I have a lot of family members that look way more Indian than I do, but they weren't lucky enough to grow up in the culture like I did. I struggled with that: Am I really Indian, or am I just another White guy? I realized that my Indian blood isn't what makes me Indian. It's the life experiences. I finally realized I *am* Indian through and through, I'm just White-skinned. I have a nephew who's Black, relations who are Asian—but in my eyes, they may as well be full-blooded Suquamish Indians because they grew up here, they're part of our community and our culture.

On my museum tours, one thing I talk about is how when the Europeans got here, they couldn't pronounce the tribe name, so they started saying it was "Suquamish." They couldn't say the chief's name either, so they were like, "Let's call him Seattle, *easy*." He didn't like it and I am sure he was like, "Every time they say my name wrong like that I'm going to flip over in my grave." That guy has got to be just spinning and flipping around all day!

There's a statue of the chief in Pioneer Square, but it doesn't say that his name wasn't actually "Seattle." What is really crazy, though, is that people don't realize there are so many Indian names in the United States—states like Dakota, a whole bunch of streets, towns, and cities. People don't really notice the influence that Indigenous people have obviously had. I mean, they had 50 percent of the medical breakthroughs** in the 1800s that are valuable today, mostly because Indians knew what plants were used for what. Even the U.S. Constitution is based off the Iroquois Confederacy. The forefathers literally looked around, saw freedom of speech and freedom of religion in Indigenous communities, and wrote them

* According to the Pew Research Center, 88 percent of White and Native biracial adults believe that passersby would say they were only White, 2 percent say they would be seen as multiracial, and 7 percent as American Indian only.

** A study found that "more than 120 drugs prescribed by physicians today were first made from plant extracts, and 75% of these were derived from examining plants used in traditional Indigenous medicine."

down. I personally am inspired by activists like Billy Frank, Jr.*** If I would tell people what to do to respect Native Americans, I would say stay more local and find out what tribes were there, where you now live. Ask your elders, to know what they used to do there in your area. It's *so* cool. It'll blow your mind.

←––––––––––––––––––––––––––––––––––––––––––––––––––

*** In the 1960s and '70s, opportunities for federal funding led tribal governments to expand programs and gain more control over local reservation policies in a national "Red Power Movement." In Washington State, Billy Frank, Jr., led "fish-ins" to regain tribal co-ownership over fishing rights promised in treaties—rights to 50 percent of the fish in the water—leading to funding for resources like the Suquamish Museum.

I love the camera. I love being in front of the camera. I love videography.

# José

**TULSA, OKLAHOMA**

If I had a superpower, I would love to be invisible.

My dream job would be as a television host.

My dream job when I was younger was first an architect, then a spy.

***My parents kicked*** me out at age fifteen. I come from a *very* Catholic, Hispanic family, and when I came out, they couldn't accept who I was. I didn't want to get into the system, and so I started couch surfing, putting myself through high school, then college, taking several on-and-off jobs along the way.

Three years ago, I went with two of my undocumented friends to a gay bar here in Tulsa. When they showed their international passports to the door person checking IDs, she went through them and asked, "Where's the stamp that proves that you're here legally?" They kicked us out, and said they would call ICE if we tried to get back in. That broke my heart completely. How can a marginalized community marginalize another community?

That was a Saturday. Sunday, I called the Dennis R. Neill Equality Center. I filed a report, talked to the executive director, and met with lawyers. Thursday, we met with the bar, which had apologized. Everything was good, but that's when my work started.

←————————————————————

As of 2013, an estimated 55 percent of the 35.4 million Latinx people in the United States identify as Catholic, which has consistently declined every year. At the same time, a third of all U.S. Catholics were Latinx, a number that is rising because of the growing Latinx population in the United States.

I am a gay, Latino, Catholic man who has survived domestic violence, and this is intersectionality at work. There is this culture within Latinos that doesn't accept gay people because of Catholicism, and then there's racism within the LGBT community, and discrimination toward people who identify as bisexual or other orientations. All the programs I start here at the Equality Center come from those intersections.

In school, I got the opportunity to host, produce, and direct my own TV show on social issues called *Tulsa Youth Talk*. Now, I'm twenty-four, I'm very energetic, I welcome everybody and anybody, and if you have an idea and want to do it, I will do whatever is in my power to help you. No idea is dumb or stupid. For example, support groups—I know that I'm not the only fifteen-year-old who got kicked out, and I believe that there should be a support group for anything—I will agree to lead it, I will show you that there's so much in this world that's so beautiful. A metaphor I use: I'll give you the keys of the car, give you a car, pay the gas, and pay the insurance. You just have to drive it.

After graduation, one month before turning the age of twenty-two, my dad reached out to me and apologized. He cried. I didn't hold no grudges, and said, "I'm nobody for you to apologize, don't worry about it." Now we talk, and he told me that anything that he does will have representation from my community. At a party two months ago, he even brought a drag queen as entertainment. I cried; I just thanked my dad for everything.

There are other families who don't talk to their kids anymore. Never. I'm very grateful and very fortunate that my dad came back around. But when people are saying, "My family this, my family that," I'm like, "It might get better, but don't hold your breath." I didn't hold my breath, I was like, "No, I'm going to do what I need to do and focus on me." Now I'm here. For some reason, that was what touched my dad's heart.

# CHAPTER SEVEN

# WE ARE ALL "NORMAL"

*T*he car ride there was hectic: *We're going to city hall! Wait, no, no, wrong way, we meant the capitol!! Is the traffic always this bad?!* We were dropped off on the opposite side of the building—actually, multiple large, marble buildings that kinda all looked the same—and we scampered through the halls, already seven minutes late to our meeting with Utah Attorney General Sean Reyes.

As we searched the building for his office, we took in where we were. The ceilings were so high that you had to bend your neck back three times to see the central dome. The exquisitely ornate marble pillars were bathed in golden chandelier light, and the floor was a "dirty" speckled marble that was, in fact, spotlessly clean. We started to notice that the people in forest-green suits walking by were looking at us—not just glances, but stares. We looked at each other, then at ourselves—our jeans, heavy breathing, ungroomed hair in lopsided ponytails. Winona uncomfortably shuffled her feet and scribbled aggressively in her notebook: *Very White. Very Republican. Lots of men.*

As we walked past doors crowded with dozens of lobbyists, hopelessly lost, we felt a hand on our shoulders. Turning around, we saw a broad-shouldered man with a face entirely framed by white-gray hair smiling at us. Winona thought, *"Oh, perfect, someone to finally help us!"* But before she could speak, the man exclaimed, *"Hey!* You two must have come from Asia! How was the trip over?"

Both of us were immediately red-faced. Priya snapped back, "Great! We just got off the boat yesterday!" A clearly unamused Winona, who nonetheless didn't want to be rude, dragged a highly agitated Priya away. We were both tired of being asked the same question—*where are you REALLY from?*—in different variations.

Twenty minutes later, we found Sean's office. Luckily, his previous meeting had run late, so his assistant declared that we were "right on time!"

Sean strode in with a confident swagger, wearing a patriotic tie and an American flag on his suit lapel. "So nice to meet you," he said, beaming as he shook our hands vigorously. He introduced the four female interns behind him, then plopped down in a large leather chair and exclaimed, with a wave of his hand, "Well, what are you waiting for? Hit me with the first question!"

We asked, and he answered, without stopping . . . for over an hour. We learned a great deal about his family lineage: how his dad, the nephew of former Philippines President Ramon Magsaysay, escaped to Los Angeles as a political prisoner, lived with Mexican Americans to avoid deportation, won an art competition with Coretta Scott King, met his Hawaiian mom, and to this day still impacts Sean's work because, in Sean's words, "to understand my principles we must understand the cultural values my dad grew up in, which he passed down to me."

Despite the fact that he wasn't too eager to talk politics with us, the way Sean spoke *screamed* pride for his heritage. There was something regal about the way he spoke,

how he leaned back so comfortably and casually in his chair like, *Yo! I'm the boss!* He made it obvious that he was not only descended from a president, but also from parents who greatly struggled to ensure that he had power. To him, that power was not a natural birthright, but an honor well deserved.

As he talked, we noticed his huge floor-to-ceiling mahogany bookshelf, filled with basketballs and flags and leather-bound *United States Reports* journals. A brown rock inscribed with the word "Dixie" sat next to a signed football and a grinning baseball player figurine. We realized that nearly every single artifact was branded with something American. They screamed pride, just as loudly as Sean, for this country.

More than anything, Sean and his office seemed to be telling us, *I belong here too.*

We were in awe—but we didn't really understand why. After all, Sean was not our favorite interview from Utah. We felt that he avoided strongly acknowledging racism, and spoke with an unshakable male authority that left us feeling seriously silenced. We didn't discuss his politics, either.

It wasn't until a few hours after we left him that we realized we were in awe, because we were *surprised.* Everywhere we turned in the capitol building, we had seen Whiteness. It was one of the Whitest places we had ever been, from the senate roster to the ceiling paintings to the skeptical passersby who just looked at us and frowned. Yet, Sean did not convey to us, in any way, that he felt out of place. He was so proud of being non-White *and* being American; to him, there was no gap that could make him belong any less to this country. So what if he was a politician of color? He made us feel that his power was as *normal* as any other White man in the building.

We definitely didn't share that experience in the capitol: we felt extraordinarily out of place, and we had been explicitly told so! Later, when we interviewed a Utah representative of color named Angela, she told us, "If I didn't have my colleague, the first Black woman elected here, I would lose my sanity." As a *man* of color, yes, Sean's experience was different, but meeting him still gave us hope, because we began to wonder—what if it actually *was* normal for all people of color to so boldly belong? To not be shamed or shut down, but instead to be welcomed as Americans just as important and deserving to be here as any other?

Our rich diversity, *not* Whiteness, should be *normal*.

Let's work to stop allowing some Americans to feel like they don't belong. Let's not be surprised that people of color, just like White people, have built up this

nation from the beginning—or have been here before us—and call it home. In Honolulu, Julia remembered the bombing of Pearl Harbor at Schofield Barracks, a largely immigrant community of sugarcane and pineapple field workers. "We were curious because we saw this plane coming down, so we ran outside. Looking down from his window, the Japanese kamikaze pilot was amazed," she said. "He's crashing to his death on 'enemy territory,' but he looks down, and he sees *all* these Japanese faces!"

We were surprised at the extraordinary confidence of Sean—but we shouldn't have been. He is just one of many people of color who are disrupting traditionally White spaces all across the country, leading a new normal of embracing and learning from one another. We must recognize people of color as part of the fundamental fabric of American life—not just our diverse exteriors, but also our diverse interior lifetimes of culture and wisdom.

We hope that you, like us, will be inspired by their stories in this chapter to imagine that, one day, no one will be approached with, *"Hey!* You must be from Asia!" Instead, let's imagine that people of color everywhere will be able to unapologetically declare, to no surprise or objection, *"I belong here too. I, too, am normal."*

# Safia

**FARGO, NORTH DAKOTA**

My role model is Ilhan Omar . . . she's a state legislator in Minnesota.

I'm really active.

I have ten siblings.

I'm five-foot-two, on a good day.

I'm a public policy major.

I've never had hot dogs or corn dogs . . . or mustard.

*I don't know* why I'm here, in Fargo, because it's cold and the air hurts your face. No one should live in a place where the air hurts your face, but . . . I'm here.

Everyone's so confused about me. I do pageants for fun, and in the Miss USA pageant, I was one of the only people of color. The judges were like, "Why is there a Black girl living in Fargo?" And a lot of the other girls were like, "Why is there a Black girl wearing a burkini* competing?" They were wearing *bikinis*, and they thought I wore a burkini because I wasn't comfortable with my skin. They thought I was ashamed, that I wanted to hide.

But no. The reason for wearing the burkini was for other girls. If another girl who was Muslim saw the burkini, she's going to be really familiar with it. She's going to think, "Wow, not only is she Black, but she's Muslim. And. She's. On. That. Stage."

At home, my parents were confused too. They were like, "What? Why is our daughter doing these pageants?" They grew up in Somalia, and I grew up in Ohio, so there's a huge gap in terms of what's expected of a woman. I was told that my place is the home, my place is in the kitchen, you know? Not strutting on a stage. Not working in political campaigns to get Ilhan Omar, the first Somali-American Muslim legislator, elected to the House of Representatives.

The point is, everything about me is apparently confusing. Nobody understood me. I started to become super self-conscious. I stopped focusing on the pageant. I started thinking, "Do the judges even like dark skin? What do I need to do? Do I have to stay out of the sun? Will they accept my Blackness? My Muslim-ness? Will they accept both together? What if they accept *neither*?"

My message is to be comfortable in your skin and to be confident in who you are. Especially in minority countries, where they advertise whitening,** you know? Remember, White should not be the beauty standard. You are beautiful in your own way, and if you're not worried about that, you have more brain power to be focused on your education and other things that might matter to you.

---

* Aheda Zanetti invented the burkini—a swimsuit that covers the whole body except for the hands, feet, and face—in 2004. In *The Guardian*, she wrote that she created the burkini "to give women freedom, not to take it away . . . it symbolizes leisure and happiness and fitness and health."

** As of 2017, companies like Unilever and L'Oréal are reported to be "cashing in on a global skin lightening and bleaching industry worth between $10 and $20 billion."

# Ronnie B.

**SEATTLE, WASHINGTON**

I met my best friend at a park.

I like to work out and box.

My music taste is very versatile 'cause I have an old soul. Favorites include Tupac Shakur, H-Town, Next, Jodeci, R. Kelly, The Temptations, Earth, Wind & Fire, Michael Jackson.

*My father means* everything to me. I feel like that term "father" gets tossed around loosely. Anybody can be a father, but my father was actually a father. He was so actively involved* in everything—sometimes it'd get on my nerves. My mother wasn't always around; I'm actually just getting into contact with her after twenty years. My father pretty much took the responsibility. Everything that involved me, involved him.

He's in jail.** He's doing about an eight-year sentence for pretty much just fitting the description of some light-skinned male who stole a cell phone. He wasn't involved. The witness even said the robber could've been White.

I talk to him every day on the prison phone, make sure that he's taken care of on the inside . . . Even though I don't need him to, he still checks up on me, too. He also plays a big part in my daughter's life.

You all should meet my daughter, Rainna. She's a character. She likes to run off and play, especially basketball. She does it for fun, but when I started teaching her, she liked it more. If I was, like, at the park and doing pull-ups on the monkey bars, she sees me, starts climbing next to me, and tries to do what I do. That's kinda the same way I was with my father.

I'm worried I'll go missing in my daughter's life, just like my father went missing in mine. When I was about fifteen, I got put on gang file. I've never felt comfortable or safe when law enforcement was around. Because you see how somebody that's Black walking down the streets, bothering no one, can be a crime suspect*** for something they had nothing to do with. So, in some of the neighborhoods I've lived in, I would just have to drive places. The other thing is, because of gentrification, it got so busy, and our neighborhoods changed so you can't even walk outside to the store or hold a barbeque. All the memories from when I was a kid—going to Jordan's and the laundromat on Cherry—those aren't there.

So many Black families are forced out of their homes or broken up. It's *messed* up.

---

\* Today, 2.5 million Black fathers live with their children, and 1.7 million don't. Black dads who live with their children are the most involved fathers of all, on average.

\*\* African Americans are incarcerated at more than five times the rate of Whites.

\*\*\* Targeting (for example, questioning, arresting, and detaining) people of color solely because of their "perceived race, ethnicity, national origin, or religion," often without appropriate evidence, is called "racial profiling."

# Standing Alone

**SALT LAKE CITY, UTAH**

I really love push-up contests.

When I drink, I refer to myself as GI Joy.

I come from a family of ten kids in twelve years. I'm number seven.

I have two little dogs I take everywhere, Meat Loaf (the artist, not the entrée) and Hailey.

*It's very polarized* here. It's people in the Mormon church versus everybody who's not.

I became pregnant at age sixteen. The Mormon church advocates for abstinence and there's no training about birth control, so I was a very naïve teenager—I would say stupid, but I was just naïve. I had no idea that I could get pregnant. The way they dealt with me . . . they suggested that I be sent away to another town, and put my child up for adoption, so that I wouldn't shame my family.

I chose to have an abortion, and they still just turned me over to the church to deal with the confusion and the hurt. They wanted me to go through "the forgiveness process." That entailed of me, a sixteen-year-old girl, going to a fifty-year-old man who I didn't know, and confessing my "sins" to him. He asked me how much I masturbated, the kind of thoughts that I had, details into the sexual acts that I was involved in, and told me

that I needed to "stay away from the Temple for a while."

My parents thought, as a lot of Latter-Day Saints people in Utah do, that the faith will take it away. I committed acts of sin, but all I need to do is go back to church, be forgiven, and pick up the morals of the Mormon church. I suffered from a lot of mental illness after all this. The church didn't take away any of my pain or guilt. I was spiraling. It was hopeless until I discovered the Native American way, which is starkly different—in a good way.

See, I *am* Native American. My mom converted to the Mormon church and left behind her Native American culture when she married my White dad. I always think: "How different would my life have been, how much pain would I have saved myself from, if my mom had not buried her Native American side? What if I knew as a young girl that mental illness is *not* shunned in some tribal cultures?"

I believe that if we had accepted more Indigenous ideas of how to treat people, and how to treat our earth, North America would have been much better. Instead, the European Christian patriarchy swept in and forced all these ideals on us: what a woman's worth is, how our minds should be treated, how our bodies should be treated.

In Utah, the Mormon church dictates all. Here, mental illness is a sign of Satan

---

**Starting in 1847, it is reported that 1,600 members of the Church of Jesus Christ of Latter-Day Saints, experiencing religious persecution, trekked southwest and settled in the Valley of the Great Salt Lake, establishing their church there. As of 2017, 62.8 percent of people in Utah identified as Latter-Day Saints.**

in you and it gets treated by seeking forgiveness. But what am I apologizing for?

I decided to become an actual mental health professional and help people the right way, but it's hard. I went from in California being able to make $80,000 to $100,000 to moving back here and making $36,000, max. It's frustrating: I have $72,000 in student loans. Plus, I'm a single mom raising a fourteen-and-a-half-year-old, so what can I do?

# Claudette

**CHULA VISTA, CALIFORNIA**

I've done nonprofit work in Tanzania at the base of Mount Kilimanjaro, where I had to hike the base of the mountain every day to the office.

I'm the only girl in my family out of five boys.

I am a certified bookkeeper.

*I come from* very humble beginnings. My mom is one of sixteen kids, and only eight survived. My grandfather left my grandmother, so she was a *single mom* with eight kids. It was a rough go of it, but my grandmother was a rock. She was my best friend and mentor in life ... she died five years ago. We grew up in Imperial Beach. The area, the projects, was run by bikers, skinheads, and then *cholos*, so we got called beaners, wetbacks, and welfare kids. I didn't understand why there was so much hate toward us.

I've been cooking for seventeen years, starting from the very bottom. My very first job was digging shit out of the drains, doing dishes while prepping. Guys don't do that. I feel like in this industry, Mexicans are called dishwashers, brown people are the prep cooks, the women are girls who wash dishes, and then the White man* is the chef. No matter how much I move forward in my career, I see guys collaborating,** doing awesome things, and I'm like, "Hey, I wanna play, I can do this too." Soon, I'm starting my own restaurant called the Matriarchal Kitchen to pay tribute to all the matriarchs in Mexico who hold the secrets to the recipes.

I've done two *Top Chefs*, the reality TV show. I did *Top Chef México* and I did *Top Chef*, which is in the United States. In *Top Chef*, I instantly felt like an outcast. I started cooking and right out the gate I made a *mole* for our potluck, and the judges liked it! But then I thought, "Oh shoot, I can't play 'the Mexican card' in every challenge. If I do, it'll be 'Oh, another *quesadilla*' or 'Oh, another *tortilla*,' and they'll make fun of me." Ultimately, that's what got me kicked off on the second episode.

Americans have a very particular way of thinking of our food, and they try to force it on you. They put us in these bubbles, but we are more than that. I am more than tacos, I am more than burritos, and I am not your idea of what my culture is.

Every culture should fight and say, "You know what, we're going to show you something different." If you're gonna do your culture right, then you do what you grew up eating in your home. You grew up

* Among American chefs and head cooks, 19.3 percent are Hispanic, 15.2 percent are Black, and 16.8 percent are Asian-Pacific Islanders. Meanwhile, many celebrated chefs—for example, three White male judges on the first few seasons of *MasterChef*—are White. In 2016, around 80 percent of the restaurant and chef semifinalists for the prestigious James Beard Foundation Awards were White.

** In 2015, 19.6 percent of the 415,000 U.S. chefs and head cooks were women. If you include "bakers," it's 34.3 percent. However, the whole food service industry is 54.5 percent women; that includes line cooks, bartenders, dishwashers, servers, etc.

eating more than what they know you as. I grew up eating more than rice and beans, so when developing my concept, my menu, I make sure that I show it. Because the second you give in to the preconceived idea of what your culture is, then we lose.

When I came back to *Last Chance Kitchen* on *Top Chef*, which gave me a chance to reenter the competition, I thought, "All right, this is my moment to try to make a mark, to try to come back, so I gotta cook *my* food." And I did cook my food. It ended up putting me back in the season, because I kept winning. I didn't hold back on spice. The ingredients I used were *my* ingredients. I cooked tarantula, I cooked beef tongue, I cooked livers. Those are ingredients of brown cultures, those are ingredients that I'm familiar with.

But let me tell you, it's not easy when you're on these shows and you have to shop at Whole Foods. Whole Foods is not meant for brown people. We call it "Whole Paycheck" because poor people can't afford it. They have the most whitewashed produce. No dried chiles, I couldn't find masa flour. I'd have to grind my own corn.

My mental blocks on the show were because of the grocery stores, the produce selection, the ingredient selection. They're just not set up for "ethnic" people.••• Actually, I hate that word, when it's like the "ethnic" aisle—what does that even mean?

They have a tiny little box in the spice section called "Mexican Blend." I'm almost offended by it. I know that *Top Chef* has the power to ask Whole Foods to offer more variety—we have chefs of different backgrounds! But all they have is the Asian aisle, the Indian aisle, and a box labeled "Mexican Blend." In competitions, they gripe at you to be yourself, but you can't be yourself. It just doesn't mesh with their systems. Okay, you want me to be myself, but you set me up for failure.

Meanwhile, growing up in the furthest town in San Diego before you get to Tijuana, Mexico, it was a borderless town. Here, we call Chula Vista "Chulajuana," because you honestly can't tell the difference with Tijuana except by seeing the license plates. People cross the border to come to work here, or Americans actually live in Tijuana because you can rent a three-bedroom house for five hundred bucks. Everything is just a really cool blend of both cultures.

←——————————————————————————————————————

••• **White people have ethnicities too (for example, your race could be White, your ethnicity Irish, and your nationality American), but by referring to only certain people of color as "ethnic," it makes Whiteness the standard.**

# Gerry

ASHEVILLE, NORTH CAROLINA

I'm a comic book nerd, for sure.

My first love is music, I do a freeform radio show here in Asheville.

I have a dog named Fernando and a cat named Esteban.

I'm a huge Liverpool Football Club fan.

*My name is* Gerry. My mom told me once she named me Gerry after a chess player she followed at the time. I used to hate my name so much. I wanted to be Quinton. I wanted to be Warren for the longest time. My entire life, I've been called "Jerry," but in Indonesia, *E*s are pronounced like *A*s, and vice versa. So my name is actually pronounced like "Garry" with a hard *G*. I've decided to push back on "Jerry." It's Gerry.

I was born in Jakarta, and I moved here as an immigrant with my mother at a year old. My mother eventually remarried a White man and had a family of their own. My parents actually used to tell me that my real father died in a motorcycle accident—which later on I learned to be not true at all. I don't really have any leads on who he is. My stepdad gave me a lot of unconditional love, but his ideological orientation is completely different from my own, and it has really helped radicalize my thinking. He is very conservative, a staunch Republican, listens to Glenn Beck, listens to Rush Limbaugh, retired from the army. There was a very specific moment during the first Bush administration: we were sitting around the house watching the news, around the time of whether or not we invade Iraq. I remember my father screaming, "Just go ahead and bomb all of them." I was like, "That just doesn't seem right." From then on, I decided I wasn't going to just assume his thoughts; I was going to try and think more critically. I'm grateful how far my own apple has fallen from that tree. There was a point in 2008 when I let them know that I was working on the Obama campaign and he actually didn't talk to me for a year. Like, when I'd visit, he'd go to his room and close the door.

I'm older than I look, and I've been doing social justice work for over ten years now. Here's a term that comes up a lot in social justice spaces: "gatekeeping." It means the role and power we wield in certain positions to control who gets invited in and who doesn't, even if it's through a social justice lens. People can be really harmful in those positions, like a self-fulfilling prophecy. Many people have good intentions, but they, and Asheville as a town, have a long way to go.

←————————————————————————————————

Glenn Beck and Rush Limbaugh are both politically right-leaning commentators. A 2014 Pew Research Center study found that while news outlets like CNN and ABC News might have the biggest audiences, the most trusted news outlets in America are actually British (for example: *BBC News, The Economist*). Eighty-eight percent of consistent conservatives said they trust Fox News, but only 14 percent said they trust CNN. The *Glenn Beck Program* and *Rush Limbaugh Show* were "more distrusted than trusted" overall by all groups.

I always have to remember the role I have in lifting up other voices that are not in the room. We need to always challenge ourselves internally, the roles we play in social justice spaces, and if you are in a position of power, how can we disrupt spaces that White people have always been the gatekeepers? In order to do so, you must be true to yourself. So much of my upbringing, I didn't know what it ever felt like to be Indonesian. Honestly, the last five or so years of my life has been a reclamation project, regaining my own power through reorienting myself. One of my better qualities—a good and bad thing—is how adaptable I am. But then I oftentimes ask myself, "At what cost is that to my own identity? At what cost is that to my culture?" I think I'm one of maybe five Asian Americans in Asheville. It's a constant fight for survival, in terms of remembering who you are. So even something that may seem tiny, like the correct pronunciation of my name—it's an important part of me and my identity.

# Eryn

**BIRMINGHAM, ALABAMA**

My favorite artist right now is SZA.

My second toe is longer than my big toe.

Right now, I am taking ballet and jazz dance at school. Going to the art school, I took ballet, modern, pointe, and Paglen jazz.

My feet are kind of smaller.

I can sing.

I'm sassy and understanding.

I like to chew gum, but sometimes it can be pretty loud.

*One day, my* ballet teacher came to me. He started asking me about my hair and whether it could be fixed. I was like, "I'll get it done," because I guess it was *kind of* all over the place? I really just wanted to go home, but he kept bantering on. He said, "Don't come back to school with dreadlocks* on your head. It's a distraction."

I was trying to keep it together and be really adultish about it, but the damage was already done. I walked out crying. I really couldn't understand how my hair had anything to do with dancing. Later that year, they changed the guidelines from just having your hair tied up, to not having any curls or "ethnic hair."

You have to understand, dance was my life. I've been dancing since I was five. It *still* is my life. I would spend days in my room after school, trying to think about how I could get the dreadlocks out of my hair. I was thinking, should I cut them? I started thinking about other things. How I'm tall, but I'm not pencil-thin. My muscles. My big butt. When I looked in the mirror, I would be like, "I just don't look like this girl, or that one."**

I was almost done with dance, but I had a passion and I wasn't going to let anybody take that from me.

I got there because of my mom, who would always say my hair is beautiful. And also because I heard this pastor talking about how your identity is found in Christ. I was just like, "God thinks I'm beautiful. Bump what *you* have to say." I started the healing process, just remembering that I am God's daughter. And then, I would listen to vibey, soul food music, this album of this girl that was being unapologetically herself. It really came in when I needed it, and when I started telling myself that I'm confident, I'm bold, I'm courageous, those things become my reality. Now, I'll walk around campus, my speaker in my

----

→

* Why are dreadlocks or natural hair considered unprofessional, militant, dirty, or distractions? In 2015, actress Zendaya wore dreadlocks to the Academy Awards, and a popular talk show host said that they made her look like "she smells like patchouli oil and weed." A quote by Paulette Caldwell: "I want to know my hair again, the way I knew it before I knew that my hair is me, before I lost the right to me, before I knew that the burden of beauty—or lack of it—for an entire race of people could be tied up with my hair and me."

←

** In 1957, the KKK burned a cross outside Raven Wilkinson's hotel window; she was one of the first major Black ballerinas. Two generations later, Misty Copeland became the first Black principal dancer of the American Ballet Theatre and was told to "pancake [her] skin a lighter color to fit in with the rest of the company."

bookbag, my shades on, blasting music with like the deadest look on my face, like, *I wish you wouldn't say anything to me.* I strut all around campus and just *embody* confidence daily. It helps me be genuinely confident.

Dance is still my life. It's what I am majoring in in college. But I'm not going to compromise or hate my hair, like I used to. I just appreciate it because it is mine. I like my hair. I finally got to a point where I can rock it just because it's mine.

# Jane
**HONOLULU, HAWAI'I**

I work very hard.

I make a good dinner.

I have three kids: Sophia, Siara, and Poema.

I'm a big rugby fan, All Blacks is my favorite team.

I love Adele.

*Because we are* such an ethnically diverse state, race is on everybody's mind and also not on everyone's mind. It's hard for you find a local person who says I am a 100 percent "this." If you ask a local person what they are, they'll say I'm a little bit Chinese, Portuguese, Scottish. The same person celebrates Japanese Children's Day, Chinese New Year, Christmas, and the Fourth of July. Everybody seems to celebrate one another. Unless you are from Micronesia. Nobody's celebrating them at the moment.

Our new immigrant group, Micronesians, wouldn't have even been on my radar if I hadn't married one. They're the latest of the immigrant population coming to Hawai'i. They're at the bottom of the totem pole. They're very visible: they look different, they dress differently, they speak differently, and they tend to be uneducated, so they're working a lot of the service industry jobs.

In the late 1940s through the 1950s, America conducted huge numbers of nuclear tests* in the Marshall Islands. The bombs were hundreds of times more powerful than the ones used in Hiroshima. So, there are now a group of islands that are nuclear-affected and have people with a very high rate of cancer. The United States made a special agreement—the Compact of Free Association—to take care of those people. The agreement was that Micronesians would get money for infrastructure, education, and health. In return, the United States gets control of the Northern Pacific, from Hawai'i to Guam— they have control of *all* that ocean space. That's the price: give the Micronesians some money, let them be allowed to live here in Hawai'i, and then the United States gets *total* military control.**

But people don't know all that. They think that Micronesians just come here for the welfare. They think they're all lazy. My husband works at the largest medical center in the state and nobody believes that he's qualified. People are always surprised. My family and I have considered moving; I don't want my kids

---

* The equivalent of over 7,200 Hiroshima-sized bombs (and larger) were unleashed in the Marshall Islands between 1946 and 1958.

** Jane's description of the United States' relationship with its territories reminded us of what Eliana from Puerto Rico had told us: "We're citizens, but we're considered second-class citizens. Second-class humans, even. We're sick of it. We want to talk about the corruption, we want to talk about the U.S. involvement, the experimentation here with people. Like, the United States bombed the Vieques Island here for practice, and now a lot of people have cancer there. Who's going to answer for that?"

being looked down upon because they're part Micronesian. But then I thought, "Why should I leave, why can't my family be an example of what you could be?" My husband's an example of what Micronesians could become. He's a role model. Every single person he meets who learns he's from Micronesia is impressed by him; they go tell another person, "Hey, guess what, when I was in the hospital today, this nurse was helping me, and you wouldn't believe it, he's Micronesian!" In his own quiet way, he's helping to change people's minds about Micronesian people in Hawai'i.

# Nastesho, Mohamed, and Hayat

**FARGO, NORTH DAKOTA**

I moved from Kenya in 2012.

I like Philosophy.

I'm interested in majoring in biology in college.

I enjoy debate.

My favorite color is black.

I read in my spare time.

I want to use science to help people.

I'm from a family of ten.

I'm a very active person—I play soccer a lot

I'm Ethiopian.

**Hayat:** When people look at me in school, they don't just see my dark skin, they also see my hijab. I just started wearing my hijab a few years back, and I feel like ever since I've tried to create this image of myself where I'm really nice to people, trying so hard to stray away from the stereotype that people have of Muslims. In the media, people only see us as terrorists. So, I feel like it's important for me to show people that that's not me, and that's not being Muslim.

I try to put forth my individuality as much as I can, and show that I'm a *person* as much as others are. I don't want a certain race or religion tied to my individuality.

**Nastesho:** Hayat is Ethiopian, and I'm Somali, so our cultures are very different. But one thing that we noticed is that people always ask us both where we're from. It didn't bother me that much because I have an accent, but what frustrated Hayat was that she only started being asked "where are you from" *after* she decided to wear the hijab. The hijab is associated with un-Americanness, so we both constantly have to confirm that we are American.

Being a Muslim and being a feminist are not mutually exclusive. You can be one; you can be both. But White feminism excludes Muslim women, just like it excludes Black women. I qualify as a feminist, and for me, feminism is about choice—it's not about one choice, it's about protecting everyone's choice. Feminism is about protecting every woman's freedom, and if you're really about that message, then you must protect Muslim women and their freedom to wear the hijab.

Wearing the hijab is a way of practicing Islam, like praying five times a day, or observing Ramadan for a month. Except, instead of praying only once in a while, my choice to wear the hijab shows that Islam is part of my everyday *lifestyle*. And my lifestyle, my religion, is not inherently unfeminist.

**Mohamed:** I get asked "where are you from?" too, but I also remember getting these questions from the police. One night I was driving, and a police officer was coming from the other direction. As soon as he saw me, he turned his lights on and followed me. I roll down my window, and he's like, "You have a warrant out for your arrest." And I'm just like, *"What?* I'm a high school junior . . ." I mean, all I do is get A's and play soccer. But he looks at me, pulls out a picture of a Black man, and he's like, "You're this person, aren't you?" He looks at me, and I look at him, and I'm just like, *"That's not me!"*

In a study by LexisNexis Academic and CNN.com that examined all reported terrorist attacks in the United States between 2011 and 2015, researchers found that "attacks by Muslim perpetrators received, on average, 357% more coverage than other attacks."

Feminism is about protecting every woman's freedom, and if you're really about that message, then you must protect Muslim women and their freedom to wear the hijab.

# Neda

**LOS ANGELES, CALIFORNIA**

I love reading books—I want to have a library one day.

My favorite music is hip hop.

I've been to Spain, Mexico, Canada, England, France, Italy, Germany, Australia, Turkey, India, Thailand, Cambodia, Laos, Peru, Hungary, and Czechoslovakia.

My other dream is to have a bunch of adopted kids, maybe be a foster parent.

I love the rain.

*We hid in* someone else's basement. They had to keep my identity a secret. The United States was giving weapons to Saddam Hussein, chemical weapons, and using it against Iranians, so at the time there was a strong anti-America, anti-U.K. sentiment both at a national level and among many of the people around me. At school, they would make me chant, "Death to America!" I would come home really distressed, really upset, because I felt like they wanted me to die—I was born in America, after all.

We eventually came back to America. I was in kindergarten, and I didn't speak English. There were a lot of Persian kids in kindergarten. They spoke Farsi, but wouldn't speak Farsi to me because they didn't want to reveal their Otherness. They were trying to fit in. Privately, if no one was around, maybe they'd talk to me. But when I publicly asked for help in Farsi—the only language I knew—they'd turn a cold shoulder.

We ended up moving to Orange County, a very White area. Previously, in Los Angeles, all my friends had the same shoes from Payless ShoeSource, they all had

→

Race impacts us right from the womb. Starting at ages three to four, children in the majority (typically White children in the United States) "show signs of implicit and explicit in-group preferences."

weird food, all of our parents were shy and not confident in speaking English. I never felt that different. But where I lived in Orange County—totally different story. They could tell the fake Keds versus the real Keds. They had nice clothes, and they had stay-at-home moms who did their hair. I didn't dress like them, I didn't look like them—I'm not even really dark-skinned, but everyone is *blond* there. It was just different. I didn't fit in. They didn't believe in me. I remember my guidance counselor didn't tell me about AP classes because she thought, *"You'd be lucky if you get into community college."*

I got used to being weird. Weird, to me, became quirky, and it became different, and it became unique, and I just started seeing it as . . . that's who I am. You don't know if it's you who's different, or just you in that space.

Music got me through that time: American hip hop and traditional Persian music. The traditional Persian music that I grew up listening to, my grandma also grew up listening to. The stories are so poetic. It's from the blood, from the bones. There's a way that it speaks to me. My grandma raised us with that music. She always thought that Iran would get better, that one day we'd move back, so if we got caught speaking English at home it was a huge deal. We had to do Farsi class, all summer, all school year long. When we'd complain, she'd say, "One day, we're going back to Iran, and if you don't know Farsi, you'll be illiterate, you'll be a bum. You have to do this."

She would insist that "this is your culture." If I was feeling particularly brave I would say, "It's not my culture, I'm American. I was born in America." I remember this one time she just looked at me, mean, and said, "You are not American. Don't think these Americans want you, either. One day they're going to round you up and they're going to say *Get out of here, get out of our country, you don't belong in this country.* Don't think for a second that you're American. You're Iranian and that's how they see you." I said, "That's not true!" But it is true, it is so true. We spoke in terms of nationality, and "American" meant White.

If you listen to Persian music, you'll understand me better. Music reflects what *is*. It shapes what is, it normalizes what is, it elevates what is. Everyone has a story, but which stories are the ones that get told? Music is that storyteller, and it's deciding which stories get told. It gets in your head and it gets in your spirit. It shapes your understanding of what it's like to be a woman, what it's like to be Iranian, what it's like to be an immigrant, what it's like to be poor, what it's like to be a certain race at a certain time at a certain location. Music is a shared experience—that's when it's at its best. I think that that is really powerful in terms of nurturing movements, rallying movements, and changing thought on a collective, not just an individual, level.

So, yes, you can view my culture as no shaving my legs, no going out, no sleepovers, no plucking my eyebrows, no dating boys—all of these things, but you can also listen to our music and understand the beautiful things. The things unbroken.

I ended up marrying a guy from America, not Iran. We don't have kids, but if we have kids, I would want them to speak Farsi, I would want them to have a Persian name, I would want them to eat Persian food, I would want them to listen to Persian music. I would want them to kind of grow up with that same duality. Yes, living in two cultures means two sets of pressures, and two sets of norms—and for some people that can be like two sets of standards that they can barely live up to and feel like they're constantly falling short of—but it's worth it. You become more flexible as a person; you become more perceptive and conscious. As a result of my experience, I feel like a stronger and better person.

# Shoghi

**ORLANDO, FLORIDA**

I'd love to have a Lamborghini.

I want to travel more in Asia

It's been fifteen
years since I moved
to Florida.

My daughter's
my world.

*When you turn* on the TV, you only see war, hunger, and catastrophe. Africa is a *continent*. It has so many countries—fifty-four recognized ones. But here, people always refer to Africa as the "country of Africa."

Most people identify themselves to a particular country—like Italian Americans or Chinese Americans. The only people who don't are African Americans. They were Negroes, then African Americans, and now Black. Even if they want to identify with us, they're not proud of their African ancestry because of what they are wrongly fed about Africa. Nobody wants to identify with people who are hungry.

I wasn't born here in America. My family has been here for a while, but I was born in Cameroon and moved to Germany when I was very young. While I was growing up in Germany, race played a huge role in my life. Although the government is trying to erase this stigma about Hitler, remnants of Nazi Germany affected Europeans' and especially Germans' thinking of nationalism. The majority believe foreigners,* or minorities , are lazy

---

→

* The term "xenophobia" refers to a fear of foreigners or unfamiliar peoples. While it is a concept distinct from racism, xenophobia "may go hand in hand with attempts to tie anti-immigrant or anti-foreigner attitudes or beliefs to racism."

people coming to profit from their hard work. The government is encouraging foreigners to move to Germany and change the mentality of Germans, but it is a very difficult process.

In Germany, the police don't respect your rights the way they do in America. Here, they read your rights, and try to make you understand why you are being stopped, and make you feel comfortable, even if they don't apologize. I still think my experiences in Germany are worse compared to my experiences in America— even though I did have this one bad encounter with the police here.

I was playing loud music when driving, and while I pulled into a gas station, behind me I saw police. They were yelling behind me to get out of the car, but my music was too loud for me to hear them. They tell you, when you get pulled over, just stay where you are, just stay put until the police officer comes and tells you what to do, so that's what I did. Because I didn't have the courage to turn down my music—I kept my hands still, I didn't want to make the wrong move—I just didn't hear them.

After a while, I was like, "Okay, this is weird. This is strange." I was expecting to see a police officer by my window, but nobody was coming, so I turned around to look, and that's when I saw the ten police officers gathered behind my car, guns drawn. I was shocked. I tried to lower my window, and *that's* when I heard them screaming, *"Get out of the car! Get out of the car!"* I was so worried I was going to be shot that day. And that's when I realized, wow, this is what a lot of people go through: miscommunication with police officers.

I got out of the car, and they just tackled me and handcuffed me. And I was like, "What did I do? What's going on?" I mean, because I was confused. I didn't know what was going on. They brought dogs and searched my car. Then they came toward me and asked, "Why didn't you get out of the car?"

I said, "I didn't hear you."

They said, "Oh, *come on,* what do you mean you didn't 'hear us'?"

I said, "I jus—I just didn't hear you."

They didn't believe me. We kept going back and forth. An officer wrote me a ticket, and he was like, "This is yours. You have to spend a night in jail." And then he was like, "In a few days, you're going to have to see a judge."

I asked this one officer, "Sir, can you do me a favor?" I said, "Why don't you go into my car and turn on my radio—the volume should be just as I had it—then close the windows and let your colleague here scream the way you screamed, and see if you can hear him."

He got into the car, and his colleagues and me screamed at the top of our lungs— like, *screamed.* He didn't move. Eventually he came out and was like, "What's going on?" He didn't think we were screaming. He looked at me, he looked at his colleagues, and he was like, "Did you guys scream?" We said, "Yeah." And his colleague said, "We were even louder than we were before."

He was very apologetic. Very, very apologetic. He took the ticket from me, he tore it into pieces. Later, he told me, "You probably would've been shot** tonight." I was like, *wow.*

I went over what happened, and started asking, "Okay, so I was exiting the car, and I was coming toward you—"

And he said, "Ah, that was really the wrong move."

I said, "Don't you know people get confused? Like, I've never been in that kind of situation. And when you see guns drawn, you just, like, panic."

---

** As of 2017, 13 percent of the U.S. population is African American, but they make up 23 percent of those fatally shot and killed by the police in the United States. Banjor, whom we interviewed in Michigan, said, "I think sometimes, in dangerous situations, I retreat to being African instead of African American." He said that people perceive him differently, often better, once he distinguishes himself in this way.

And he said, "Well, I guess our safety is more important."

That's what he said. He said *their* safety. So if I did not turn around, maybe shots would have been fired. I was like, "Wow. For nothing." He said, "Yeah, unfortunately. Unfortunately, it happens every day."

When we were interacting like friends, he was a cool cop, but I don't know, that's when I realized that the police are afraid: they are not the only people with weapons. In Europe, only the police are allowed to have any weapons. You have police brutality, they fight with people, but they don't shoot. I've never heard of a police officer killing somebody in Europe. Never. That day, I knew that it could've been worse, but it felt like a misunderstanding. I don't know if it was so much racism or police brutality, as much as America's gun culture.

# Louise

I am happiest when I can cook and I love to make pastries and cookies.

My husband received six Purple Hearts, one Silver Star, and two Bronze Stars.

I like to ballroom dance.

I enjoyed working as a legal secretary for thirty-eight years.

*I was born* in Seattle on April 25, 1926. I was going to graduate in June 1942, at sixteen years old, from what was then Broadway High School. But the war started with the Pearl Harbor bombing on December 7, 1941, and two months later, the president issued Executive Order 9066— meaning all persons of Japanese ancestry would be removed from the West Coast.

My parents had two large grocery stores, and at first we thought only they would be incarcerated, while my older brother and I, as American citizens,* would stay to manage the grocery store and take care of my three younger siblings (my oldest sister was married in Minneapolis). After the order, we didn't really know what was going to happen to us . . . but it turned out *all* of us would have to move and leave everything behind. We were desperate, the public knew we had to leave, and we were exploited, naturally—we sold everything, including up-to-date equipment and electrical slicers and ice cream freezers, for a total of $2,000. After their humble beginnings, think of what that did to my parents and their dream to get a better life for their kids.

------------------------------------------→

* Two-thirds of all interned Japanese Americans were native-born U.S. citizens. Louise added that citizens and noncitizens alike were "shocked and ashamed Japan had invaded America."

The first ones they took were from Bainbridge Island, on March 30. We were uprooted from Seattle on May 14, and they told us to meet at a certain spot at 14th and Jefferson. We took a taxi there because my dad had already sold his car, and we got on a bus with one suitcase and all of our bedding.

It was one month before my graduation.

The first place of incarceration was the Puyallup Fairgrounds. We were behind barbed wire, but my family was fortunate enough to be given a barrack room. Others were housed under the grandstands, and to sleep at night, they first had to clean out the stalls of the horses and animals. Ten families lived in one barrack. You could hear everything down the line—people crying, babies crying, people arguing. We were all squeezed in for months.

I remember for one whole week they gave us Vienna sausages in a can every night for dinner. Everybody got sick. The proximity of the bathrooms was at least one block or two blocks, depending on where you were living, and one night there was so many people with diarrhea that they all were running to the bathroom. It was a human necessity. I remember hearing a commotion, and I looked outside, and those people were being met by soldiers guarding the top of the grandstand with machine guns ready to shoot. They thought we were rioting. It was cruel.

In August, we were sent by coal trains down to Minidoka, southern Idaho, which was really desolate country. They couldn't have found a worse place; we had dust storms practically every day. It would storm, and you would be walking in mud all the time. All of the ten concentration camps** had terrible conditions like ours: out in the desert, hot and cold, nothing but sagebrush all around us. The weather was totally foreign to us; you had never experienced that kind of cold. We stayed there for four years, until the end.

We had to create a city for ourselves, for self-preservation. Everybody took whatever job they could—firemen, policemen, security, cooks. I'm proud to say that the residents created a more livable condition for us. They made gardens and they farmed and they dug up the land so they could find water. They grew all these vegetables and raised animals like chickens, so we didn't just have to eat terrible things like mutton.

I also had no skills at sixteen, I hadn't even taken up typing, and so I took a job as a waitress in a hospital mess hall. My mother took a job as the seamstress for the hospital, and my dad as security for the block. We accepted our way of life just because, culturally, we're very obedient citizens,*** and our parents came to America so that their children could become educated as good citizens in the mainstream of America. I think back now, and it's amazing that we did everything that they told us.

---

** It is reported that President Franklin D. Roosevelt called them "concentration camps" himself. Another internment even more frequently ignored than the Japanese internment: Lola, a Yup'ik (Alaskan Native) woman, also told us that, in 1942, the U.S. government "took people from the Aleutian chain, put them into isolation camps during World War II, and no one helped them." The United States had evacuated approximately 881 Aleut Native people against their will to internment camps almost two thousand miles away from their homes. Their stated purpose was to protect them from Japanese invaders, but they were largely neglected and left without access to basic living needs like water, housing, and sanitation long after the Japanese invasion ended. Some 118 Aleuts perished, while less than thirty miles away, all of the seven hundred German soldiers held at a prisoner-of-war camp returned home.

*** A pattern emerged in the camps: Japanese-American internees were fiercely loyal to their country, conducting U.S. flag-raising ceremonies and encouraging purchase of war bonds. This may be because deference and obedience are more common cultural norms in Japan than the United States, but perhaps more so because Japanese Americans wanted to "prove our unquestioned loyalty." Plus, dissenters were sent to a "special camp" at Tule Lake, California.

I met my future husband in the camp. At the time, he was around twenty years old, and I knew he was the love of my life. But he left the camps in February 1943, about a year after the executive order, when the government decided that they needed more soldiers and came into the camps looking for volunteers. They had created a segregated Japanese-American army unit called the 442nd Infantry Regiment combat team. Actually, like other Americans, a lot of our draft-age boys had gone to volunteer for the army at the start of the war, but they were rejected and told, "Your 1-A draft status has been reduced to 4-C, meaning alien no longer eligible to go into the military services." So one year later, my future husband was thinking: *This is my chance to show my loyalty . . . not as an enemy alien, as a nonalien.*

A lot of our boys did volunteer, which created a turmoil inside our camp because our parents thought their sons would be used as cannon fodder. There were rumors that it would be suicide to sign up. Many boys got kicked out of the house and had to sleep in the laundry room until they could patch over their differences with their families. We saw that as a turning point in our experience being incarcerated; my husband said that volunteering might make the difference of whether we could *ever* get out of the camps. Many boys were just sitting around and anxious to do *something.*

They wanted 5,000 men—3,500 from Hawai'i and 1,500 from the ten camps on the mainland. Around 10,000 men volunteered total. I would guess from each camp on the mainland, they wanted 150 people—and we had over 300 volunteers. They suffered a very heavy casualty toll . . . They went into places that other American troops were not able to conquer, and so they had many more injuries and killings in action than the average guy. The 442nd—the "Purple Heart Battalion"— became the most decorated unit in World War II for size and length of service.

About the time that they were recruiting soldiers for the 442nd, they started easing up restrictions for us to go out—we could be cleared by the FBI if we had a sponsor or specific purpose—and most of us wanted to go east. So in June of 1943, I relocated to Chicago. I proposed I would go to business school to learn to type, and then get an office job, but the whole time I was wondering how my parents could possibly send me to school when we're living in the camp with three kids and no income.

The office job gave me something to look forward to. None of my friends could go with me because they hadn't graduated yet, so I went by myself. I wouldn't let my children go through that experience, but I did what I had to do.

I did find a job in an office, and after three and a half years, my future husband came back. He had been in Europe fighting

World War II. He had been injured six times, and they told him he should work with his hands because he would lose his hearing eventually. After we got married, we stayed in Chicago for a year so he could go to vocational school for air-conditioning and refrigeration. When he graduated, though, it was hard to get a job, and all the places he looked for a job said, "No, we don't hire Japanese."

My, he was discouraged. So he said, "Let's just go back to Seattle." By then, 1947, they had closed up the camps and people were starting to go back. My sister also had come back from Minneapolis and found a regular apartment for us—so we count ourselves lucky, because many people didn't have a place to live and crowded into the Japanese cultural center. My sister had sponsored my parents to live with her, because when they went looking for their possessions from the former neighbor who had offered to take care of all their sofas, beds, and washing machines before the war, there was nothing there. The guy had sold everything. Many people were exploited like that. We all had to start over again, even though our parents have been in this country for thirty years and built up their life. They bought a dry cleaning business; my father learned how to press pants and my mother did alterations as a seamstress.

We lived frugally, because that's what we were, Depression kids. My parents were finally able to send my sister to Juilliard. And then they could send my older brother to nautical school. He had gotten kicked out right after the war started because they thought he might be involved with espionage. Can you believe, though, that with the incarceration of approximately 120,000 Japanese people on the West Coast, there was not one single case of sabotage or espionage?****

But we still suffered the same discrimination as before, and my husband still couldn't get a job. The American public didn't even know all that we went through—that our boys had fought in the war, were a major part of the war, and contributed to the fact that America came out as a winner. It took many years for people to start recognizing that we were good neighbors, took care of our property, and worked hard.

Now, I have three daughters, four granddaughters, and three great-grandchildren. My children ask, "How could you have let them do that to you? Why didn't you protest? Why didn't you demonstrate? How could you not be angry and resentful?" Well, we just didn't do those things back in those days. I told them that I look forward instead of trying to think back, because psychologically it would be detrimental.

---------→

**** This is documented for all Japanese-American citizens *and* noncitizens.

Most people really didn't talk openly to our kids about our experience. But one time, *we* had to. On December 7, our daughter came home from school, we're around the dinner table, and my husband says, "Well, how was your day?" She says, "I hate Pearl Harbor Day." And we say, "Why?" She said, using a racial slur, "Oh, because the teacher talks about 'the Japs' that invaded Pearl Harbor, and the kids all look at me, and think that my father was one of the causes of the war." I said, "Well, honey, you should be proud of your father, because he was a hero in the army during World War Two." She says, "Oh, I thought he fought for Japan."

That was a pretty ironic twist for us, like, *oh my gosh, what have we done?* So then we realized that we were making a mistake by not telling our children what we went through. It's such a long story, though, that we had to talk about it over a number of years.

I'm still learning, too. When I was around fifty, the president sent people to take testimonies from personal survivors, and I went to listen to the hearings in Seattle. I was so fascinated I had to take three days off from work. I didn't realize half of the things that people were going through, like my friend who had a baby in camp while hospitals lacked equipment and skilled workers. People were sick, and died because of lack of care. I realized I had to give my parents more credit.

Our boys formed Seattle's Nisei Veterans Committee Foundation because Japanese people couldn't get into the American Legion or Disabled American Veterans clubs. We gather here for lots of things because we Japanese Americans are very concerned about the repeating of history that we're seeing. For example, we see Mexicans and Muslims taking the brunt of discrimination, and so we're very supportive of the immigrants. We have an upcoming panel with Japanese Americans and Muslim Americans together.

I still feel that America is the best country that we could be in. We are fully loyal Americans, the same way we felt when they incarcerated us.

# CHAPTER EIGHT

# DIVERSITY IS NOT THE GOAL

*W**ho knew* that New York City would have something in common with Council Bluffs, Iowa? Council Bluffs was only a twenty-five-minute drive from our host's home in Nebraska. On the Lyft ride there, we scrolled through our phones, scrambling to find last-minute information about the place, debriefing each other every minute or so. "Council Bluffs was named after an 1804 meeting between the Lewis and Clark Expedition and the Otoe tribe," Winona said, not taking her eyes from her phone. "It's ninety-two-point-six percent White," Priya said, looking up now, locking eyes with Winona. Silence.

Our Lyft driver, Tarana, was young, maybe twenty-five years old, with a green-black *"With God"* tattoo on her left wrist. Black kinky curls slid out of her baseball cap and grazed her eyes. While we spat facts out at each other, she was swaying to Drake, muttering lyrics to herself and not paying any attention to us. *"She must be used to strange passengers,"* Priya thought.

Looking down at her phone to double-check the directions, Tarana furrowed her eyebrows. "Um, there is nothing here, ladies. Where am I supposed to drop you off?"

"Uhhhhhhhh . . ." Winona looked through her window, frowned, then twisted to look through the front windshield. A flat, cracked main road stretched infinitely before us, showcasing not-so-glamorous buildings spread far apart: a gas station, a fast-food restaurant, and some run-down shops. Farther along the road, behind yellow, patchy lawn, the same buildings seemed to repeat themselves. Over and over and over again.

After a few seconds, Winona's eyes lit up and she pointed excitedly at a grocery store. "There! There!"

Tarana flicked on her indicator and took a turn into the grocery store parking lot, which was littered with abandoned shopping carts. A few plastic bags somersaulted in the breeze. Stopping her car in front of glass double doors, Tarana looked around suspiciously. "Actually, I'm, uh, going to wait around here until you two are done. It's . . . safer that way."

We thanked Tarana profusely and headed toward the grocery store, promising to be quick.

Inside, the air-conditioning and fluorescent lighting hit us with a blast. It looked like any ordinary grocery store, except for the staring—at us. "All we need is three or four interviews," Priya whispered to Winona, slipping the camera strap around her neck and beneath her ponytail. "We got this."

We've interviewed twenty-four people in one day before, but we've never been more exhausted than when we finally interviewed two people in Council Bluffs, Iowa. Nobody—whether it was the mom piling tubs of ice cream into her shopping cart, the couple browsing the pasta aisle, or the store manager busily scanning items—wanted to talk about race. We couldn't find a single person of color to interview.

"No, our daughter is best friends with a minority girl. Some do, but we don't got

problems with anybody. We treat everyone equally."

"I'm White trash, but I treat everyone the same! I've got friends of all different races. Which friends? How many? Well, uh, I've got one Arab colleague. Great guy."

After thirty minutes of hopeless "non-interviewing," we left the grocery store. When the automatic double doors closed behind us, we were relieved. Tarana looked relieved too. She waved at us in the parking lot, mouthing *Get in!* through the tinted car window.

"You couldn't find *anywhere* else to go grocery shopping?" Tarana asked, raising an eyebrow as we buckled our seatbelts. We laughed. "No, no, we weren't shopping," Priya said, quickly explaining our project as Tarana drove.

"So what did the Council Bluffs folks say when you interviewed them?" Tarana asked.

"'I have a friend of color, so I'm not racist,'" Winona said.

Tarana smiled painfully. "Yep. Thought so." After a few moments, turning onto the highway, she added, "Well, you all are from the New York City area, right? It's so diverse up there, it must be much better than Iowa or Nebraska."

Absentmindedly, we nodded.

Three months later, we were living in New York City. During one meeting on the eleventh floor of a skyscraper, someone told us, in awe, "I can't even imagine what it must've been like to travel to such remote places. I mean, places like, I don't know, the middle of *Iowa* must've been . . . just . . . You must be glad to be in New York City. I mean, we're so diverse here! New Yorkers treat everyone equally."

Priya caught Winona's glance. We had heard those same exact words before.

It's easy to think that New York City is the opposite of a place like Council Bluffs, Iowa. After all, New York City is only 43 percent White, whereas Council Bluffs is 92.6 percent White. But people we interviewed in *both* places were complacent about diversity. In Council Bluffs, people paraded their one colleague of color, as if proof that they weren't racist. It didn't matter that that colleague probably couldn't ever hold actual power in the company, which was likely run by all-White executives. In New York City, people bragged about the city's diversity, without realizing that, at the end of the day, a hugely disproportionate number of the city's African Americans got off the subway in Brooklyn, Mexican Americans in Queens, and Chinese Americans in Chinatown.

If you're in a diverse place, ask yourself: Where do most of the people of color live? Is that area perceived as "safe"? Are its public schools as prosperous as the ones in, say, the more White neighborhoods? Just because New York City is more diverse than Council Bluffs doesn't mean that it's more racially harmonious or equitable. In fact, New York City has the fourth highest level of residential segregation in America.

Diversity isn't enough. And even among diverse populations, it's easy to get stuck in a mind-set of stopping the work at just "treating everyone equally." Treating people "equally" won't set right centuries of racial discrimination: "What me, a Black woman, goes through isn't *equal* to what a White man goes through," said Treniya in Atlanta. Pursuing equality is *not* enough. What we want to achieve, instead, is *equity*.

Nick, whom we met on the Pine Ridge Reservation in South Dakota, told us that the best definition of equity he had heard came from an eighth grader named Kyle. Kyle said, "I noticed that kids on reservations don't come to school because they're embarrassed that they don't have shoes to wear. And I notice that some kids have really bad shoes, but at least they *have* shoes. Equality is a truck showing up and giving out only size 8 Nikes. Equity is a truck that shows up and has a size shoe that fits everybody. That way, everyone can walk around." In other words, equity acknowledges inequalities. Equity focuses on the just and fair distribution of resources and access to opportunities.

From the stories in this chapter, we hope you'll realize how—whether it's in the most diverse metropolitan areas, like New York City, or a mostly White rural town, like Council Bluffs—diversity and equality are not enough. They shouldn't be the goal. Instead, for now, equity should be.

Aaron G.

WASHINGTON, D.C.

I am a fan of X-Men comics.

I love weddings.

I also write plays!

I make podcasts for fun.

I write poems.

*To me, race* is a political construct that is used over history to justify an unequal and inequitable distribution of power, social sanction, and resources. Race isn't real, right? But if the system perceives you in a certain way, you internalize that, and then race becomes very real.

I grew up in a small town in Colorado, called Falcon. I was also raised as a Baha'i, so to be non-White, non-Christian where I grew up, it put you at the outside of a lot of circles. There are two times in my life where somebody said that they could no longer be friends with me. One, he was a very conservative orthodox Mormon who said that "Black people are the mark of Cain, you're going to hell, I can't be friends with anybody that's going to hell." Then, there were other folks who have thought I was going to hell because I wasn't Christian, and I wasn't baptized. They stopped being my friend, too. Yeah, this was seventh grade.

We grew up with a lot of what people in the coastal cities are afraid of now. You see this a lot in D.C., there are swastikas and KKK and the n-word painted places, and people in D.C. really freak out. But I grew up with that, that was just standard from my childhood. Any bathroom you went into had a swastika, and the n-word written, and something about not liking Mexicans, it was just standard bathroom writing.

I did not enjoy a large part of growing up in Colorado Springs, so when I got a chance to go to the University of Chicago, I took it and left. I was always a very nerdy, academic kid, so I loved the idea of going to a school full of nerds. My great-grandfather had been a janitor at the University of Chicago, and he had learned to read at the University of Chicago so that he could sign his paychecks. There was something really cool about getting an English degree at the same school.

In 2014, when Michael Brown was killed, there was like a bunch of big rallies in D.C., and I just started going to them. As part of Black Lives Matter DC, I started posting events for Black organizers and politically aligned Black people to meet and build relationships and talk about rights. I was doing a lot of art at the time, and podcasts, and installations, in addition to my paid organizing. I saw these patterns and realized that, simply, our *human* needs aren't being met, and I think that fuels a lot of what we call "racism." Real structural situations—wealth gaps, the police— further this narrative, this fake narrative of White supremacy, and that then gets internalized in interpersonal relationships. If we want to overcome all of these, what I

In Genesis 4:15, God places a visible "mark" of some sort on Cain for murdering and lying. While this is a perversion not written in the Bible itself, "as early as the fifth century, Cain's curse was interpreted as black skin."

call "logics of domination," we have to do it on multiple levels.

First, you have to look at the inner work. You have to heal from your own trauma so that you can actually engage with the reality, loving yourself so that you can be constructive with others. Then, there's a lot of relational work that has to happen, actually building transformative relationships with other people and recognizing that people aren't their identities. Then, you focus on the systems. How systems perceive us, put us in a different position in society, and our social location actually determines our experiences—it determines what resources we have access to, where we have power and where we don't. We have to come up with some way of building relationships across these differences in social locations in which we can see each other as humans. Part of the work of getting free is relearning how to love each other and forming authentic relationships.

What we need is not a revolution where one group of people takes power from another, but we need to actually transform how we think about power, and how we interact with each other. It's a process of building social power, building personal power, and transforming the way power is wielded, and that has to do with inner work, relationship work, but also organizational work.

# Isabella

I'm moving to Singapore for college, because— why not?

I play the mandolin.

I've climbed a significant number of 14ers, which are mountains over 14,000 feet in elevation.

As a child I didn't know how to say no to anything so I ended up playing the harp for years.

*I have kind* of a weird family. We are entirely Hispanic, and what's not usual is both of my parents got graduate-level degrees from Stanford. So, I grew up in an intellectual, well-off family, compared to what most people imagine for Hispanic people. In the seventh grade, my class rank wasn't number one, and I remember my dad telling me I *had* to be number one. He said that my classmates probably don't know another Hispanic person, so I would be the image they had of Hispanic people for the rest of their lives. No pressure, right?

I went to a private boarding school, which charges high fees that only the White families can afford, which made it tokenization* central—from its administration to its students. In classes, we'd have discussions about race or read books about race, and all questions would be targeted at me. I was the only one expected to talk.

---------------------------------------→

\* Tokenization—the symbolic effort to be inclusive to minority groups, simply for the *appearance* of being nonracist—can exist on professional and personal levels. For example, if people of color are hired to be the "face" of a company trying to be more diverse, while White people maintain authority, that's a problem because the actual power remains with the White people.

This year, during my gap year, I lived in Bogotá for a semester working at a school. As someone who's Hispanic, living there with European, non-Spanish-speaking, White women was . . . well, interesting. I constantly had to authenticate their experiences through my speaking Spanish and being brown. Because I existed, they felt *validated*—like they weren't just a couple of White tourists.

Translating continuously was frustrating. I had to translate for strangers in bars, who weren't even talking to me, but were talking to my White friends. I felt like my only role was *in service* to them. So I was tired of that, and I decided one day that I wasn't going to help navigate—I just wanted to go along with the flow, to be normal. The long story short is that I let my White roommate navigate for a day, and we ended up trying to go to a volcano, failing to go to a volcano, and having to actually hitchhike our way back. The whole day basically went to shit. At the end of the day, I apologized for not helping out more and suggested that next time we take a tour. My White friend said that she didn't want to take a tour because she wanted an "authentic trip." And *that's* where the problem was.

The problem was coming in as a foreigner, or White person, and assuming that you *deserve* an authentic experience.

It's like, huh, why is there this feeling in White people that they belong everywhere? Meanwhile, *I* feel like I can't belong anywhere!**

---→

**  Ta-Nehisi Coates said this (referring to White people using the n-word): "When you're White in this country, you're taught that everything belongs to you. You think you have a right to everything. . . . You're conditioned this way. It's not because your hair is a texture or your skin is light. It's the fact that the laws and the culture tell you this. You have a right to go where you want to go, do what you want to do, be however—and people just got to accommodate themselves to you."

# Katja and Gadisa

**OMAHA, NEBRASKA**

I let my son do my hair sometimes.

My favorite motto is "Do not withhold good from those who deserve it when it is in your power to act."

I have an American Ninja Warrior course in my backyard.

I like diving.

Mangos are my favorite fruit.

I was born in Ethiopia.

I love to run.

My sister Kiya and I love marshmallows.

*Katja:* When you adopt, you are now a conspicuous family, you don't all look the same, and you'll be noticed. I was at a parade once, and someone yells, in front of my kids, *"Did you foster or adopt?"* Why do people just yell these things out to strangers in public?

I'm teaching my son a concept: I don't want him to look at his skin, and think "yuck." My son always draws himself with brown crayons, but other families have said to me that their adopted child doesn't recognize that their skin is brown. If my kids hear "Ethiopia," they scream proudly, *"We were born there!"* Some other parents lack insight that their children need connection with their roots and with people who look like them. When we go to the library, we purposely get books with a lot of diverse characters. If every book has White people in it, and your kid is Black, there's something unspoken conveyed. If every teacher is White, and your kid is Black, that also has an impact.* We invite people of every color into our home too. We pursue diverse friendships. I am very intentional about surrounding my kids with diversity, but living in Omaha, it's not as simple as it might seem.

See, North Omaha is the Black community, South Omaha is the Hispanic community, and West Omaha is White. I grew up in West Omaha, the White community, and I remember that there were over six hundred people in my graduating class, but only six Black people. I thought there must be no Black people in our city. I remember during graduation, they were like, "You are ready for the world! You're prepared!" but I was like, "Crap, I'm not prepared!" I felt lied to by my community, by the adults, by my parents, by my church, by my school. I was like, "No one even told me there's a Hispanic or Black community in this *town*. That's embarrassing!"

There used to be a law that Black people can't live past a certain line, and while

---

* A study found that having just one Black teacher in third, fourth, or fifth grade reduced low-income Black boys' probability of dropping out of high school by 29 percent.

** A recent study shows that three out of four neighborhoods marked "hazardous" in red ink by the federal Home Owners' Loan Corporation from 1935 to 1939 are more likely than other areas to comprise lower-income, minority residents today. Marking these neighborhoods with red ink was the practice of redlining, or "the discriminatory pattern of disinvestment and obstructive lending practices that act as an impediment to home ownership among African Americans and other people of color."

that's changed, homogeneous communities were established and just remain that way** today. This place is so segregated that there's hardly any crossing over between races. So when people have opinions on race, they're often based on almost nothing of real-life experience, they're based off the things they see on TV.

I know a lot of White people who just sit back and go, well, I don't see any people of color here, so it's not my fault that my friends are all White. But you can't do that. If you're passive, you're still part of the problem! I was a teacher for seventeen years in North Omaha, and my school was 99 percent Black. One year, I baked brownies each week and dropped them off at one of my students' houses, met their family, and let them know that I was so glad that their kid was in my class. Because I noticed that you're in this Black community, and the parents drive on this side of the street, and the teachers stand on the *other* side of the street to welcome the students, and there's no crisscross!

One time, I show up at this home—I call ahead of time, of course—and I get there and the mom had dinner ready for me. She made tacos! And I was like, "I cannot believe that you are giving me dinner!" And she's like, "I can't believe you came and brought brownies!" I bought these brownies for a dollar a box, and that was the best dollar that I ever invested, ever! Any time I had to communicate with those parents in that whole year, they saw me as an advocate, someone who is for their child. *That's* an example of how I built relationships with diverse people, and my kids see the fruits of that. I want to pour my love out.

*Gadisa (Katja's son):* Well, I was born in Ethiopia. Well, one time there was a little baby born in Ethiopia, and he was so precious, he was smiling and laughing and his mommy and daddy were far away, missing him. One day, they got a message that said, "Come get your baby!" They jumped and they shouted, "Woo!!" They were so excited. They got on an airplane and flew-w-w to Ethiopia, they picked up their baby and they hugged him and they kissed him and they held him. And he squeezed them! And they loved him! And that baby was me! Yeah, yeah, I was that baby! My sister was not born. My sister loves to eat marshmallows.

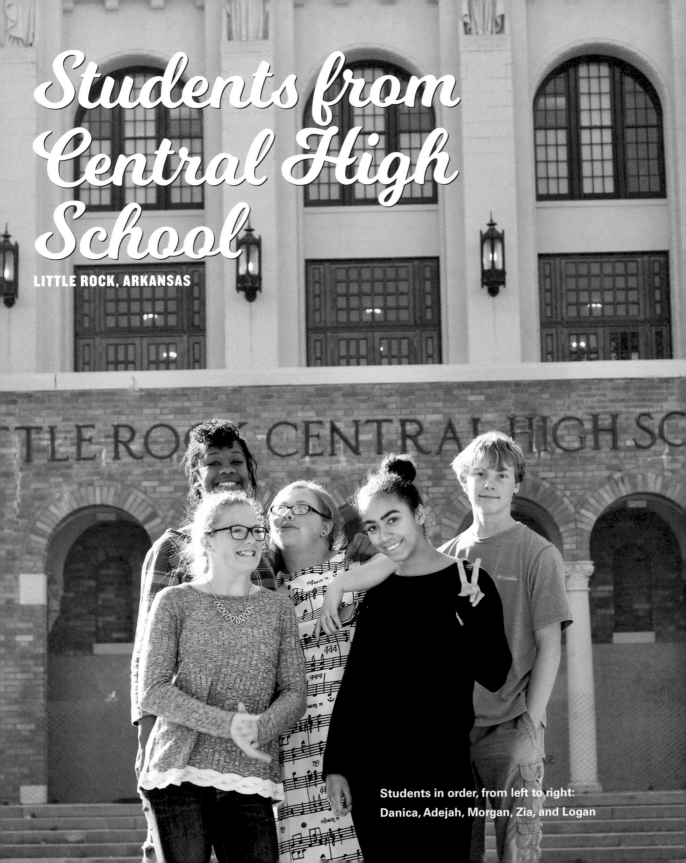

# Students from Central High School

**LITTLE ROCK, ARKANSAS**

Students in order, from left to right:
Danica, Adejah, Morgan, Zia, and Logan

***Morgan:*** At this school, you don't really think about the history. You know, what you think about is, "Crap, there's too many people in the hallway." I guess if you're just standing around, and it's real quiet, you might think, *"Oh my God, this building is like ninety years old and sixty years ago all this crazy stuff\* happened."* But, to be honest, it's not really surprising to me.

Central is *not* segregated anymore, but it's *not* integrated either. At lunch, you will see where the White kids eat on the patio, and you'll see the Black kids eat in the back of the cafeteria. You see a lot of the Hispanics gathering together. And if you walk through the hallways, you'll see a lot of, like, the Asians eating in the physics classroom. You go to the regular classes, and it's pretty much all Black and Hispanic. You go to the Pre-AP classes, you have some Hispanic and mostly White and a couple of Black students here and there. And then you go to the AP classes,

←————————————————————————

\* **In 1957, nine African-American students attended the formerly all-White Central High School. Although other Black students were simultaneously desegregating other schools around the same time, Central High School was the most prominent national example of the implementation of the May 17, 1954, Supreme Court decision *Brown v. Board of Education*.**

and they're almost all White or Asian. We don't mix.

***Stella, the Librarian:*** Like, My church is mostly White, but I have gone to Black churches, and I like them, but I think everybody tends to just go where they're comfortable. That's what happens here.

***Zia:*** I think that at Central, people are segregated by race because of the way neighborhoods are in Little Rock. So I-630, the highway, it's pretty much a clean cut of where Black people live, which is around Central, and then where White people live is on the opposite side of I-630. So when you grow up in that environment, you obviously become friends with the people you grew up with. My dad is Black, and my mom is White. Growing up, it's been hard to find a place or a balance between being Black and being White. If I had to choose one race to identify with, it would be Black, because the way I see it, I can't really identify with being White. You know, because I have some melanin! I'm not perceived as having White privilege.

***Morgan:*** I am White. That's definitely been a step up in the world, you know, being born bright red. I used to go to a school where I was one of ten White people, and so I'm not going to say that reverse racism** is a thing—that's complete crap—but I will say that going to a school where you are the minority kinda gave me a taste. At that school, I wasn't allowed to talk about civil rights, even though that's something I'm really passionate about. I wasn't allowed to play sports. There was this whole ostracization of the ten White people. It felt weird.

*Adejah:* My mom, she's Black, and my dad is 50 percent Choktah, Native American, he's from Mississippi. Being Black and also taking rigorous AP classes is really hard. I'm already a minority, but the demographics in AP classes versus regular classes are just crazy. People don't expect me to go outside my—I don't know—of what they believe is comfortable for me. It makes you want to stick with what people expect me to do: sports and dancing, I guess. I don't know, it makes me

———————————————————→

** As Sam White said best in the 2014 movie *Dear White People*, "Black people can't be racist. Prejudiced, yes, but not racist. Racism describes a system of disadvantage based on race. Black people can't be racist since we don't stand to benefit from such a system." In other words, even if a Black person is prejudiced against a White person, the White person will still be supported by all our sociopolitical systems, and that systemic racism won't be "reversed" anytime soon.

really uncomfortable. Really, really uncomfortable.

I guess that since my dad is, like, half Native American, that means I only have 25 percent in me. Since I only have 25 percent, I'm not allowed to own any land on the reservation and some tribes won't claim me. When I was thirteen, I had to apply for a certificate, and I got rejected a bunch of times because I don't have the right amount of Native blood. I feel a lot of rejection from everywhere right now.

*Morgan:* I want to branch off of what Dejah said. Central High School is really Black, around 55 percent, but when you get to AP classes, there are four Black people in a class of thirty people. There's a stigma that Black people are not going to do well, and you can kind of feel it when you walk into a room. I feel like I have to prove myself, like I have to work harder to be better than the White people in my class just to be considered on par with them.

*Logan:* My story is like the absence of a story. I was fortunate to have grown up in a family where race has always been an open thing. But I do get frustrated when I go duck hunting, and some of the people around me are not as open about race.

*Danica:* I came from Utah, and everybody is White, but if you aren't White, nobody cares because racism is not a thing out there. When I was little, there was one girl in my neighborhood and she was Black, but she hung out with all of the White little girls. We were best friends! People just cared what was on the inside. I think that racism is a choice. You aren't born racist.

**Morgan:** I think there are two very different types of people at Central. Dejah and I are different, but it doesn't matter to me because I love Dejah, she's my friend. But then there are people who're like, "We're all the same and blah, blah, blah." There are people who understand the differences, and then there are people who are—it's the whole, "I'm not racist" thing, you know? "Oh, I'm not racist." "I have a Black friend," or "I listen to Black music," and it's like, *no!*

# Angela

**SALT LAKE CITY, UTAH**

My favorite person is my grandma.

_The Bluest Eye_ by Toni Morrison is my favorite book of all time.

I'm a foodie.

My friend and I find dive bars and document them.

*When we talk* about equity, a lot of the people still have this ideology that if you pull yourself up by the bootstraps\*, you can accomplish anything. That's not true. As a person of color, how do you move your way up into positions of power? You could be the smartest person in the room, but if you don't have connections, and you don't have those opportunities to interact with people who hold those positions of power, you just won't get access to certain things.

For me, even as a person of color, I've benefited from privilege. Privilege is how I'm part of the Utah House of Representatives today. When I got my first job in the mayor's office, it was because of another person I knew there, who was also big on social justice issues. Working there, he saw this job open, and he felt like I had the qualifications. There might have been three or four hundred people who had the same qualifications, but I had someone on the inside advocate for me, and that's a lot of what communities of color don't have: that person on the inside to advocate\*\* for them.

So, now, as an insider who's really an outsider, I'm always thinking about advocating for the voices that aren't there. I do my best to make sure I open those doors for other women and other women of color. I look forward to working with young people who have an interest in the political process. I've been fortunate to have interns from diverse backgrounds and lived experiences. And once they've finished interning for me, I do my best to keep in contact. I landed one intern a job in city hall, another now works for the county mayor. My goal is to get those women involved in the policy, and get them some

←

**•** "Those misinformed citizens who ponder why Black America has not lifted itself by its bootstraps should be aware that when the Black man was brought to America by slave traders he had neither boots nor bootstraps. . . . For over 300 years the Black man in America has been isolated from the so-called 'bootstrap' culture." —Dr. Benjamin L. Perry, Jr., inauguration speech as first Black president of Florida A&M University, 1969.

←

**••** A study cited in *Harvard Business Review* found that 70 percent of White participants' jobs, "past and present, had been landed with the help of friends or relatives who were in a position to provide inside information, exert influence on the candidates' behalf, or directly offer job or promotion opportunities." In her book *The American Non-Dilemma,* author Nancy DiTomaso calls this practice "opportunity hoarding" and argues that the "enduring racial divide is sustained more by Whites' preferential treatment of members of their own social networks than by overt racial discrimination."

experience so that one day they can run for office. When I leave office, I want the person who replaces me to be a woman of color from the neighborhood who actually understands the demographics they're representing. I want the people of my district to have somebody who looks like them, and can relate to them, and understand their issues, representing them.

If we don't start seeing more people who look like me in positions of power, I don't think we will ever get rid of the stereotypes. I remember once my friend and I went shopping to try on some suits because I had to do a presentation. When we were walking out of the mall, security came up to me and said, "Empty your bags," and I was like, "Why?" and he was like, "Well, because those girls think you took something." I told him, "I didn't steal anything!" And he said, "I don't care, empty your bags." Another time, I was on a double date, and we got pulled over for no reason. The cop made the guys get out of the car. He asked if they were gang members, and I was like, "Well, aren't you really violating procedural rights?" because I thought I was really smart, as a freshman in college, and he told them, "Tell that girl to shut up, because if she doesn't shut up, then I'll find a way to arrest you."

Remember I was talking about my first real job working for the mayor? People would always assume that I was the front desk staff.

# Eric, Josiah, and Galen

**WHITEFISH, MONTANA**

My nickname and name all through middle school was Pickle.

I play guitar and trumpet.

I used to have really long hair.

I lived in Tanzania for three months.

I do cave survey research.

I was born in a cabin.

I sing.

For a long time I wanted to be a professional extreme sledder.

I'm in a jazz fusion band called "Gimmick."

This is the first year I've gotten my hair cut just the way I wanted it to be.

I competed nationally in telemark skiing.

**Eric:** I've lived in Whitefish, Montana, my whole life. It's 96.5 percent White. I love when I go to Seattle and I see people that aren't White, it makes me very excited. When I travel and go to an airport, and I see a person of color, I do find myself staring a lot. Mainly out of just, like, I don't know, curiosity. At our school there's one African-American kid this year, and he really stands out.

**Galen:** I was born in North Fork, in a cabin. As Eric already said, this area is not known for its racial diversity, but the one piece of racial diversity that affected my early life would be that of Native Americans. With all the racial ignorance that I have, the one thing that I can claim is that I have this little bit of Indigenous knowledge. My parents have a lot of connections to Native Americans. My birth was actually blessed with a traditional Native American ceremony. Recently, my father had to go through some cancer surgeries and one of his friends performed a Native American ceremony where they try to release the toxins from an individual.

I'd not really encountered much beyond that, though. My junior year I decided to take an exchange year to Norway. It's a country full of White people with blond hair and blue eyes, but recently due to geopolitical issues there's been a lot of immigration to Norway. I remember at one point sitting with my host family, and my host mother was a very, very kind person, and generally was actually very liberal, but she was talking about how she was so disappointed that all these immigrants were coming to Norway and taking up places at universities. It was really awkward because I was sitting there as someone who was planning to immigrate to Norway, who was planning to go to university there and I was saying, "Why do you think that?" She realized her mistake and said, "Well I wasn't talking about *you*." In that moment I realized that "you" was White people.

**Josiah:** I'm not like these two, I've never been outside of the country, and I've spent most of my life in Whitefish. I have only been mildly affected by it, I have a very nonracist* opinion toward other cultures. The happenings that have been going on in Whitefish with the

---

* **Consider the language of "nonracist" versus "antiracist":** To be nonracist implies passiveness (which can include being a bystander), while "antiracist" implies *actively* fighting against racism. If you're privileged and passive, you're still part of the problem because you remain a beneficiary of an oppressive system.

neo-Nazi** mishaps were really surprising to me when they happened. I didn't realize that we had such a racist group of people in our population. I feel like we've got a bad brand sticker on our town now because of it.

*Galen:* When I was an exchange student in Norway, all this business with the neo-Nazis was going on. It was so weird watching it from abroad. I was sitting in my room and my host family came up and they said, "Your town is in our Norwegian print newspaper!" I was sure they misread it or something, because our town is so small. And they said, "No, look here, neo-Nazis invade Whitefish, Montana!" My hosts were disappointed because, you know, their country was invaded by Nazis.

*Eric:* We talked about it a lot in our classroom at school. Richard Spencer

→

** **Richard Spencer, a well-known White supremacist, is a part-time resident of Whitefish, Montana. The Daily Stormer, a neo-Nazi website, promised a 200-person anti-Semitic march in Whitefish on Martin Luther King Jr. Day, which never actually happened. According to the Southern Poverty Law Center, 954 hate groups are still active all across the United States.**

wanted to start up a White supremacist utopia here essentially, and he pretty much created a nationwide thing in just this small town.

*Galen:* I feel like that's the terrifying thing—Whitefish is not special. We don't have an exorbitant amount of White supremacists, but yet, Richard Spencer was able to come here and make an army of White supremacists. I think honestly he could've done that in just about any small town in the United States, and, I don't know, that's to me really the terrifying thing. The ability of it to be re-created is really possible.

*Josiah:* I'm a Christian. I should love everyone and not distinguish any real difference between them and treat everyone with respect. Personally, in our schools, we have a very, very positive environment where everyone is treated equally. It's easy to say, since we're all generally White, but I still think that even if we had more diversity in our school, we would still treat people the same.

*Eric:* I don't think Josiah's wrong at all. There was a student here a few years ago, who moved away my sophomore year, and his father was Black and everyone liked him. He won this award in our eighth grade class for being a really cool person, and I think it shows we have a lot of respect in Whitefish for different cultures.

**Galen:** I really agree with that, but I think even the respect you were talking about to the few students of color wasn't even proper respect. Because they were, like, the token minority. At least that's what I saw—people were basing their respect for those people not on the fact that they were really awesome people and really interesting individuals who had powerful personalities, but on the fact that they felt like they needed to be racially savvy.

**Eric:** Right.

**Galen:** I think that even that type of "respect" can be really ingenuine sometimes.

# Patience K.

COLORADO SPRINGS, COLORADO

I like to write.

I like to ride my bike.

I have three kids.

I'm from Utah.

I like cookies-and-cream ice cream.

*I'm of three* different cultures—my father is from the Congo, my mom is second-generation Mexican American, and my mom's mom is of English and Welsh descent. I grew up in an impoverished community of color in Utah. Everything was extremely Mormon, which was seen as a kind of purity. My father originally came to the United States not speaking any English, and *somehow* he just connected with my mother! I don't feel like I've been accepted by any one group, and I've really had to learn how to connect with people in order to just have relational needs met.

Socioeconomic status and race have been extremely connected in my life, even down to the food I eat. Many communities I see every day are either food deserts or food swamps. In food deserts,* folks live at least a mile or more from a grocery store, but that's compromised by their low wages and lack of transportation. Food swamps are areas of town inundated with fast food restaurants, convenience stores, and just unhealthy, high-calorie foods.

This is so important, because if this is the main staple of your diet, it will

dramatically affect your health outcomes in the long run. There's a study about how, within our city, there's a life expectancy gap between the south and north of town. That gap is *16.1 years*. They call it high areas of Poverty Index—often the communities of color—and low areas of Poverty Index.

Food equity** matters. We redistribute fresh and healthy food to neighborhoods, but we really also have to deal with these systemic roots of poverty. Like, what are the underlying roots of poverty? Low wages. Economic injustice. Structural racism. When you look at the history of our

---

* About 23.5 million people live in food deserts. Nearly half are also low-income. Latinx, Native American, and Black communities are two to four times more likely than Whites to lack access to healthy foods.

** One study shows that the difference between the longest- and shortest-living groups in the United States is thirty-three years. This isn't just because of food access. Looking at another driver of health disparities—the lack of insurance—a 2002 report found that racial and ethnic minorities constitute about one-third of the U.S. population but make up more than half of the 50 million people who are uninsured. Another study concludes that "the combined costs of health inequalities and premature death in the United States were $1.24 trillion" between 2003 and 2006.

Furthermore, among all food workers, 21 percent of Black people, 24 percent of Latinx people, and 38 percent of Asian people earn subminimum wages, compared to 13 percent of White people.

country, you see that wealth didn't just happen. It was produced generationally. The same thing happens with poverty. Wealth was able to be produced by having land, being able to cultivate that land with free labor, turning it into industry. If you had no land,••• as many people of color didn't, you had no means to build wealth over generations and generations. You have cycles of poverty. We still see that today.

←--------------------------------------------------------

••• In history classes, we usually learn about the "40 acres and a mule" promise in 1865 to give every freed Black family forty acres of land. What we don't learn about is that President Andrew Johnson reversed it after Lincoln was killed—and gave the land back to former Confederate owners. Later legislation also lacked implementation plans, and for decades it was very difficult for non-White people to own land.

There's a study about how, within our city, there's a life expectancy gap between the south and north of town. That gap is *16.1 years.*

# Sione

SALT LAKE CITY, UTAH

My favorite singer is Lauryn Hill.

I'm a big film geek.

I like grapes but I hate anything flavored "grape."

I really want to go to New Zealand.

People always think I'm twenty-five, but I'm really nineteen.

*I was born* in Redlands—a small town in California. My dad is an immigrant from the Pacific island of Tonga. My mom is from America.

My dad actually came to the United States on his Latter-Day Saints mission, and while he was living here, he couldn't envision himself living in any other place. He met my mom and they got married. I have three little brothers. We later moved here to Utah, which is a little bit more diverse than where I used to live. I never met somebody with the same name as me until I moved.

I think the most difficult thing about growing up as a Pacific Islander is not having enough representation . . . not seeing you. I can't see anybody, not even on TV or in movies, that I could want to be like. My dad and his siblings all worked construction jobs. Every Pacific Islander I met when I was young wasn't really in a position of *power*.

If our people *are* present in the media, we are super misrepresented. We are seen as lazy or violent or only good at sports. So many people first see me or one of my brothers and say, "Hey, do you want to join our football team?" It's a misconception that I don't have anything else to offer the world.

It made me really want something more. That's why I lead a peer leadership club and class called People of the Pacific in my high school. It opened my eyes up to how much I was limiting myself, and how I let other people around me affect what I thought I could do. I was introduced to so many powerful Pacific Islander people in America: like Eddie Aikau, Haunani-Kay Trask, Mau Piailug, even Dwayne Johnson.

I want to be a role model, but I don't know if I can. Basically every Pacific Islander says, "Family over everything," so many of our students drop out of school. I really value education, but since my family is always first, there were situations where I had to be 100 percent with them and so my grades suffered. I got detentions for being absent so much. When it comes to our assignments, many of us who are first generation are on our own because our parents won't be able to understand them.

Although I'm taking a few years off just to support my family, I'm proud that I got into college, and that I even got some scholarships. Maybe that will set me on a path to being not just Tongan, but somebody with power who can be a role model for others.

←——————————

Often Pacific Islanders are cast in the same general "model minority" category as all Asian Americans, but only around 18 percent of Pacific Islanders have a bachelor's degree, about half as many as the general population.

# Matt

**PORCUPINE, SOUTH DAKOTA**

When I'm not working, I raise heritage breed dogs on
the eastern side of the reservation, and chickens.

I've got a six-month-old son
who is named after Macklemo[re]

I'm originally from Louisville, Kentucky,
a place that loves college basketball.

I spend my free time cutting
wood and building homes.

I was a vegetarian for ten years.

*My grandparents were* pretty racist. I didn't know any sort of word for folks of color other than the n-word for a while. Without a doubt, you have love and respect for your grandparents, because they're your grandparents, right? But honestly, they existed in a place of fear for anybody non-White. I remember in high school, living in Kentucky, the woman I dated was a Black woman. My granddad saw her, and said, "Who's that little n-girl?"

You really can't legislate compassion, caring, empathy, and that's a lot of what folks, especially White moderates and White progressives, look for: a check box at some point in life to say, "Look at me, showing compassion! Look at me, caring about race!" I believe that what it really is, is the way that you choose to wake up every morning and live your life.

I left Kentucky in 1998, when I graduated from high school, and since that time have been involved in the fields of education, community work, housing, and now work here at Thunder Valley on the Pine Ridge Reservation, which is the intersectionality of that education and community work and housing coming together.

There are a few different things that we try to do here. One is that we teach young folks to build homes for fifty to a hundred years down the road. The second part is to focus on continuing education. About a quarter to half of our kids come to us without a GED or a high school equivalent. And then the third piece: social-emotional focus. We can go out and teach anybody to swing a hammer, or continue their education, but if you choose to ignore some of the challenges that are presented just by existing in a high poverty area like the res, then you know most individuals aren't going to be successful. So, we do equine therapy with horses, talk therapy, and sweat lodges for that social-emotional healing.

Regardless of whatever community of color that I am living in, institutionalized power, from the federal government to local policies, is typically stacked against folks of color—it doesn't matter if you're Native, doesn't matter if you're a refugee, doesn't matter if you're a person of color in Kentucky. Our systems are not designed to take power out of the hands of largely White men who hold it. I work with Native youth, usually eighteen to twenty-four years old, to help them take back some of that power. As a human, as a citizen of the United States, as a White man, that's my duty.

←——————————————————

Pine Ridge has the lowest life expectancy in the country (66.81 years), and the lowest per capita income ($8,768), ranking as the poorest county in the nation.

# Jennifer M. and Felice

I'm a private investigator who specializes in mass shootings.

I speak brave, terrible French.

I joined Instagram just to follow Drake

I will beat anybody at karaoke.

I make really good banana bread.

I love Prince.

I love Jay-Z and cried the first time I saw him in concert.

*Felice:* At first, I hated her.

*Jennifer:* Hated.

*Felice:* I was twenty-three.

*Jennifer:* Which is her excuse for everything.

*Felice:* That's true. I made a lot of bad decisions at twenty-three. But, literally the night that I met her, she was sitting in the lap of a poet—a person I refer to as my arch-nemesis because we just totally did not get along. And I was like, "If you are that close to somebody I don't like, I cannot possibly like you."

*Jennifer:* We got close eventually. I remember, around the time I had cancer—

*Felice:* Oh, I know the story you're about to tell! Can I say it? So we went to this breast cancer awareness book reading thing somewhere in the West Village, and afterwards a woman came up to her and she was like, to me, "I have a reading series, called Sisters Black Like Me. I would love to have you come read." And I was like, "Awesome." And then she turned to Jen,

and she said, "I would love to have you come read, too." And Jen said, "Sure, yeah." And then we just died laughing.

*Jennifer:* We looked at each other and I said, "Do you think that she doesn't—"

*Felice:* I was like, "I think she knows."

*Jennifer:* Race is, for us, one of the things we are asked the most often. We're like, what is happening to us? Why are we always assaulted, almost, with this question?* Because I'm White and Felice is Black, we are demanded almost to speak directly to that. Why can't we speak to another topic and just represent an active intersectional friendship? We are two women who started out as strangers and became sisters. We had the surety of our friendship as men passed through our lives, through family changes and career changes. Our friendship has been a kind of transcendent place. A refuge really for both of us, I think.

*Felice:* I was teaching a workshop on Fire Island one summer. And I was probably the only woman of color there that was not a nanny. And I was working

---

* From Ophelia in Maine: "My race is just so 101 about me. I have these elementary conversations with people about the basics of who I am—explaining who I am, why I am, how I am, when at the same time I could be having a conversation with somebody else about, like, my hopes and dreams. I wish I could just tap out sometimes."

with just the most privileged children in the world, and I was being called the n-word by strangers on the street. I remember just being like, I want my sister, Jen, with me. Regardless of her race, because she knows me better than anyone. And I know she's going to be like, "Whatever you need, I'm here." Even if the world sees me as this limited racialized identity, I have somebody on my side who sees me as a full human being.

*Jennifer:* I live in Brooklyn, in a largely Black neighborhood. One time, I was walking home, and a man, who probably was on drugs from the way he was walking, screamed at me in the middle of the afternoon, "What the fuck are you looking at, you fucking cracker?** Get the fuck out of Bethesda. You don't belong here!" And immediately I was drenched in sweat and walked home. And I was in tears and Felice was the first person I called. The next time Felice came to my home, I was like, "Hey . . . uh, want to go walk around the neighborhood?"

*Felice:* Get it? Because she wanted to show them she had a Black friend, ha-ha.

*Jennifer:* Sometimes people will ask me, "What is it like to be a woman writer?" And I'm like, "I'm a writer." I'm not going to suggest that I transcended womanhood, or race, but I don't always want that hanging over me.

I think it's refreshing that we don't talk to other people about our races. We don't owe that to anyone. Because I think you see us and expect for us to sit down and start talking about race, how we're friends *despite* Felice being Black and me being White, but Felice and I are just best friends. We talk about what best friends talk about. We talk about men. We talk about God. We talk about work and being a writer and living in New York, TV, cops, and cops shows, lots of cop shows.

---

** Although originally used to refer to poor White people, assumedly shortened from "whip-cracker," "cracker" today is used "as an epithet for bigoted White folks."

# CHAPTER NINE

# IF YOU WANT TO HELP, HEAL

Spring 2017, half a mile away from each other, in the darkness of a sleeping town, two alarms simultaneously began blaring loudly at three a.m. The two of us woke up. We had only slept for a few hours. Priya, slinging a heavy backpack over one shoulder, dragged herself into the car, then to Winona's house—or, the next day, vice versa. Together, until school began, we would clank away at our e-mail inboxes, drafting cold e-mail after e-mail, getting the work done to actualize our gap year, while the sun rose behind us.

We thought then that we understood exhaustion. We didn't.

Four months later, we were just leaving the dinner table with our wonderful host family in Morgantown, West Virginia, when Priya prodded Winona's shoulder aggressively and urgently. We were nearing the end of our journey's second leg, and we had been on the road for over a month. We still had two more cities to go—Baltimore, then D.C.—before we'd take a short break at home. On the stairs down to what was formerly a miner's basement, Priya whispered, *"I. Have. Dots. All over my right arm."*

Winona abruptly stopped, turning around and causing Priya to stumble right on top of her. *"Ohh, myy—"* she began, eyes wide open. *"Priya, then why are you touching me right now?"*

"I don't know what it is!" Priya whimpered, retreating a few steps back.

We huddled in the basement and hatched a game plan: we would wear long clothing, avoid the children, and cancel some of our interviews. Over the next two days, as the condition grew worse for both of us, we would spend most of the time pathetically curled up on our twin beds, itching uncontrollably. Later, our doctors deduced it was *likely* a bed bug attack, but at the time, we guessed it was poison ivy. Over the phone, Priya's dad proposed an allergic reaction to unfamiliar laundry detergent; Winona's mom claimed divine intervention. They all told us we had been on the road too long, and we needed to go home.

The truth was, we really wanted to go home. We loved hearing dozens of stories a week from so many people, and for them, as well as for the people who would eventually read their stories, we would never change a thing. We also felt so grateful, *all* the time. Yet our bodies had never felt so weighed down; not only physically, but also emotionally—we felt utterly exhausted. Our mysterious bodily ailment only heightened our awareness of that exhaustion, one that felt very different from waking up at three a.m. in high school, because it came from a very different place.

For the past month, every hour, every day, we'd meet a new stranger, most often a person of color. We'd ask for their most personal and most vulnerable stories. While many were hopeful, many were heartbreaking. On our fourth day traveling, in Seattle, we interviewed a Japanese internment camp survivor, then a college student who lost her entire childhood neighborhood *and* home to

gentrification, then a man whose father had been wrongly incarcerated, all in a row. Our very last day of the trip, in Charlottesville, Virginia, Heather Heyer's mom showed us videos of her daughter laughing only weeks before Heather was killed in protests. We listened to men who had been shot, children trafficked and abused, ordinary people of color beaten on the ground. During and after each interview, it felt hard to breathe. Our hearts physically felt more and more tense. We had our own experiences too: being explicitly called foreign in every other state, being reminded over and over of our own memories, being scared for our lives in rural country among staring White men with guns.[*]

One mentor, hearing our experience, gave us the language of *"secondary trauma"*—emotional duress from listening to and wanting to help others who had experienced trauma firsthand. We realized that hearing up to twenty-four stories in a day might be too much. And even if it wasn't, at least we had to do a better job of taking care of ourselves, of *healing.*

We learned the art of self-care. We journaled often, we dug into music and art,

[*] Perhaps some of the exhaustion also came from traveling, and from being with one other person for over 720 hours consecutively. Winona, by the way, talks in her sleep. And Priya, in Morgantown, decided to hide all of the anti-itch cream for self-usage. Sigh.

we sought conversations with our hosts outside of race, we occasionally took an afternoon off to visit a museum exhibit on another topic. To activists around the country, we began to ask, "How do you sustain yourself, how do you heal, doing this work? Isn't it emotionally exhausting?" Many would chuckle. "*Obviously*," a Black woman told us in Vermont. "I hate talking about race. I'm tired of it. But we have to do it. Tapping out of racism, out of this work, is not a privilege people of color have anyway."

Audre Lorde once wrote, "Caring for myself is not self-indulgence, it is self-preservation, and that is an act of political warfare."

Those next few days in Morgantown, we deliriously and melodramatically shared our greatest dreams with each other: to hug our moms before they tucked us into bed, to wake up to home-cooked Chinese eggs and Indian *dosa*s and dig in greedily with chopsticks or hands, to easily *breathe* the air of a town familiar to us, to *not* talk about race for just one day. To feel free was *not* to adventure, but to be home, to feel safe, to feel loved. We needed that to heal.

We ended up huddled in our beds, watching *Titanic* next to a box of tissues and untouched Vietnamese takeout. We postponed Baltimore and D.C. to leg three of our trip. When we returned home, our mentor would remark, "You two came back as different people: I feel a much greater *heaviness* within you."

The effects of the potentially-bed-bugs condition** healed within one week. It takes *much* longer to heal from the heavy, emotional sting of injustice. Many people of color—who may already experience racism and then have to relive it in conversation, or defend themselves when others don't believe them, or be called on to speak on behalf of their whole race—can and do experience a very real, tangible exhaustion. We haven't found this type of fatigue to be as acknowledged or validated as it should be. We even noticed it way back in high school: during any classroom conversation about slavery, civil rights, or non-White people in general, more often than not our teacher *and* all our classmates would turn to the only person of color in the room for answers.

All the people we've met who are affected by trauma on a daily basis, all the activists working full-time to face and bring down racism—we find their resilience extraordinary, their strength unimaginable to most of us. Their propensity for self-care is not a matter of preferred choice; it is essential. Just as a preflight safety demo will tell us to "place the mask over your own face *before* attempting to assist anyone else," just as the well-known saying goes, "Do not set yourself on fire to keep others warm," activists like Sandra Kim from D.C. will

←

** We still aren't sure what it was.

tell us that, for them, "healing work and activism work are one and the same."

Remember that the necessity for healing does *not* mean that responsibility solely falls on marginalized folks to fix themselves. Rather, we must always place responsibility for change on the oppressive systems in place. All of us are affected by the toxicity of racism, and we all have a duty to do something about it. Let's take care of ourselves too, so that we can get the work done. If you want to help, heal.

# Kimmy

**HONOLULU, HAWAI'I**

My favorite tattoo is on my arm and I still have to finish it.

I love school, that's one of my favorite things.

I love to visit my friends who are in prison.

I love going to the beach.

*I was born* and raised here in Hawai'i. My biological mother was sixteen years old and living in a girls' home in the hills of Kailua that was meant for "bad girls." Shortly after my mother gave birth to me, she gave me up for adoption.

I was adopted into a pure Japanese family, and my new mother and grandmother were very prideful. They emphasized that I had to be with someone in the culture. I was molested at the age of seven, and my Japanese mother chose her boyfriend over me; she didn't believe me, and I became an outcast. From then on, I was treated differently, and it broke me. She didn't know how to love or how to give hugs because her mom never did that to her. So, she didn't teach me how to have a good relationship. Everything she projected on me, I later projected on my kids. I allowed the generational curse* to continue. I went to prison. My mother went to prison. My brother was in prison. My biological dad was in prison. My two sons, my second oldest son and my third oldest, are both in and out of prison.

As my childhood progressed, my mother became verbally abusive. I ran away and made a life on the streets. Prostitution, stealing, you name it, I did it. It took a hold on me. I met people and started using drugs at eleven years old. Eventually, I ended up in a detention home. I ended up in the place where my mom gave birth to me. Shortly after leaving at eighteen, I got

pregnant. I was so desperate to feel loved and fill that void in my heart. My baby's dad came from an abusive home too, and we both had trauma, so we always clashed, we always fought. My baby came premature: three pounds, two ounces.

The relationship didn't work out, and I had a baby with another guy, then three more babies from another guy. In all of this, I wasn't thinking about my kids. The *drugs*, people take drugs because they want to numb that pain, fill that void. Ice was my number one drug. I eventually committed a lot of big crimes and ended up in prison. I was trying to find myself and love myself at the same time, and I carried the heaviest shame and guilt.

Today, now that I have a clear mind, I know what to do. I hope one day my kids can see me for who I am today and not who I was before. My third son, who is hooked on pills, still tells me that was because of me and his dad, because of the trauma.

After a year in prison, I got out and went right back to drugs. Next thing you know, I went back to prison again, but escaped and got trashed, and went back to craziness. In 2003, I came back to prison, spending a lot of time in lockdown because I was high

←————————————————

* **By the 2010 census, Native Hawaiian/ Pacific Islanders made up 10 percent of the island's population, yet 39 percent of the prison and jail population.**

risk. In that time, I went into a faith-based substance abuse program where I learned about myself spiritually and found God. I started to cry for the first time; I was like, "Oh my gosh, I'm so horrible." I would always blame my mom, and I realized really my mom didn't put a gun to my head and say, "Hey, smoke this pipe right now." I realized[**] that everything I did in my life was a choice that I chose.

One of the wardens at the prison really believed in us. He said, "Kimmy, when you walk through these gates, you are forgiven." I couldn't understand that. I had hurt so many people. My change was happening when I went to these programs, because the warden helped us find a place of healing. If you don't heal while you're in prison and take accountability for what you do, like, you're still stuck in that rut, you're most likely gonna come back to prison.[***] In prison, I was even put in some leadership positions, and they helped me to grow and hold people accountable and do amazing things.

It was a miracle that my forty-year sentence was reduced. I finally left prison in 2014. It was hard for me, but eventually I found my biological parents—and I wanted to go to school before I found them. There were grants for people that were Hawaiians, so I had to actually go into my adoption records and get proof that I am Hawaiian. From there, I looked into my adoption files and found my mom, my biological mom. I learned that she died shortly after she gave birth to me. At the age of eighteen, she got shot execution-style because she was in a gang. I learned she had a twin sister, my auntie, who used to follow my mom around. My mom was on drugs and going on the run, and my auntie got scared, so she just stayed home after. My mom later told her, "I want to come home," and my auntie told her, "I'll be waiting for you." She never did. When I

---

[**]  In a 1983 foreword to *This Bridge Called My Back*, Cherríe Moraga writes on building a U.S. women of color movement: "Coming to terms with the suffering of others has never meant looking away from our own." At the same time she adds, "We must acknowledge that to change the world, we have to change ourselves—even sometimes our most cherished block-hard convictions . . . If the image of the bridge can bind us together, I think it does so most powerfully in the words of Donna Kate Rushin, when she insists: 'stretch . . . or die.'"

[***]  A study of 660 persons released on parole in Hawai'i between 2005 and 2006 found that 1) Parolees averaged 56 total prior arrests and 24 convictions per parolee; 2) LSI-R scores (a rehabilitation assessment tool) predicted recidivism fairly well; and 3) A little more than half of parolees failed on parole within three years.

reunited with my aunt and shared these stories, I felt acceptance and learned who I really am. Just recently, I met my biological brother and he was crying as we shared family stories together.

Discovering my roots has really helped shape my identity. As a kid, I didn't want to be Japanese and I didn't want to be Hawaiian. My identity was really messed up, because if you don't know your roots, then eventually you're just going to make something up. My passion today is with the women in the prison through the Pu'a Foundation. Hopefully I can inspire them not to fight, not to be angry, not to be resentful of their past. I fought my whole life and it didn't get me anywhere. That's why I like the queen, Queen Liliuokalani of Hawai'i. People spat on her, people betrayed her, and she stayed humble; she was beautiful, quiet, she was super smart. She wanted the Hawaiian people not to be angry, but to forgive the White men for real.

We need to come together, and the only way we do that is if we stay humble. We can't fight against each other. We've been fighting all these years and we're not going anywhere. There's so many people that are hurt and broken by the past. We can't directly heal anybody, but hopefully by sharing our stories, people will think about it or be inspired.

# Javier

SANTA FE, NEW MEXICO

I enjoy date nights.

I love road trips.

I eat red chiles at my mom's house.

My favorite time of year is fall.

*I was raised* in a multigenerational family that has mixed ancestry—early conquistadors as well as Mexican and Native American heritage. New Mexico* is very much a blend of cultures in that way. My family's also very traditional and Catholic.

In high school, I didn't know anyone who was gay, and I didn't know how to come out. My world was very conservative; the church created a huge fear. I'm a person of faith, and I didn't want to walk counter to God. Even when my two cousins died of AIDS, the silly chatter was whether or not they'd have a spot in heaven.

At the same time, in high school I was introduced to leadership. I was president of the senior class, then president of the student body, then I went to Boys State [an American Legion program]. I was the first in my family to graduate from college, largely because my brothers helped out and took on extra jobs. Shortly after graduation, I had the opportunity to run for the county commission.

There, I met a girl; we ended up getting married and having two beautiful girls. I felt like it was tradition, getting married and having kids. There are lots of people like me who keep their true selves secret. The option to come out hadn't really presented itself, but my sexuality was becoming more front and center in my mind, and I was starting to understand that I could no longer bury it. I had two daughters, and I was living a lie. I knew that if my wife and I stayed together, it wasn't going to be good for them or for us. I went through the process of coming out in two stages: first, coming out to my family, as a father and husband, and then to the community, as the mayor.

When you come out, the sky really becomes the limit. There's nothing people can use against you. You're fully participating in your life. Ultimately, the whole process of coming out has made me a stronger father for my daughters.

Today, I try to minimize how much of my sexual orientation leads to policy. For example, during my campaign, I spent time with the trans community. It was hard to understand, but that became my real first education about the issues they face. In my first state-of-city address, I had a trans youth give the pledge of allegiance, and I

$\longrightarrow$

* As of 2017, Hispanic people made up 48.8 percent of New Mexico's population, Native American people were 10.9 percent, and non-Hispanic White people were 37.5 percent.

** Nearly two-thirds of transgender students avoid school bathrooms because they feel unsafe or uncomfortable.

spoke about creating safer places in the city with gender-neutral bathrooms.** It was about a sixty-second statement in a forty-five-minute speech, but the next six to eight weeks were all about how the mayor was allowing perverts to come into the bathrooms. Well, I believe Santa Fe should be inclusive—truly welcoming and understanding—for everybody. Did I do that because I was gay, or because I was responding to the needs of the community? I think I was doing a bit of both.

I'm hoping that my presence in office, as a Hispanic gay man, sends a message: if you're put in a position to improve the lives of people, you should do it.

# Aubrey

**LOS ANGELES, CALIFORNIA**

I love Greek and Egyptian mythology.

I am obsessed with dogs. Most of my Snapchats are of dogs on campus.

I can rap Eminem's "Love the Way You Lie."

I love Jollibee (a Filipino fast-food restaurant).

*My family filed* papers in 1992, before I was born, for citizenship in the United States. In the Philippines, my parents reminded me at least once a year of the possibility that we might go to America. I loved my home and I didn't want to leave my grandparents, my dog, or my friends. So I told them I'm not going. I didn't want change.

But when the papers for citizenship came twenty-two years later, I realized that this was my opportunity to establish a strong family relationship and live with my dad. At the time, for *seven months* a year we wouldn't get to see my dad while he was working at sea on a cruise ship—or even talk to him because of a poor phone signal.

It was really hard to let go. Mostly, I lost my dance community, which really put me in a bad place. My mind went to areas that it shouldn't have. Asian-American communities plow through our struggles. This mentality causes us to continue to work, even if we are breaking down, turning down our emotions or neglecting our physical health, because we tell ourselves we're not "successful" yet. In my family, we don't talk about depression or anxiety.

UCLA was the only school I applied to as a dance major. That's not really accepted into Filipino culture—because of my family's migration story, people had thought applying as a political science major, to eventually become an immigration lawyer, would have led to more "success."

But here, I found dance again. I became super vulnerable. I wasn't afraid of my emotions. I embraced my mental state and health. Dance has saved me in so many ways. Hip hop is so inclusive, and it's not about aggression, or fighting back, or backlash for the social struggles we go through; it's all about love and life and even the unity of similar community conditions faced within the African and Latinx and Asian-American communities. Dance is there for everyone.

I usually say this, "Bloom where you were planted." You can't bloom as a flower if your soil is toxic. You have to find your own sunlight, your own sources of water, your own sources of happiness, because at the end of the day, what really matters is you. If you are not happy, you can't spread joy to the community. If you follow your

Thirteen percent of all Americans contemplate suicide in their lifetime. Among U.S.-born Asian-American women, that number is 16 percent, higher than immigrant Asian women and U.S.-born Asian men. The 2007 data show female Asian Americans ages fifteen to twenty-four were second only to Native Americans in their rate of suicide deaths. All Asian Americans are less likely to get help for any mental health problems than White people.

parents' dreams, I don't think you are going to be effective as a community member. Your boundaries are your quest. Just think of your limitations as a challenge, as your lifelong quest to overcome—because even though Asian Americans are part of the model minority group, "success" is not a finish line we are supposed to cross. You should not be talking about the end game, but instead the process.

# Evelyn

I write children's books.

My granddaughter helps me write my books.

When I was a preschool teacher, I impersonated Elmo to calm the kids down.

My husband is the love of my life, we have been married for twenty-seven years.

*The housing projects** were terrible. They had low-income families—including my mom, dad, my four brothers, and I—squeezed into two- or four-bedroom apartments in row houses. There was a lot of oppression, violence, gang warfare, prostitution, and drugs, and it took a lot of work to not get involved. I remember playing in the playground and being worried that a whole family of fourteen people would come jump on me. I still have the emotion of running out of the playground and into our apartment to be safe.

I remember how, since there was no awareness for getting medical care for sicknesses, my mother didn't go to the doctor until she had stage four breast cancer. Nothing could be done.

When she passed, my then-boyfriend and now-husband decided that we had to get out. We didn't want to raise our children in that violent environment. We didn't want our girls to have a bunch of babies and have no focus on their future or education. We've lived in the suburbs for twenty-five years.

It was scary times when my family lived in the projects, but now it's even scarier. People feel unprotected and unsafe, but have no choice because they can't afford** to live anywhere else. Regular people don't have access to trailers of guns worth millions, so who is dumping them in our community? People don't have anything and will use the guns to kill themselves out of desperation. Same for drugs: we do have dealers, but who is their source and why are they killing *our* families?

I wish people would communicate. The government could organize a forum in the community to figure out what people fear and need, rather than turn their backs on the people that need the most help. If we can come together, hear both sides, not be scared about backlash, then there will at least be less negativity, because people know that somebody is going to take action.

To people who are struggling in the projects around the country: if you are a

———————————————————————→

* The projects go back decades—in 1933, during a housing shortage, the government created suburban houses specifically for "White, middle-class, lower-middle-class families," pushing Black people into city housing projects. A good book to learn more: Richard Rothstein's *The Color of Law.*

** There are more Americans living in high poverty areas (where 40 percent or more of family incomes fall below poverty line) than ever before. That number nearly doubled between 2000 and 2013, from 7.2 to 13.8 million.

believer in Jesus Christ, trust that he is going to be a provider for us. Jesus Christ helped us to have a better life. There have been numerous occasions when I should have died, but his angels kept me alive. Keep on trusting that he will heal our bodies, communities, and minds. He is in control and will turn the situation around. [If you] believe this is the best you can have, you will never have anything better. Be encouraged, get an education, and fight for your dreams and your family . . . don't let anyone stop you or tell you that you can't, because you really can do it.

**Alok**

OLATHE, KANSAS

I love playing cricket.

My favorite color to wear is black because my mom told me it makes me look tall.

I have two bumps on my forehead from when my mom dropped me when I was two months old.

I love playing pool.

*I was born* in 1985 in Hyderabad. I came to Kansas City in 2006 to do my master's in electrical engineering. Like every Indian kid, all the best memories obviously involved playing cricket. Race and religion stuff was unheard of. I remember Hindus and Muslims had different festivals, but you never said, "This is my festival, that is yours." We went to each other's houses for all of them.

The transition was pretty smooth here; it just felt like going from place A to B. We met in groups in Hyderabad who helped us plan for the move. A cousin picked me up from the airport, and my brother lived in Dallas. We never distinguished that we are going to a country that doesn't recognize us. We never thought of it that way. The notion hasn't changed for us.

Right after "the incident,"* a lot of people asked me if my view of the American dream changed. When I said no, it did not change, not many understood where I was coming from. The support that the community gave actually strengthened my belief in the American dream even more.

There's nothing new that I can talk about with the incident that hasn't already been reported. It's a one-off incident that shouldn't have happened. We were just having a regular conversation, and it was a bad day for the gentleman and so he took his anger out on us. We were at the wrong place at the wrong time.** We've got to keep moving forward.

We still continue to believe that this is our country, this is our home place, this is where we bought our homes, and this is where we are raising our kids. We call two countries our home. One of my White friends here in America self-proclaims to be the godfather of my son, Arjun. So if

---

* On February 22, 2017, Alok was hanging out at a local bar after work with a friend, Srinivas Kuchibhotla. A White man who came in first shouted at them abuses like "sand niggers" and "get out of my country," before shooting them both, injuring Alok and killing Srinivas. According to the South Asian Bar Association of North America, "South Asian communities are being targeted in a way that we have not seen since immediately after 9/11."

** We were awestruck by Alok's positivity. We were also reminded of others we met who struggled to avoid self-blame and victim-blaming, thinking that they deserved to be hurt because they did something wrong. A psychology study of the "just-world bias" shows that, because our brains crave the predictability of good being rewarded and evil being punished, our culture tends to unfairly blame victims of injustice.

something happens to me, he's going to take care of him. Before the incident and after the incident, we still continue with the same: Best friends. Family. That's it. Nothing else.

After what has happened, though, I definitely am more attached to my son. Having a kid is a blessing for sure. Your perspective changes a lot. We're in a blessed state, having the opportunity to hold him, change his diapers, all that fun stuff. I'm writing a letter to him right now that does include what happened that day. It is my responsibility to let him know from my own words, and help him understand the diverse culture we have in America while he's young.

Future plans? I don't know, man. I've just got to prepare myself to change the diapers even more. Just give me that strength.

# Karen

**GARY, INDIANA**

I played point guard on my high school and college basketball team.

I love rap music.

I have a twenty-three-year-old daughter who's now a mother and tells me what to do.

I love to travel and party.

*During the time* that I grew up in Gary, it really transformed to a predominantly African-American city.* I went to school with folks who looked like me, I worshipped with people who looked like me, if I was shopping in the city, it was around people who looked like me. I also had two active parents. While it was comforting, and my teachers were clearly interested in my well-being, what it created for me was an artificial environment. I was in a community created out of segregation.

I went to Harvard for undergraduate and law school, and it was culture shock. I had a roommate who liked punk rock! Another roommate was on the crew team—I had to look it up. I understood most of them went to more challenging schools** than I did, but I was still confident. It helped me to understand the importance of having diverse experiences as you grow up.

When I came back, I saw Gary through a different lens: I understood an over 80 percent African-American city was not normal. I worked in the prosecutor's office again, and I was one of probably three African-American lawyers. Even to this day, I'll go to a meeting with the attorney general along with other mayors, and it'll be all White men and two women, both of color. My childhood, education, and career as an attorney and in government has allowed me to talk about race very comfortably, to look at a list and say, "I don't see any people of color on here. Why is that?"

I often think that people are more sexist than they are racist. You know, sometimes men of color will say, from a biblical standpoint, that they would prefer not to have a woman lead. Even if they say to me now, "You're a great mayor," they still operate in that manner. When I was practicing law, *every time* I walked into this judge's courtroom, he would say, "Is it Freeman *or* Wilson?" about my last name. I'll say, "It's Freeman-Wilson." He kept asking. You have to let a whole lot of stuff roll off your back.

←————————————————————————————————

* White flight during the 1970s meant White people moved out of Gary, furthering an already heavily racially segregated northwest Indiana. Karen explained how in 1967, Mayor Richard G. Hatcher was elected and "people were afraid of having an African-American mayor."

** A clear example of systemic racism is seen in our education systems, where the level of education you get often depends on where you live. Karen told us, "It's one thing to say, 'No one ever called my child by a race-based slur" (interpersonalism) and another thing to say that it doesn't matter if you're born in Gary or Munster or East Chicago or Schererville, you will get the same quality education" (systemic racism).

On any given day, somebody complains about something, multiple times. Even when I go to church, a lady gives me a list of things on her block. To hear it all, you have to have an inner faith and vision that these are just problems we are still working to solve. We are a diamond in the rough, and I know we are full of assets—I mean, we're at the intersection of four major highways! Our Achilles' heel was just an overdependence on a steel industry that broke, and we're reshifting our economy now. When you Google the city, a lot of things that pop up are about poverty and violence. But over time, organically and increasingly you'll see positive things like our ArtHouse. There are so many examples of good people informally supporting each other every day.

I love the resilience of the people of Gary. We have been challenged, but folks see it for what it is, and they try to change it: they keep going to work every day, keep investing in property, in community. That's what resilience is all about.

# Darren and Dom

**PORCUPINE, SOUTH DAKOTA**

I like hunting and fishing.

I love baseball—go, Yankees!

I enjoy babysitting.

I love dogs.

I was a water protector with Dom for four months.

I enjoy good vibes.

I have a great personality.

I'm just overall a good person.

**Darren:** We're brothers. We're enrolled in the Oglala Lakota tribe, and me and him, we're spiritual. We do the Sun Dance.* We go to ceremonies, sweat, everything that a Lakota does. There's music, a lot of prayer songs, four direction songs, and ceremony foods, buffalo heart and kidney . . . We're still learning a lot about our culture.

**Dom:** We'd like to show other teenagers our ways, how we look at the world spiritually.

**Darren:** It's so powerful—if you guys have ever gone to a sweat ceremony, you'll see stuff that nobody else in the whole world will ever see. It can't be explained. It'll just change the way you live, you'll *know* there's a higher power. Before I got introduced to the spiritual stuff, I was out there. I was a bad kid, I was out there

→

* The Sun Dance is one of the most important ceremonies for the Lakota people (and other Plains Indians), considered a time of renewal. According to one writer, "The dance represents the people's participation in the life of the cosmos itself." Darren also mentions sweat lodge ceremonies, which are meant to "help the vision quest seeker enter into a state of humility and to undergo a kind of spiritual rebirth."

drinking and doing drugs. A lot of youth who don't participate are like that, and thinking about suicide. They just have to know they are not alone. We go through a lot of hardships on this reservation— there's poverty all over, there's no jobs, I have a lot of friends that have just given up hope.

**Dom:** Well, if we're going through a hard time, we know we usually go to sweat. It cleanses your soul, makes you a better person.

**Darren:** There's also a lot of hardship and suffering in the Sun Dance. We pray together, and miracles will happen. Last year was our first year participating in it, in Thunder Valley, and there's a thing called "piercing."

**Dom:** Yeah, you get flesh wounds from the Tree of Life: you hook yourself up to the tree, and you dance and you pray. Whenever you break off from the tree, that's where all your prayers go and your flesh goes.

**Darren:** I pierced twice last year—one was for my dad, who's going through a lot healthwise. We lost our mother at a young age. Sun Dancing helped my family get through all the hardships.

*Dom:* People don't know it, but prayers[**] are actually really strong. And it brings us together as one, makes us thankful that we still have our ways despite all the genocide in our past. We celebrate still being here, and still knowing our tradition, our language. We practice the ways of life, so we can pass it down.

*Darren:* Some days when you're broke, you're sitting there thinking, "How can I get off the res?" I have connects in Victorville, California, and I'm gonna start working up there, but I'll always come back for Sun Dance and stuff, 'cause this is our way of life and we can't lose it. What I want is just for our ways of life to be there, because it's so important for the Lakota people.

*Dom:* Sometimes I feel like we're stuck here, but I enjoy being here because it feels like home. I love this place, I grew up here, I know pretty much everybody, and I feel like I belong here. I wouldn't want to be anywhere else, because our language is dying down and our generation has to keep it going.

←——————————————————————————

[**]  While there is a huge diversity of spiritual practices and beliefs across Native Americans in the United States, in many tribes, spirituality is extremely important in both daily life and in healing from trauma. One study of Navajo patients found that 62 percent had been treated by spiritual interventions from Native healers in the past.

# Ophelia

**PORTLAND, MAINE**

I'm an award-winning pumpkin carver.

I once got to play music with Yo-Yo Ma and the Silk Road Ensemble. I play the piano.

My favorite part of the Oreo is the outside, not the inside.

I'm currently the president of CAFAM, the Chinese & American Friendship Association of Maine.

*Growing up, what* I remember most vividly is this pretty universal experience of being a third-culture kid. My parents immigrated from Hunan, a province in China, to the United States about a year and a half before I was born.

To me, being an Asian-American person is not a hyphenated identity. I don't like the usage of the hyphen in "Asian American" because I am fully both. I don't really feel as though "Asian" is an inflection, or a flavor, in my Americanness—my identity is fully in both camps at the same time. For a lot of third-culture* kids, or at least in my experience with ABCs—American-born Chinese people—you are never completely at home in the homes that you attempt to make. And that's okay. Those spheres that I think I can, to some degree, inhabit, I don't inhabit them. But I get to peer into them: what it's like to be an Asian person, what it's like to be American.

I honor and respect my parents' journey, while my relationship with my parents is still a little complicated. It's largely been a combative relationship, with an underlying understanding that we really love each other. There is no doubt in my mind that our value systems are different. For example, while this was never the largest source of our conflict, when I went to college, I got my nose pierced with a brand-new best friend. I had a debit card at the time, and my parents had the password to my account. They were like, "What is this seventy-dollar charge to this tattoo shop? Don't let me see it." Even now, if I decide to go back home, I'll take it out just out of respect for them. You know, redecorate my face. Another thing: my parents still have a sense that "nonprofit" means "no profit." I think that they have a little bit of sadness knowing that the money that I make will never be able to provide for them in a way that I want to be able to. Lucky for me, I have a younger brother who can handle that. I think.

I do have a very strong sense of filial piety,** and at times my sense of filial piety to my parents can come at odds with my filial piety to my community: to the people who have made it possible to live a strong and authentic Asian-American experience, and, as a queer person, to queer activists. My parents see those pieties as largely incompatible.

---

* This idea is also described in Homi K. Bhabha's writing about the hybridity of a Third Space, so that "we may elude the politics of polarity and emerge as the others of our selves."

** Chinese culture is heavily shaped by Confucianism, and in Confucian philosophy, one of the most important virtues and duties is "filial piety," an attitude of respect and obedience toward one's parents and elderly family members.

When I first started dating my wife, Hayli, we realized there were a lot of cultural differences between us and our families. Her family is from Rockland, approximately two hours north of here. They're *Mayflower* people, meaning their family has been in Maine since the *Mayflower* landed. I absolutely adore parts of their culture, and some other parts . . . could use a little bit of updating. What I've come to realize from the experience of reconciling my wife and my family, myself and her family, is that one of the best witnesses for change has been us living our authentic lives.*** I can give my parents articles, books to read, cite facts, but I don't think anything is really a substitute for hard work that the heart has to do, and finding ways to love people when you didn't think it was possible to do so. The only viable, sustainable bridge-building I've seen happen is living, letting people see that your life is beautiful and that you have so much confidence.

We've been married for two years now, and we'd been together as a couple for several years before that. It has taken my family a very long time to come from where they were then. This last Christmas, we decided to come back to see my parents. It was a pretty painful experience, but at the same time, I really commend my parents and my wife for being able to reach across the aisle to each other. Hayli is a very blunt person. She said to me, "Write me a list of ways that I can prove I'm a good Chinese daughter." So I wrote her a list. When she saw the list, she said, "I don't know if I can do this. This is, like, a really intense list." But there was her opportunity to demonstrate some of that love in ways she does not usually. At the same time, on my parents' side, one of the more beautiful moments was when Hayli sent my parents an e-mail, something stupid like, "Hey, this is the windshield wiper brand I think you should buy." She called them by the names they chose to go by: Lily and Zack. I would call my in-laws by their names, too. But my mother called me one day and said, "I was really hurt that your wife didn't call us 'Mom and Dad.'" She was all fussy about it. I was like, "Oh. That's really sweet." It meant a lot. My wife decided on calling them "Ma and Ba," like "Mom and Dad" in Chinese.

*** Trans actress and activist Laverne Cox said in the *It Got Better* docuseries: "Telling the truth to myself about myself is awesome because it's just a relief. I don't have to try to be something I'm not—I can just be. Who you are authentically is all right. The shame is what kills you. Believing you are unworthy of love and belonging—that who you are authentically is a sin or is wrong—is deadly. Who you are is beautiful and amazing."

# Ples and Azim

I like tennis—I was a tennis champion in high school.

At one point I had dreadlocks down my back.

I like to dance.

I like to travel.

I walk backwards to exercise, and do yoga in the morning for ninety minutes.

My nickname is Butch.

I like golf.

I maintain a collection of precious stones and rocks from every place I've ever traveled.

*Azim:* I met Ples soon after I lost my son, Tariq. He was a university student and worked as a pizza delivery man on Fridays and Saturdays. He was lured to a bogus address by a youth gang. One of them was Ples's grandson, Tony. Tony was fourteen years old and given a gun by the eighteen-year-old gang leader. In the gang initiation ritual, Tony shot and killed my son. He was only twenty years old.

It brought my life to a crashing halt. Extremely complicated to lose a child. If I had been there, I would have put my body between the bullet and my son without even thinking. I went through all the emotions; I was even suicidal at one point. I didn't know how to go home without my son.

I am a Sufi Muslim, and I meditate two hours a day. My mother was very spiritual, my dad was a businessman. I grew up with equal emphasis on my spirituality and my career, and that's what saved me.

I began to see the enemy as not Tony, but rather a society that forces many young kids to fall through the cracks and then choose a life of crime and gangs and drugs and alcohol and guns. It's a big problem: we lose* sixteen kids ages twelve to eighteen every day, and another two hundred are arrested and go to prison.

I reached out to Ples. We both lost a son, because my son died, and Ples lost his grandson to the adult prison system. Tony is thirty-seven and still in there. I can't bring my son back, you can't get Tony out, but the one thing we can do is make sure that more people don't end up dead or in prison.

Actions have consequences, and we can all make good and nonviolent choices. At the same time, we can all choose forgiveness instead of revenge. If you're being bullied, remember that bullies need help too. You can't destroy dark with dark. You go into a dark room, turn the light on, it's no longer dark. You can't destroy hate with hate, only love can do that. Revenge is the precursor of every new act of violence. There's a great quote from Gandhi along the lines of, "an eye for an eye, soon the whole world is blind." We love each other, we support each other, and we respect each other. From conflict, you can find a brother.

*Ples:* Azim's heartfelt and very compassionate, forgiving response to the

---

* According to the Brady Campaign to Prevent Gun Violence, in the United States, 47 children and teens ages zero to nineteen (and 342 people total) are shot every day in murders, assaults, suicides and suicide attempts, unintentional shootings, and police intervention. Homicide is the second leading cause of death among U.S. fifteen- to twenty-four-year-olds.

murder of his son was very much an answer to my prayer. When I found out that Tony was responsible for the murder of Tariq, I began to focus my meditation and my prayers in a way that sought guidance and opportunity for me to meet Tariq's family, especially his father, Azim, and express my deep, deep condolences for the loss of his son at the hands of my grandson. I wanted to commit myself to him and his family in any way that I could, in any way that I could.

Azim punctuates the reality of the violent society that we as Americans live in. Tony grew up in a household with his maternal grandmother's family. Many of the males in that family were gang involved. Tony actually experienced the aftermath of one of his favorite cousins being murdered by rival gang members.

←

** As of 2012, 55 percent of crack users were White, and 37 percent of crack users were Black. Yet, Black people were "21.2 times more likely than White people to go to federal prison on a crack charge."

But these societal forces don't just exist in ghettos where Black and brown people live. Look at the opioid epidemic in this country. It's called the opioid *epidemic* because it's mostly young White people. It's not called a *war* on drugs.** It's a therapeutic, societal approach—the way they look at people who are affected by taking OxyContin. It's way different than throwing police on them and throwing them in jail because they happen to be Black or brown.

I don't see any difference at all—none—between an addict who's addicted to pharmaceuticals and an addict who's addicted to whatever the hell they're addicted to. It's all addiction. It's all very hurtful. It's all very harmful. But in our society, in our wonderful society, we make these distinctions. We deal with them very, very differently. It has to stop. It has to stop. It makes the entire society dysfunctional. We must focus on wellness building for particular people in particular places instead of focusing on wealth and health building for the entire nation. As Americans we should all want that.

# Hermon

LAS VEGAS, NEVADA

I was given a Rastafarian namesake by my Rastafarian community.

I am a musician. I've been in reggae bands, jazz bands, avant-garde crazy experimental bands, metal bands.

I love matcha green tea.

I have a couple bad-ass sci-fi movies to write.

*I ran for* Congress as a progressive Democratic Socialist for the purpose of including more diversity in the House, because my particular background—being Iranian-Korean-American—has never been represented. You gotta have people who understand the culture, the dynamics, the history of those regions and diasporas to be able to actually push for diplomacy.

I basically suspended the campaign as of a week ago, on February 2, 2018. I'm coming from a pretty raw place. I was all in and I just punched on the brakes. I'm still navigating a lot of my own existential processes right now.

I'm a first-generation child of immigrants. My mom came from South Korea, my dad from Tehran in Iran in the seventies, and they both barely spoke any English. Farsi was my first language. I don't know how they actually got about making me, but I think there's maybe a few places in the world where people who have such disparate backgrounds can meet and be able to raise a family and consider themselves the next generation of this place, America. From a young age, I was always navigating these hyphenated hybrid identities that made me feel like I was an anthropologist. In a way, it distanced me from my own self; I can observe the cultures that I am part of without fully being recognized as of those cultures. It's a lifetime journey to figure out where I fit in the world.

Iranian and Korean cultures, for me, had a lot of parallels because they're both old world cultures, while American culture is still quite formative, still developing, in a constant process of becoming.* We have the ability to shape that reality; that's the beauty of America. Of my identities, being American was where I saw the greatest contrast. I remember the first time I saw my father cry: I went up to him at six and said, "*Bâbâ,* why do you speak so weird?" The tears came right in front of me. I understood for the first time how much race actually affects people's life experiences, their feelings and emotions.

My campaign was a very public, very frontal process. In a way, I was part of a very fringe political ideology that wasn't really mainstream until Bernie Sanders's run, which enabled mainstream Americans to think, "Okay, has capitalism gotten us to a point where we need socialism now?" I couldn't say I am a

---------------------------------------------→

* Frederick Douglass in his well-known speech, "What to the Slave is the Fourth of July?," said: "The eye of the reformer is met with angry flashes, portending disastrous times; but his heart may well beat lighter at the thought that America is young, and that she is still in the impressible stage of her existence. May he not hope that high lessons of wisdom, of justice and of truth, will yet give direction to her destiny?"

socialist straight up, because I have people who have five-bedroom homes. I have to say it another way, like, "Seven out of ten Americans live with less than a thousand dollars in savings."

To me, people are like, "Who the heck is this guy? Is he Latino? Is he—what the fuck is this guy?" That confusion forces them to be a little bit more fluid in their thinking, because they can't pin me down to one particular group, and then I can talk about the issues being intersectional on economic, racial, criminal justice, environmental lines, you name it. Everything was so inherently intersectional that I didn't even need to talk about the keyword "intersectionality."

We each have agency, a relative power to effect change in our community. You can think of it in concentric circles: your personhood; the next ring is family, friends, and partners; and then outside your acquaintances, your colleagues, your community at large; then your region, your country, et cetera. But then there's the structural part of it: economic policies, justice policies, housing policies, race, your own skin, the resources we have access to.

Those structural barriers made me step out. The moneyed interests are so fucking strong, even in the Democratic Party. They want to maintain the status quo. My own structured agency was so limited, given the power of the structure. I found myself being pushed to the edge, getting exhausted to the

point that had I continued all the way to the end, I wouldn't be the same person. I would've felt crushed by this mountain that is the establishment, that is this political machine with all its levers of power, with all its institutional memory, with all its huge amounts of money behind it. It's a huge system** to fight.

I didn't mention that one of the prime motives for me to do this was having lost my father. Losing my father was, for me, losing a part of myself. I had a crisis of self, of "who am I in this world without my father, who is my cornerstone?" All these dark money groups put tens of millions to propaganda campaigns, and I was thinking, "Oh my God, I had just lost my

←————————————————

** The United States is built off capitalism, but in a Spring 2016 Institute of Politics poll among eighteen- to twenty-nine-year-olds at the Harvard Kennedy School, only 42 percent supported capitalism, 33 percent supported socialism, and the majority rejected both ideologies. Typically, those who supported capitalism were more likely to be college graduates, White, male, from the South or West, and members of the Republican Party. Socialism was supported by eighteen- to twenty-year-olds, Democrats, Clinton voters, and Hispanic and African Americans. A similar poll in Spring 2018 found 64 percent of young Americans have more fear than hope about the future of democracy in America.

father," Muslim ban comes out, rubbing salt into the wounds, and I was like, "I'm gonna fucking run for office, this is bullshit." My people have been vilified since I was born—I was two-thirds of the "axis of evil" during the Bush administration: North Korea, Iran, and Iraq. I'm gonna push back with a seat at the table. Excuse my French, I'm not a candidate anymore, I can say that.

I'm still trying to fight that system, but doing it from the inside at this point in time would've led to death by a thousand wounds, even just in the general attacking of my family. Now I'm trying to do it in a way that's life-affirming, and not life-threatening. Maybe this was for the better, to not continue. I don't know. I'm still grappling with all that.

# CHAPTER TEN

# LET'S ALL GET TO WORK

"*R*ocky," Winona interjected, half an hour into our interview. "How do you know all these stories, if no one else in the community does?"

"Well, I do a lot of research, I read a lot of the old newspapers. People tell me things; I'm a local," he responded. He uncomfortably rubbed his few remaining white hairs. "Well, I can't say *local*, because my folks moved here in 1948, so I'm not *really* a local. But I want this museum to be very personal, a place for stories, not just a storage house for the artifacts. I want people to get the full story."

Priya had frowned skeptically at Rocky's resistance to identify as a local in Sundance, Wyoming, despite having lived there all his life. Although our two sets of parents did not know each other until a year into our friendship, they had moved, separately, from much larger U.S. cities to Princeton in 1999 because of their jobs. Shortly afterward, we were both born in the same Princeton hospital, three months apart. Today, we'd unabashedly call ourselves Princeton locals.

We came to understand that Sundance culture is very different. Rocky didn't consider himself *really* local because the "local" families had been there for *centuries*. Nestled in the northeastern hills of the least-populated U.S. state, the easy-to-miss town of 1,182 people rarely sees transience; most of the ranches have been run by the same German, Italian, and Scandinavian families since they chased out the "heathen" Lakota people after 1874. "The White families were taught to fear the Lakota, to hate them," Rocky, the curator at the Crook County Museum, told us. "That never really left . . . Sundance was built to be a wealthy, White town."

A historian by training, Rocky had spent the past few years digging up his town's racial history, an endeavor necessary because *no one* else he knew had even tried. One story from the late 1800s particularly makes him mad. Of the three Chinese laundries that used to be in town, only one stayed for a while. The owner was a Chinese man, and the White Sundance residents all agreed that he was making too much money. The Chinese man said, "I live here, I'm a good citizen, I'm giving it back," but they still wanted him to leave, and threw him in the middle of the streets, poured beer all over him, and called him a drunk. An article called "What Shall We Do With Him?" in the February 12, 1896, local issue of the *Crook County Monitor* wrote,

> We fear that it has become a serious question as to what steps should be taken to permanently remove a crazy Chinaman from Sundance. Parties here have paid his transportation to Spearfish and Deadwood a number of times, in the hope that the people of his blood in those cities would care for him, but like a counterfeit coin the Chinaman invariably returns . . . The Chinaman is in a pitiable condition and should be sent by the government to his native land for treatment.

They eventually got rid of him by calling up an insane asylum in Denver to take him away, saying they were afraid "this gentleman gone mad" was going to harm somebody in town. "You know, the good ol' White supremacy thing," Rocky finished, sighing.

After leaving the museum, we picked up our lunch at Wild West Espresso, where the lady at the counter asked, by name, about the children of every passing customer. Two interviews later, we stomped our way through the snow to the medical clinic—which had slightly over or under ten employees "depending on the day"—and Priya asked the front desk where we could find a person of color to talk to. "Uh," the woman said, hesitating for a few seconds. "I believe the two Black people are out of town today."

Prejudice was not exclusively confined to race: a police officer we interviewed named Adrian told us that queer people were scared to come out after "what happened to Matthew Shepard," a gay University of Wyoming student who was brutally tortured and left to die in 1998. And in his experience, it didn't take much for hate to spread. His family had stopped talking to a cousin who unthinkably dyed her hair purple.

Rocky seemed puzzled when we told him we were much more interested in hearing his story, rather than, say, the "marvelously infamous" local story of an

American criminal, the Sundance Kid. He was extremely proud of his hometown history, yet he was also honest, often brutally so. He wasn't perfect—for example, he commonly referred to local Natives as the "Sioux," while some Lakota people in nearby Rapid City had told us it was an offensive term meaning "little snakes," given to them by their foe, the Ojibwe, and normalized by European fur traders. He admitted without prompting, "I might still have blinders on." Nevertheless, the extensive information in the museum and walking tour brochures made it clear: this history buff was *extremely* determined to pursue truth and justice.

He had applied what we call a "Racial-Literacy Lens."

We hear this question all the time: *If I want to show up in this messed-up world as antiracist, what should I do?*

The world already bestows us with answers. Organize the walkout! Call your senator! Donate to a nonprofit! Importantly, VOTE! But, while inspiring and necessary, these models of activism also encourage us to ask: Is that *all* we can do? And even if we do join in and post emphatically on social media about how much we love *Black Panther* or Oprah's Golden Globes speech . . . is that enough?

A framework we propose: put on your Racial-Literacy Lens. In other words, look at both yourself and the world through a racially literate filter, *self*-activating first to become a more effective activist for others.

The formula has three steps, or "the three Cs":

1. **Be Conscious.** *Are you actively aware of race's impact?* Rocky didn't realize until later in his life that Sundance had a racist history. He listened, and he learned. He thought about it often afterward. He walked through the same space and had a completely different experience, just based on his consciousness.

2. **Be Critical.** *What are the specific problems?* Rocky knew no one in Sundance had easy access to a presentation of the full history.

3. **Be a Contributor.** *What are the best solutions you can pursue?* Identify the skills and resources you can leverage for social justice, and do the work. Rocky was already a curator. He decided to reflect that full history in his museum. (With his friends, he also never talked about Sundance the same way again. Remember: Solutions can be big or small, innovative or preexisting. Small acts matter too.)

This formula also applies to us. We started learning about race in Princeton. We became conscious. We realized that our teachers weren't given the tools to teach about race. We were critical. We created a story-statistic model and a textbook. We were contributors.

To recap: Racial-Literacy Lens = Consciousness + Critique + Contribution.

An important note on the formula—the term "racial literacy" can be misleading, perhaps implying that we must only *become literate about race.* We really think of "racial literacy" as shorthand for racial *and* intersectional literacy *and* leadership. As you read in "Our Richness, Race and Beyond," race and other identities are deeply intertwined; our lens should not be limited to racism. And *literacy* is meaningless without *action*: remember, just *thinking* about cooking won't put any dinner on the table. However, if everything we just mentioned was in the formula, we bet you wouldn't remember it. Plus, we believe that the focus on *becoming literate about race* as a first step will more naturally lead to the rest.

Think about the stories that have impacted you most so far from this book. Maybe it's Claudette, who had to cook Mexican food on *Top Chef* with one spice bottle of "Mexican Blend." Or Kao Kalia, who writes to write her Hmong people into existence. Or Butler, who taught us names from the Civil Rights Movement we should've known all along. How do they change your *consciousness*? Your *critique* and perspective—on textbooks, on

migration, on history? How will you *contribute* in your own community from now on?

The people you'll meet in this chapter have asked themselves the same or similar questions.

We can all apply the Racial-Literacy Lens to any space we inhabit. We need it in academic spaces, like classrooms or museums; we need to keep the lens on at our family dinner table, at the amusement park, and at the counter of our favorite small business. We're not asking you to completely change your life, but rather, reframe it. If every person used their Racial-Literacy Lens, imagine how much we could disrupt the injustice we see everywhere—together.

We *implore* you to turn racial literacy into a daily practice.

Make it a habit to ask yourself: *Am I applying my* Racial-Literacy Lens?

Using the Racial-Literacy Lens doesn't necessarily make you an "activist." Many full-time activists command an awe-inspiring level of commitment, training, and knowledge (and this is just one proposed framework among the many solutions they and others are developing today). But options for everyone to engage in activism go past just career or side volunteer work. It's not like you're an activist *or* a dentist, an activist *or* a cashier, an activist *or* the president—activism doesn't have to be a prescription for just a few or a title you assume, because to stand against all forms of injustice should be a human duty, no matter what your profession is. We can and should all work together to break down our entrenched systems of racism. Ordinary individuals *just* like Rocky can be ears and microphones for justice.

Sharing our stories of race and identity can change the world. Let's all get to work!

# Sybil

**LITTLE ROCK, ARKANSAS**

I studied in Japan as an exchange student through the Experiment in International Living.

I was president of the Rockefeller Foundation.

Writing was a thing I loved best in college.

Some people have said to me, "I thought everything was okay after the Little Rock Nine." Did they think we were just singing and dancing afterward?

When we lift one story up—like that of the Little Rock Nine, or Rosa Parks—there are other stories that get pushed back. You don't see that there are a thousand or thousands of unnamed people who were engaged in the struggle, who made sacrifices, who put one brick on a road that took a billion bricks. We are a culture that loves icons and heroes. When so many young people ask the question, "What can I do? I can't be like the Little Rock Nine!" it's because we created this sense that that's what it takes to create change. Your name doesn't have to be known for you to be important. The Little Rock Nine were the warriors and every war has warriors, but every war also has foot soldiers. If not for the foot soldiers, the war wouldn't be won.

My role was as a foot soldier.

When I was growing up, I was constantly reminded that all of us needed to do something, to do my part in the struggle. You have to understand the context of what it was like for parents to train their children to not go to a bathroom that is not for the colored, to not drink from water fountains because you could cause problems, to not look White people in the eye, because, if you're an African-American boy and you look at White women, you could be lynched.

My parents raised me as a hydra-headed monster, to be aware of the present, living in a segregated society, but also to keep hopes and dreams alive. Previously unavailable jobs were opening up for African-American students, and we needed to speak well, to be disciplined, to be well-educated, to dream big dreams and know that if you don't get to the moon, you might get an armful of stars.

I lived in a house that was built by Grandfather. It was at the corner of 7th and Park, seven blocks to the north of Central High. As a part of my house, he built a grocery store. On the adjacent northwest corner was an Anglo grocery store, Grant's—if you were Negro, you went to my parents' grocery store, and if you were Anglo you went to Grant's. Half the block up was Negro, and the other half was White. So my neighborhood was segregated, but not segregated. I saw White people, and my parents were friends with some of the neighbors. For example, one of our Anglo neighbors, the Harrises, didn't have a car, and when it rained hard, my father would drive the oldest son to high school. When the father was away in the military and the family hadn't gotten rations, my parents gave them groceries until they could get money and then they would go to Grant's. I don't remember ever being in their house, though, sitting down in their living room.

When I was six years old, my grandfather thought it was very important for me to be out and doing a paper route distributing a newspaper owned by Daisy Bates, the *Arkansas State Press*. My grandfather drove me over to other Negro neighborhoods so that I could sell my paper. I sold Girl Scout cookies, I took piano, ballet, and tap, I was taught to be a good citizen. I learned to step up and be engaged. I had the type of confidence to get stuff done. My parents felt that having poise was very important.

I became a student volunteer to be screened for Central. You were interviewed by an all-White male screen board. They told my parents they were surprised at how poised I was. I was admitted by myself in the tenth grade. I graduated in 1962 in a class with 544 people, and I was still the only African-American student.

I went to the church that the Little Rock Nine went to. My parents were friends with their parents. Being able to go to Central High School was seen as one of the major breakthroughs to break out of the chains of segregation, yet strangely enough, people did not talk to the Little Rock Nine, or ask them what their experiences were. I think there was this understanding that people needed to have normalcy in their lives. When I went to Central, people only encouraged me to do good and work hard.

At dinner, my parents would say, "Let's talk about school." Most days the same thing happened: no one would talk to me, for three years. Once or twice I had accidents where I was kicked, or someone spat in my face. People called me the n-word about five million times. The National Guard left after nothing happened the first day, and the struggle changed, became physically threatening. The first day ended and nobody spoke to me, it was just a shunning. Not a person greeted me. Believe me, I was in the same homeroom with the same people for three years. The only person that muttered one word to me was someone who said, "It's your turn to read the Bible."

I have taken young people who come to Little Rock on civil rights trips, and I am struck by the young African American, full of venom and rage. Change will not take place if you are always enraged, if you decide that violence is the answer. I think that, instead, doing well is the best revenge. Look at the long gain. Do not believe that what is happening to you is the most egregious thing that has happened to your people: you were not born in slavery, you did not live during Reconstruction, you did not live during Jim Crow. Don't place yourself in a position that keeps you from having a good life, from having a position that will be able to enforce power soon. I have been able to make a difference at the right table, not as an angry woman, but as a person who believes higher education can create a fair place.

This is a million-year problem, I believe.

My expectations are of being able to savor the changes that take place, not to be complacent about it, not to make myself crazy about it, because I will not see in my lifetime what I would like to see.

←--------------------------------------------------------------

On the "Angry Black Woman" stereotype, a Black student in Trenton, New Jersey, told us, "It shouldn't be a stereotype—I don't even think that's possible, because everybody gets angry—but I mean, it makes sense that you'd get more angry when you go through more stuff."

# Ron W.

HONOLULU, HAWAI'I

My daughter is fluent in both English and Hawaiian.

My daughter coined the phrase "more funner."

I spend most of my time in historical archives.

**Something that we** need to highlight right off the bat is the idea of your traveling to "all fifty states." Most of my colleagues don't consider Hawai'i a state of the United States. They literally consider Hawai'i as a nation that's occupied by the United States. There were people who devoted their lives, gave their professions, to keeping their nation independent. So to erase that by just talking about it as the fiftieth state is problematic.

We must platform the Native Hawaiian voice. But it's not only about their words, it's not just translation, it's about hearing it with a cultural understanding. I went on a class trip to Tahiti with my language *kumu*, or teacher, and one of the students said to our hosts, "Cool shirt." The host *took off* his shirt, wrapped it up, and put it on the student's bed. So there's this generosity and this inherent idea of nonpossession in Hawaiian culture. Cultural differences like these are what you must understand, so, as a Hawaiian studies professor, I can't be disconnected from the actual people whose history I'm studying.

Thirty years ago, everyone talked about Hawaiian history as, "when the White missionaries arrived, brainwashed Hawaiians, and then stole their land." I have a problem with that. What about Native agency? For example, I came in thinking that Christianity was a tool of the White man that they used to put down Native Hawaiians. That's not what happened. When you look at the records,* you realize that many people took on and *used* Christianity as one of their primary tools to fight for the independence of their nation.

Niihau is an island off the coast of Kauai. It's a privately owned island, and Native Hawaiian only. The Sinclair family bought it in the 1860s, and they've preserved the Hawaiian culture and languages that are there. That's the biggest group of Native speakers we have, and the permanent population there today is somewhat less than a hundred. People are not allowed to visit in general, and folks who leave have to ask permission to come back. I was blessed to visit their church a couple years ago. I sat in a *church* with them, and there's not a person around who would argue that they're not about as Hawaiian as you can get.

---------------------------------------→

* **Puakea and Kau'i, two activists we met in Hawai'i, are working to translate 114 years of newspapers from Hawaiian to English, only 2 percent of which has been translated before. Kau'i said, "The history I knew was largely influenced by the missionaries who took over the preexisting government, and to erase what was there before was part of the plan. If you could not speak Hawaiian, you could not access those records, "those truths, so they didn't let us speak Hawaiian for a while."**

They're also *very* Christian. Everything, like you go to the grocery store, and they're like, "Jesus be with you."

That's when it hit me, like, how prideful of *me* to look at *them* and smile and be like, "Oh yeah, they're brainwashed." There's a complication about where Christianity lies in the Native identity. I mean, look at the American South—many civil rights movements were all sprouted in the churches. In academia, however, we generally want to create the story that you can be hard-core Hawaiians, *or* you can be Americanized Christian Hawaiians. So I had to snap out of that *"I know better than you poor people"* mind-set that I think a lot of historians are in.

When I went to do this work on the church, it wasn't the story•• I wanted to find. I literally went into my dissertation saying, "I want to tear apart the Christian church." The easy thing to do is tell the best story, the most effective story that gets people fired up. But what my *kumu* encouraged was for me to tell the truth. And it was worth it: When I gave this presentation about Christianity, this Hawaiian Native man stood up, and he said, "This is the first time in thirty years I felt like I didn't have to hide my Christianity to be Hawaiian. Thank you."

At this university, University of Hawaii Mānoa, the latest figures are 6 percent Hawaiian or part-Hawaiian faculty. Native Hawaiians are 21 percent of Hawai'i. People are like, to me, a White guy, "What the fuck are you studying *our* history for?" Or sometimes I'm called "a fraud." And I can understand that. When I was an undergraduate, good Hawaiian friends of mine said, "I wouldn't want a *haole*, or White person, being my teacher." I completely understand that too.

Even if you're White, think about it, and you'll see how race impacted your life from the beginning. When I was nine, ten years old in the seventies, I used to get Ku Klux Klan flyers in my mailbox. They'd say, "Come to our meeting next Saturday." I also remember my dad's best friend was the chief surgeon at this medical center, he was African American, and he used to take his son, Jack, me, and my dad out hunting all the time. In Arkansas, you just kind of go out, and whoever's property you come across, you ask their permission to hunt. My dad went up to this trailer house to ask permission—we stood back—and the guy said, "Yeah, you can hunt here, but not them niggers."

•• **Pew Research Center reports that Hawai'i, in 2015, was 6 percent full-Hawaiian, or 21 percent including those who are part-Hawaiian. Research shows that the Hawaiian death rate dramatically increased after European colonizers arrived: one in seventeen Native Hawaiians died within two years of Captain James Cook's first visit in 1778. By 1800, the population had declined by 48 percent, and by 1840, 84 percent.**

So, with that understanding and childhood, I guess I didn't really have an option to "not care" about race. It always bothered me. I always cared. When I came here, I knew that I could never live here, I could never study this land's history, without understanding and getting to know the Indigenous people first.

One of the cultural protocols is that you don't teach or you don't write or you don't do anything without responsibility and privilege being given to you by your *kumu*. You can get your degree, and it doesn't matter. Your *kumu* must say, "You should do this." And so, when my *kumu,* Dr. Haunani-Kay Trask, asked me to teach, for me that was not only my privilege, but my responsibility.

Everything I do, as a White guy in Hawaiian history, is still a constant evaluation of my positionality. It always is and always should be.

# Tiara

**PITTSBURGH, PENNSYLVANIA**

I love dogs—pugs are my favorite.

I have a YouTube channel with my boyfriend.

I like to do makeup, this is my favorite look.

I've lived everywhere in Pittsburgh, in every area pretty much.

*In senior year,* I was a co-cheer captain with my friend Treniya. Something racist happened in my school, and that's when me and Treniya looked at each other and agreed—*we're taking a knee at the next football game.*

Right before the game, we told our girls, "Hey, listen, this is what we're doing, you don't have to do this if you don't feel comfortable. This is what we're doing, because it's what we believe in." Our coach, a White woman, made it clear she didn't *really* support it, but she said she didn't care what the two of us did. We told our school too, so they'd be prepared when the backlash came, even though we didn't have to. They said, "Okay, whatever, it's your choice."

There were thirteen or fourteen girls on the team, and probably half took a knee, even some White girls.

Our goal was to cause a conversation. We wanted to get people in Coraopolis, where our school was, to realize that racism exists. We did start that conversation, and supporters did come out with stories saying, "This is what happened to my child at Cornell High School," but we didn't expect that there would be so much more hate.

Right after, everybody was after us. *Fox News* picked it up, it went nationwide. Some of the cheerleaders completely took back what they did, and then we got the blame because we were the captains and we "forced people" to take a knee. The school got so many death threats, and the phones wouldn't stop ringing off the hook because people from across the country called in saying we should be suspended or expelled. This mother with four kids from Beaver County called and said she was going to come to school to beat us up. On Facebook, people from the Moon Township area posted that our parents are on welfare, we should be lynched, and we should be raped. They took our season away for cheerleading, because it was unsafe. They took our homecoming away too. Even though the superintendent told us personally that he understands and is proud of us, that he supports us, he was also agreeing with the other side.

You could tell there was a huge divide in the school, Whites against Blacks.* People

---

* **A national survey for ESPN found 72 percent of African-American respondents either strongly approved or somewhat approved of the NFL player protests, while 62 percent of White people either somewhat disapproved or strongly disapproved. Within the NFL, in 2018, thirty-one of thirty-two team owners voted for the policy to ban on-field protest or demonstration during the national anthem. At least 70 percent of NFL players are Black. Only two owners are people of color—and neither are Black. In fact, of all ninety-two major U.S. professional sports team owners, only one is Black.**

were mad at us and said, "No, there's other ways to protest!" What other ways could create such a large conversation?

Treniya and I were torn for a good minute, because we made things rough for the football team. But I'm not gonna apologize. We didn't do anything wrong. We stood our ground. Still, we were two high school seniors, and we got nervous. We started to watch where we're going. My parents didn't want me to go walk the streets by myself, and I had to quit my job at McDonald's because of the harassment. My dad got some people to be our security. I started to get really bad anxiety. I would go to therapy, and remind myself everything is in God's hands.

So many people, including a lot of Black people, don't understand why you take a knee. Even my mom, who's White, said to me, "You're half White." I asked, "If I get pulled over by a bad cop, is he gonna care?" She didn't understand it until I put it like that. She has no idea what people of color go through daily.

If more people understood, maybe they'd understand why we would take a knee. For example, I grew up with the n-word being thrown out. Even my fully White sister once called my stepdad the n-word. My family moved schools because people made fun of our White mom getting with a Black man—my great-granddad disowned her when she got pregnant with me. Lots of people ask me things like, "Ew, why is your top lip darker than your bottom?" And you know how Nicki Minaj is shaped? Many Black men think we should be shaped like an hourglass. Well, that's not how real life works. I'd get made fun of because I'm Black and don't have a butt. My first boyfriend, a Black guy in seventh grade, told me for three years, "You're not White, but I mean, you'll do for now." I straightened my hair constantly, and dressed how *they* dress, the way he liked it. I changed myself completely to be with somebody who didn't even respect his own race. And that's just getting started. We have to talk about these things.**

---

** These experiences aren't exclusive to Tiara. One of our very first interviewees in our high school told us that, after her first kiss, the boy whom she shared it with told her she couldn't tell anyone, because he didn't want word to spread that he had kissed a Black girl.

# Lua and Family

DELAND, FLORIDA

I'm a certified yoga instructor.

I'm vegan.

I'm the only girl in a house full of men.

I've run one half marathon, and that will never happen again.

I used to own a hedgehog named Dude who hated my husband a lot.

I grew up on an Indian reservation.

**Can you talk** about your childhood, before you lived here?"

"Terrible."

"Can you talk about it?"

"No. I don't wanna talk about it."

"That's your choice."

"What about today?"

"I like Reed, he's my favorite."

[laughter]

"You wanna know what I like about you, Reed?"

"Ha, that you two are super silly together?"

"Aww—"

"This is a heartfelt moment."

"What are some of your favorite moments together?"

"On the couch."

"What?"

"You remember? When we made the fort. Sometimes we play on the PlayStation together! Yeah, *Reed*! You tripped, that was funny!"

[laughter]

"We just went on vacation together."

"Bowling, hiking, football—"

"We didn't play football!"

"Yes, we did, in the big field."

"Frisbee—"

"—snow-tubing, falling on the water river . . ."

"It was scary."

"It was not."

"No, it was not."

"I went fast, so I screamed."

"So did I."

"You missed it—"

"—oh yeah, the funniest part, I missed it, I went into the *other* lane!"

"He—"

"It was the first time you went on there."

"He slipped into the other side, where there was no slide. He slid downhill, and got stopped, because the snow stopped. Then he went back up and told me not to go, then he went and slid the other way."

"How come your favorite stories are all about each other getting hurt?"

[laughter]

"You fell into the water? You don't remember that?"

[more laughter]

"What's it like having four kids in the house instead of two?"

"It's crazy—"

"Yeah, crazy."

"Nonstop noise."

"Is it fun though?"

"Yeah, it is."

"How is it different with two brothers?"

"Well, it's quiet with just us two."

[laughter]

"Oh, no, with us two, we're not quiet."

[laughter]

"Wait, guys, can we play hide and seek?"

"Hmm. Maybe."

"Can you describe life—"

"Reed doesn't have a life!"

[laughter]

"Ohhhh!!! Wrecked!"

[laughter]

"Are you guys really good friends?"

"Yeah."

"Hmm, sometimes. Sometimes, Graeme, sometimes."

"We're really good friends."

*"Frenemies!"*

"We're friends, but enemies."

"Why enemies?

"Why not?"

[laughter]

"No, we're friends all the time."

"Aww."

"We're like Rumpelstiltskin, that's basically the whole reason why."

"I think that's an inside joke, I don't get it."

"Frenemies!! Or should I say, brothermies. My friends are my friends, my brothers are my brothers."

"That's deep."

[laughter]

*Lua (the mom):* I grew up in South Dakota, on a Lakota reservation, with a lot of foster kids in my house. My two sisters who are Sioux were adopted. I always kinda thought that if you have extra space or ability in your home to take an extra kid, you should consider doing it.

We've had kids of all different religious backgrounds and ethnicities and ages and races in our home. I always try to be sensitive to what's culturally different, but actually, as kids, at least in our house, there hasn't been that much difference. They want to play, they're not naturally very judgmental, they're very inquisitive, and they ask a lot of questions. Right now we have two foster sons.

I've always felt a responsibility raising my two biological White sons, actually—to raise them to understand and do something about their own privilege, to set a good example of what feminist, inclusive White men can be like. The big difference that I do see with raising African-American males is that sometimes, when we're out, people expect more or are more frustrated by my Black kids than my White kids. Behavior seems to be more judged of my Black kids.

For us, foster care has been very hard. Kids have all kinds of traumatic experiences. For example, their home is so unstable that they can't live there anymore, and they're separated from their parents.[*] Graeme, my biological son, has said before that he couldn't even imagine what it would be like if he and Reed only saw us once a week for an hour. You don't know how long you're going to have them; you have to deal with whatever plan the state has. On the good side, when you show kids a loving home, good role models, or how you

---

**•** **This separation process is extremely traumatic. Racial bias is also reflected in this decision by social workers: Black parents are more likely to be deemed unfit, and have their children removed, than White parents. Black parents are also disproportionately likely to be reported for abuse.**

can solve disputes without violence . . . you see such progress in such a short period of time. They just want love and attention and consistency; they want to be cuddled with at night. It's cool for our own kids to be grateful for it, meet kids from different backgrounds. It's been a great growth experience for our family.

There are more kids in this county who need foster care** than there are foster parents. They're kids who belong to the community, and someone needs to step up and do something about it. To be cheesy, they're all our kids, in this world. But I mean, I really feel that way. They are all our responsibility.

---

** In the United States, 397,122 children are living without permanent families in the foster care system.

# Protim

**NEW BRUNSWICK, NEW JERSEY**

My greatest desire is for my daughters to outdistance me in every way possible.

If I have nothing to do whatsoever, I will either watch something related to cooking or I will cook.

I'm in my forty-first year and I still regularly ask myself what I want to be when I grow up.

**On the schoolyard** of Lindbergh Elementary School in New Jersey, I had a scuffle with a friend of mine. It was second or third grade. He was White. His name was Ryan. I was one of two non-White children in my school, but my family were the only Indians in town, actually. We got into a fight: pushing, shoving. But the thing that hurt the worst was when he told me to go back where I came from, and called me "Hershey Boy."

After the fight, my dad, Baba, picked me up to take me home. Just as we stepped onto Union Street, he stopped to say this: "Be careful how much you want to be like them. They'll never accept you, and if you try too hard to be like them, we may not, either." In that moment, I felt something leave me. It wasn't because Baba was wrong, it was because his words felt like a prophecy. For over thirty years, I have walked in a world between worlds.*

Another moment I remember is a Fourth of July night in junior high, at a friend's house. We were all lighting fireworks, and I noticed that my bundle didn't have a bottle rocket like the others. In my town, bottle rockets were also called "nigger chasers" and weren't just fired into the sky. They were fired at Black and Hispanic kids from the school across town. That night, at the end of our firework celebration, one I thought was one of the best nights of my childhood, I noticed all of my seven other friends were starting to light their bottle rockets and point them towards *me*. I saw it coming and started darting away. I could feel the sparks skip off the sidewalks and hit me. I realized that in my community, I was "nigger."

I developed an anti-Indian hatred. I hated what I was and what I wasn't. I hated how Indians were satisfied—even happy—to not ruffle feathers or say anything "wrong." At home, they'd complain, "America this . . . America that," but in public, they accommodated everyone. I was constantly frustrated at how badly they wanted to fit in, all while that's exactly what I wanted, in my own way. Years later, I married a White woman who called my parents "Baba" and "Ma," and took lessons to learn Bengali. She said, "I want to understand your world." Good for her; I didn't.

After a decade on Wall Street, where it

---

* A study called "East Meets West" in the *Journal of Family Psychology* found that Asian-Indian immigrant parents who had a separated or marginalized style of acculturation—adopting White culture—reported *higher family conflict* than those who had an integrated or assimilated acculturation style. When there was no acculturation gap, adolescents also had higher self-esteem and less anxiety.

was finally "cool" to be Indian as long as I "played the game," I went to seminary and became an ordained Christian minister. Upon graduation, I became executive director of a faith-based nonprofit at Princeton University. This season awakened things that had been sleeping for years. At Princeton, we pursued the empowerment of students of color and the engagement of on-campus racial issues. Seminary. Princeton. Theological studies and university students, together they gave me the motivation to not only pursue justice for others but to re-embrace my Indian identity, interact with formal learning on race and intersectionality, and activate my activist spirit. It had always been hovering. Finally, it had somewhere to land.

Nevertheless, I left Princeton and joined a charter school network in Newark. The work of justice here is definitely not as "sexy." It's more in the trenches, maybe more reflective of what many communities of color face in urban America. Here, while I'm still very connected to a racial conversation largely dominated by White and Black populations, my focus has shifted toward finding a significant niche for Asian Americans, Indian Americans. I consistently ask, "When will other people grant Asian Americans with true 'people of color' status? They often have a derivative identity that is dependent on which perspective they adopt in the White-Black binary. However, Asians' own identities

are often overlooked. We are yet to be fully embraced for who we are, especially within our racial identity and the work of racial literacy.

While the Indian-American and the African-American struggles are not the same, to paraphrase James Baldwin, I have become more conscious and much angrier.** I'm angry that Black voices are silenced by White systems and structures. I'm also furious at how Indians, Asians, immigrants, and non-Western voices are silenced by many in the West. In a very surprising way, this tracks back to Baba's caution from years ago: "They'll never accept you." It's just that "they" is bigger and more complicated than I could've imagined. Hegemony is real, and sadly, many people of color are joining the project of Whiteness by rejecting and silencing other people of color, including Indian Americans.

However, Baba didn't just say "they." He also warned that "*we* may not [accept you]." I have no idea about how to talk to my parents about race or anything like it. I'm not just Indian, I'm a Hindu Brahmin, and I've gone through the sacred *upanayana* thread ceremony. From the perspective of

←—————————————————————

** James Baldwin once famously remarked, "To be a Negro in this country and to be relatively conscious is to be in a rage almost all the time."

ethnicity, religion, and class, I've been given the script for academics, career, and family. None of it involved disrupting the status quo for some high-minded ideals. It certainly didn't involve me going to seminary. It certainly didn't involve becoming a Christian activist, so much so that Baba's first response to the news was, "How do I explain this to your grandfather?" That's our generational worship and honor-shame culture talking. Baba asked that *after* my grandfather had been dead for twenty years.

Right now, I'm trying to hear what's coming from both sides. I'm trying to embrace both and then reject both. "Chew the meat, spit out the bones" kind of mind-set. I feel many children of immigrants have some version of that, whether they are Persian American, Indian American, Korean American, or whatever. Honestly, I think these days a second-generation Indian American has more in common with a second-generation, say, Chinese American, than they do with the first-generation Indian American. It full-circle tracks back to what my dad said all those years ago on the playground.

I've been fortunate to gain language and categories for understanding myself and challenging my people. We Indian Americans need a reboot, a reset. We need to reimagine success as something more than model-minority doctors, engineers, and the like. It's fine. Be that, but not while being so compliant, so apathetic, so riskless. This is a tremendous opportunity. What we need is for people like my two Indian-American daughters to imagine that it's not only *acceptable* but *expected* that Indian Americans would be involved in racial and intersectional work . . . as courageous risk-takers and masters of new disciplines.

**Danya**

**LAWRENCE, KANSAS**

I studied Spanish abroad in Barcelona and visited ten countries last term.

I adore cats, but my favorite animal is the sugar glider.

I went bungee jumping in Switzerland.

My favorite place in the world is Paris.

I recently discovered these dark-chocolate-and-coconut-covered almonds from Costco. So good.

*One of my* dad's best friends, Uncle *Aziz, was a doctor who moved back to Syria from the United States because he wanted to help with the war effort. He later died in an airstrike.*

*There was this guy I met when I was fourteen, and had this summer fling with, like puppy love, kind of. We fell out of contact over the years and he crosses my mind from time to time because I don't know, and have no way of knowing, if he is alive.*

*One time, people showed up outside this mosque in Texas with AK-47 assault rifles to protest. There were little kids being dropped off! I said it was inhumane. (People weren't happy with this piece. The comments said things like, "Why don't you and your family get back on their camels and go home.")*

These are all stories I've written about. In sophomore year, I switched from pre-med to journalism, and I started to write about experiences I had with the Syrian War. I used to go to Syria all the time, and I started writing to humanize the war, to show that it's not just the numbers and the people dying,* it's not this foreign, faraway thing. Real people like my family are being impacted, in the United States and abroad.

---------------------------------------→

* The total death count is over half a million, including more than ten thousand civilians in 2017 alone.

I got used to using myself as this platform, using my journalism skills to share my stories. I accepted that people aren't always going to agree with what I say or who I am.

I was born in a suburb of Kansas City, and that suburb is 96 percent White. Both my mom and dad were born in Syria and immigrated here when they were eighteen and twenty-five. I was raised Muslim, and I am Middle Eastern, but I didn't really view myself differently until 9/11 happened. That day I remember we got sent home early from kindergarten, and I could see the smoke billowing out of the buildings on TV. The next day, my parents came home from work with two different stories. My dad's name is Ayam, and he said people were weird to him at work, but he wasn't sure if it was in his head. My mom is a doctor and she was working as a respiratory therapist at a hospital. When she walked into work and everyone looked at her . . . one nurse stood up and gave her a hug.

Growing up, I felt like I was in a constant limbo of sorts. I wanted to fit in with the other kids, but also balance the culture and religion at home. I felt like I was living two lives, or that I was a fraud. I felt shameful that I spoke English and Arabic with my parents. In high school, I was a cheerleader, and I wore the cheer uniform that showed my legs and arms, but you're not supposed to do that as a Muslim. My dad would always try to get me to go to

Sunday school, but I didn't want to be associated with going to a mosque. When I went to the mall, I knew there were all these older women judging me. At the University of Kansas, I'm in a sorority . . . there's only two other Arab girls in Greek life here, as far as I know. It'd be exhausting when I went out in high school, because I wouldn't drink, but also because when people are drunk they'll often ask, "What are you?"

When I was younger, my guy friends would often make bomb jokes. My younger brother's friends always ask him if his uncle is Osama bin Laden, and I had a friend who would get a Snapchat from this guy every single day with the 9:11 time stamp. It's really disheartening to see how Muslims and Middle Eastern people are dehumanized and lumped with this horrific attack in which Muslims and Middle Eastern people died as well.** You just kind of get used to those things, and get thick skin, even though you shouldn't have to. I just take them with a grain of salt and move on.

I've started to realize that people don't know what they don't know, so you have to show them through your stories how you've lived your life. I wish people wouldn't be so afraid to have those conversations, and wouldn't be so afraid of offending each other. These conversations might not be the most pleasant experience, but I would rather have you ask me than have you not know, and for that to manifest into fear or resentment . . . If people understand me, they'll understand my culture, and that will make things easier in the long run for everyone.

←

** An estimated sixty Muslims—including emergency responders, businessmen, cooks, and airline passengers—died on 9/11.

# Steph

**BOSTON, MASSACHUSETTS**

My dad was a Chinese Elvis impersonator.

I learned how to play Super Mario from my mom, who was the first one in our family to beat the game.

In my free time, I like to do neon sculpture.

I have been paid as a DJ: DJ BIG SPOON.

*I was raised* by a single mom; she's Korean. I don't feel particularly attached to my Chinese side because that's my dad's side, and he was never around. I grew up poor, my family was on food stamps for a while. Most people don't think of East Asians as having that kind of life experience. But, at the same time, I suspect that my life is easier because I'm not an African-American woman in tech, and so my inclination is to acknowledge my privilege. Even as I acknowledge that the model minority narrative is false, I want to also acknowledge that Asian-American women and men have a higher median income than many other people of color.

My mom continues to sacrifice a lot, and she takes care of my sick brother. She never really spent that much time at home with us; she was always working. She worked three different jobs. One job was a minimum wage job, so she had to work two jobs in addition to that to make enough money. She basically raised the three of us on a salary below twenty thousand dollars a year.

I remember the day that she showed us our new apartment when I was little. We had been effectively homeless, and we finally got a place of our own. It was a really ugly apartment. Kinda dingy, dirty, small, and it had one bedroom that all of us would share—we were a family of four. My first reaction was like, "Oh, this is not that great," but my mom, she turns to us, smiling, proud, so oblivious about it, and she says, "Isn't this amazing. This is *ours*. This is *our* home." In that moment, she redefined home for me. I think that's why I have never actually valued making a ton of money in my life. I value purpose and jobs where we can try to chip away at the inequality that exists in the world. She—my mom—showed us that you didn't need all the "bells and whistles" for home to be a home. Home is family. The values that she instilled in us in that moment carried through.

Addressing the inequality in clean energy stems directly from my personal experience. I feel like I got this privilege that very few people get—a good education. Our nonprofit specifically works on deploying solar to everyone, focusing on low-income to moderate-income access. We do things like invent a new credit score

---

Steph's the cofounder and CEO of Solstice, a tech nonprofit trying to make solar energy accessible for every American. She's acknowledging how, as of 2015, Asian women held 5 percent of computing jobs while Black women only held 3 percent. The 2010 census estimated African Americans to be 12.6 percent of the U.S. population and Asian Americans 4.8 percent.

for energy, which qualifies people, rather than using the FICO credit score, which is a discriminatory system.

I think that our society is obsessed with entrepreneurs and entrepreneurship. It's seen as this idea of: young person goes and starts a business, and then offers the world a service it wants, and it's all very sexy. Really, entrepreneurship is an act, not a profile. In my mind, it's a verb, not a noun. Entrepreneurship can happen whether you are a CEO or whether you work as an administrative assistant—and I have been both in my life. There's nothing more entrepreneurial than the immigrant experience because you give up everything, because you are forging a world that you can't see yet; that you can only imagine. Those were the values that my mom instilled in us, and I've seen it with all immigrants.

*I grew up* in a very small, quiet, conservative rural community here in Nebraska. It's about two hours from here. When I was very young, a lot of the Pawnee Indians would come back in the summer and put up their tents, and I learned how to Rain Dance with them. Everything closed at six o'clock, completely shut down. Nothing. There are streetlights, but no stoplights. I mean, very small town.

So when I went to college, it was my first real opportunity to have close friends from other cultures. I met my husband, who's African American. Every day is an awesome opportunity to find out more things. But it isn't just about eating soul food for me, or hanging out with White people for him, it's about understanding the world so much better, because I can see through my eyes *and* my husband's, and vice versa. God kind of picked us to be something different, an anomaly, you know? An opportunity to make a difference. It's phenomenal.

So when we were blessed with twins, from the get-go, we have said to them, "You guys are something that Mommy and Daddy could never ever be." Because I can't be biracial. I'm a fifty-three-year-old White chick. And same thing for Dad. I mean, he's the most phenomenal man—except for my dad—I've ever met, but he can't ever be biracial. So we just said to our kids, "You are the beginning of a whole new genre of people. Go. Go be that voice. Be a leader."

Most kids that come here, to this school, have been in a "behavioral compromise"• at a different public school. That might be a fight, or having an illegal substance in school. It's something bigger than just skipping out on classes. This school offers an opportunity for kids to still stay in school once being kicked out. I'm the school counselor.

If you look over there, most of those pictures on the wall are from students over the last ten years of my life. I know for a lot of teachers it's like, "Hey, I ran into so-and-so who graduated a while ago. They had a nice car and they took me to lunch." Well, that's not the same future that a lot of my students have. I'm just always happy to *see* them—and see they're *alive* . . . That's pretty huge. I've been to more funerals than I ever wanted; horrific things. I go into the jail every week and visit kids that didn't have somebody rooting for them. It's hard. Lots of kids ended up in jail. Many of them are dead. Many of them have been murdered.

You know, I've heard some of my students say, "Dr. Busby ain't White, dude."

$\longrightarrow$

• **As of 2013, Black students are 3.5 times more likely than their White classmates to be suspended or expelled. A nationwide study showed that one in four Black students with disabilities were suspended at least once (compared to one in eleven White students with disabilities).**

What an honor that is, to not have to just be seen as White, by physicality. For so many of our kids here, so many kids in all communities, they have never had the opportunity to trust White people. That's the truth. Some kids just need someone to be able to see for a second, or to just take a breath of what they're breathing, because life just can be so heavy.

For example, have you ever seen the movie *New Jack City*? It's pretty horrific. Wesley Snipes was in it, and this drug dealer took over this apartment complex and turned it into a drug ring. So the place where I tutored, that's what the neighborhood kids called it: New Jack City, because of drugs and prostitution. Right in the middle of it, we started a tutoring center. Here I would show up in my car and waltz across the common area. At night, sometimes the police would come to the door and say, "We're going to lock the door from the outside. Don't open it, or you're in trouble too." And I'd have to take all my tutoring kids in the back corner. We'd hear somebody pounding on the door, shots firing . . .

I got out of my car one day and started across the parking lot. This guy approached me and tried to put his hands on me . . . and, suddenly, just like that, there were three or four guys I didn't even know who came off

the porches to help me. They were the drug runners of the neighborhood. It was a high gang neighborhood, and they were the lookouts. They saw that he was harassing me. They came and got him and said, "You don't *bleep* with the church lady! She's here for the kids!" How cool is that?

I go to bed tired every night, but I know I'm doing what I'm supposed to be doing. I mean, what could feel better than that? Anyway, I think it's important for me to say too that I'm not the answer here. I'm not some sort of savior.** I'm simply a mediator, that's it. I'm not the answer for anything, except just to be here and to be consistent.

←——————————————————————

** The White volunteer who saves "African kids," or the White educator who inspires a classroom of kids of color—these are all common media portrayals of a "White savior." Why is it problematic? It can seem more so to convey the power, superiority, and kindheartedness of the White person, rather than the unjust system itself. Shermaine, who worked in a public charter school in D.C., told us, "There was a heavy Teach for America presence there, and I witnessed the aftermath of teachers who were interested in building their résumés rather than being invested in teaching."

Purple's my favorite color, maybe just because it represents royalty and death.

# Monique

**LOS ANGELES, CALIFORNIA**

I started a soulmate journal when I was seventeen, and I gave it to my husband on our wedding day.

I have a dog named Zoli.

# I'm from South Carolina,

from this city that was one of the last to take the Confederate flag down from the state capitol. When I went through a private high school, I was one of a very small population of people of color. From my childhood, one memory comes to mind: I was in this car with a group of kids. We were just driving, and then someone cut us off on the road. The boy in the front seat next to me called that person the n-word. He didn't see them, but that's the word that he chose to use. I remember being weak inside myself, hiding inside of myself . . . I think I made it okay so that I didn't have to see what it really was.

Looking at my career as an actress today, *High School Musical* was the stand-out thing that put me on the map. I remember reading the role of Taylor McKessie, and I believe in the script she was going to be a tall blonde. I remember when I was called back to read for Taylor, hearing the words she was saying, actually having this thought: *"Oh my God, I've never seen this girl on television."* Funnily enough, the other two people who were called back for that role were Asian, which stereotypically on television is more perceived as right for the role. I thought,

*"What an incredible opportunity it would be to portray someone who is the smartest, who looks like me!"* That became part of the spiritual fiber of that role. I wanted it for that reason.

Previously, and especially in the beginning of my career, the roles that I would go out for were very much stereotypical, and primarily, if not entirely, sassy. That was the thing, like, "Oh, sassy Black girl!"[*] And truthfully, I didn't really challenge it that much. I think I was bothered by it, but I didn't know what I would do with those feelings anyway. I feel like I had this perception that White was better.

For me, my role was significant. I think it might be one of the greatest honors when girls of color come up to me and say that I was their favorite, that "seeing you, validated me being smart, validated who I am." It was huge to get to play the smartest girl in school—someone of high intelligence and character—and be Black. That, for me, is the whole point . . . to be embedded in a girl of color's memory as a real and attainable vision of what she could be in her future.

Race was not a platform to speak on, but something to embody by being Black.

[*] The stereotypical "sassy Black woman," especially on reality TV, is dramatic, loud, aggressive, and angry—often insulting Black female intelligence. When asked how best to describe how African-American women were portrayed in the media, the adjectives most cited in a study of five hundred women were "argumentative" (60 percent), "lazy" (46 percent), and "corrupt" (45 percent).

That's the difference: this isn't something that I talk about, because I don't feel necessarily the most qualified, I haven't done the most research. However, I think it's embedded in how I walk through the world, the choices that I make. Fast forward to today, I am actually walking out the vision and the dream of that moment.

I want to give credit to the fact that there are some incredible artists out there, exceedingly more conscious than I am. That being said, I think that the industry as a whole, and people as a gross generalization, are incredibly irresponsible with our platforms . . . especially when a popular song is racially insensitive or misogynistic, I don't think that many artists and actors are aware of the impact that they are making, or necessarily care.

I'm always looking for connections between our issues, so that we can feel like a stronger human force without diminishing the fact that our individual struggles are very valid and very real. For instance, I have a production company, run by a Black woman and a Latinx woman. Previously, I would just say, "Oh yeah, I have a production company." I've realized that, wow, it is something that we are two women who have a production company.[**] It's even more something that we are Latinx and Black women. Let's be intentional in what we're putting forth into the world, the same way people have been intentional about what they've taken from other people. We have to be aware that our contribution is significant. I do own a production company. I am an advocate for women and girls. I have a beautiful Black family. And I am walking out the expression of being the most beautiful, truthful, eclectic Black woman I can be.

My advice to young girls of color? Stand in your truth. Be brave. Sometimes these experiences happen to us because only through them would we be required to find the voice within us. I would have loved to have known what would've happened if I'd spoken up or gotten out of the car. By excusing it, I perpetuated it, but I had an opportunity to be brave. And that bravery doesn't mean to be combative either. It's not to be like, "I'm going to pick a fight." It's to ask questions: "Why did you say that? What did you mean by that? What makes you feel that this is okay?" To actually be present for the possibility for change.

← ⸱⸱⸱⸱⸱⸱⸱⸱⸱⸱⸱⸱⸱⸱⸱⸱⸱⸱⸱⸱⸱⸱⸱⸱⸱⸱⸱⸱⸱⸱⸱⸱⸱⸱⸱⸱⸱⸱⸱⸱⸱⸱⸱⸱⸱⸱⸱⸱⸱⸱⸱⸱⸱⸱⸱⸱⸱⸱⸱⸱⸱⸱⸱⸱⸱⸱⸱⸱⸱⸱⸱⸱⸱⸱⸱⸱⸱⸱⸱⸱⸱⸱⸱⸱⸱⸱⸱⸱⸱

[**] In 2017, women accounted for 19 percent of all executive producers and 25 percent of all producers among the top-grossing 250 films. Very few of all these producers are women of color.

# Kao Kalia

**SAINT PAUL, MINNESOTA**

I can always pinpoint my husband's nipples, doesn't matter how many layers of clothing.

I love to fish, but I have never caught a big one.

My heart stopped beating two years ago and I died and came back to life, so I've only been alive for two years.

When I speak Hmong, I feel like I'm singing.

I love hot water.

*I was born* in a Hmong refugee camp in Thailand. Men with guns kept us inside. White missionaries who came with Bibles tried to recruit and convert us by offering candy to the kids. It was fairly attractive when you live in a place where you only get food three days a week. But I hated it, because they also took your pictures. They wanted you to stand by yourself really straight. That was my first initial reckoning with the fact that the Hmong had no power, that I was living in a borrowed space.

When I was six years old, my mom and dad heard that there were people being transferred to Laos, but bombs were being dropped so whole busloads of people would explode. They made a very heavy decision to come to America. They heard there was a place called Minnesota that was very cold, but you did not need to have a lot of skill to get work in the factories. And there were schools.

I am very close to my siblings. They're my team. My only goal in life is to live and to keep them living, so that I can die first. My biggest sorrow would be if I had to bury any of them. My first friends in Minnesota were from the refugee community—our school bus would drop off all the White kids, and then all the kids of color would get off at the projects. Young White boys would come to the projects and yell epithets at us. One of the first things that I learned was the middle finger. I came back home and I asked my mom, "What is this thing, is it a greeting?" and she pretended

not to know, as if the ignorance could protect us from the world that we lived in.

I was a selective mute for many, many years. I grew up not talking about Hmong and not talking about all of the secrets that I thought I had to keep. That Mom and Dad worked the night shifts, that my sister and I had to take care of the younger kids after school until midnight. I knew that if any of my teachers knew, they would call child services and that we would get taken away from our parents. I realize now that until I talk, every little girl who comes home to take care of her siblings late at night—a part of themselves are held captive inside. The courage to talk about this happened when I became a writer and public speaker.

I do creative nonfiction. I can position myself within the bigger history books. I can sit and talk to you not as a writer or as an Asian American alone, but as a Hmong American writer working from the poverty line. Positionality—an honest reckoning of who you are in the world and why you are in a space at that time—is key for me. It is honesty.

My people have been decimated* by the American government, two-thirds have

---

* In the late 1960s, during the Vietnam War, the American government recruited Hmong in Laos to fight with them against communism. Hmong soldiers died at ten times the rate of American soldiers in Vietnam. Since Vietnam was taken over by Communist leaders in 1975, over 150,000 Hmong have fled Laos.

died in a war or have been slaughtered in its aftermath, and we have been deleted from the history books. We are people without a place on the map, and it is hard. In Thailand, Chinese corporations are using Hmong graves to get bones to be used as medicine. In Laos, all of the mountains and the hills that the Hmong lived on have been purchased by gold mining companies. Hmong people in the jungles run from a war that history books have declared over since 1975. Hmong people are being persecuted in Vietnam, sometimes because they want to practice Christianity. In America, we are one of the most linguistically isolated and impoverished groups.** The Hmong heart inside me weeps. I can feel it, the heart that has no space to breathe in the world. It cries. It reinforces to me the importance of the work that I must do and the life that we must live. I do believe that this profession is a calling.

I have always known that you find the very universal in the very personal—that is where humanity lives—and so strengthening my views of the world gives me more confidence to speak from a place of conviction. My strong convictions were first learned in that camp, then in the housing projects and neighborhoods I lived in. But I think that until we can really tell our stories from where we are positioned, until we can really back each other up with all of our fullness, we aren't really fighting on the same team.

I'm in this position where, because we are new to so much, because I am one of the first published writers telling the stories of Hmong, whether or not I want to, I work in the field of representation. I have to be aware of the dangers of this representation. We are continually in the process of writing ourselves into being.

I have a four-year-old daughter and identical twin boys who are two and a half. My daughter goes to school a block away from where Mr. Phil was—Philando Castile***—who all the children loved because he was very kind. It was really heartbreaking to explain why he was gone.

I try to teach them Hmong language in my house. Language ties me to my culture. I love the way that it makes me feel when I

---

** People often mistakenly lump all ethnic groups from Asia in with the "model minority," when, in 2015, 28.3 percent of U.S. Hmong compared with 12.1 percent of all Asian Americans were living in poverty. At the same time, Kao Kalia made a note that she "would not feel so brave in America without the Asian Americans among her. It is not a coincidence that a Japanese American, Karen Tei Yamashita, was one of the first writers to extend a hand to me."

*** Philando Castile, a thirty-two-year-old Black man, was shot seven times and killed in his car in the Twin Cities town of Falcon Heights, while his girlfriend and her daughter stood witness.

speak; you can feel the reckoning with the ghosts. My kids have Hmong palates, so they like the kind of foods I like. We like crispy pork and chicken skin a lot, and boiled pork bones with greens. It reawakens, it's healing, it's comforting; when I smell it, I know it is home. Hmong women are also known internationally for embroidery, so I make it a part of their life every day. Some people call them costumes but they are not that, they're just clothing. There is a story of cultural genocide in China, that a long time ago our written language was outlawed. So the Hmong women and girls embroidered their language into their clothing. For maybe a hundred years, people could read it, but then eventually it just became beautiful shapes and flowers. My daughter told me yesterday that she's not scared because she believes that Hmong embroideries keep vampires away. Probably not true, but very cool! She believes there are powers in these things that remind us of who we are.

My name, Kalia, means dimples. My grandma gave me a happy name because I was the first kid born after they made it to the camp. She called me the girl with the dimples, or the song with the dimples. My mom told me when I was a baby, I would hear a song and start laughing . . . so the song became real. I think I have an incredibly beautiful name. I don't know

how it will match me when I am older, because sometimes this world has made me more angry than joyful. It is hard to be joyful when you live in a city where a killer walks on, and Mr. Phil is gone. I am going soon to the Stillwater prison, because my number one fan club is the men from jail. Whenever I go, it is like a reckoning with everything I love and everything I hate all at once. My Black brothers and sisters are going through so much. In my line of work, I do not know how dimply I get, but I think in general I am a very joyful person, I have had to be. So I live to love. I love flowers, my whole house is filled with orchids, I love to see them bloom, I love beautiful things. My children are delightful, that helps too. The song can't die, my name cannot die, even when I do.

I do not think I'm going to see racial justice in my lifetime. I know that it is likely that I will leave three interracial kids in a very racist world, but I want to leave them with the knowledge that their mother really tried to build a better place, not only for them but for all of the kids who are unlike them. I think that it is a really important thing to do.

The burden that I take up, I am not in it by myself, and that gives me hope. That's enough, otherwise we can never die, and eventually I would like to die. Eventually I would like to rest.

# HOW TO SHARE YOUR STORY

We hope this book has persuaded you that talking about race can improve—or, at least, enrich—your daily life. If starting that conversation sounds tricky, the following ten conversational norms may help.

## 1. Do your research ahead of time.

A conversation about race probably won't be constructive if you haven't ever thought about race or your own racial identity. Reading articles and books like this one to reflect on the ways that race impacts all of us, learning common terms and systematic concepts, and connecting it back to your own place in the world—that's work that should be done individually or with trusted friends *before* the conversation. Finding language for lived experiences is useful for both White people and people of color.

## 2. Don't make assumptions.

Remember you can *better* understand but not *fully* understand a person's experience, because you haven't lived it. Be humble and vigilant about what you don't know! Avoid making assumptions about someone else's story. Oftentimes, these assumptions can unconsciously involve stereotypes, biases, or the false narratives of racial history that most of us learned in school.

It may also be helpful to not assume everyone did their research, and to compare and agree on definitions of common terms like "racism" and "privilege."

Finally, do not assume that everyone will "process and engage with information about race" in the same way. Courageous Conversations about Race, developed by Pacific Educational Group to achieve racial equity in education, created the below compass to show four different ways people deal with race:

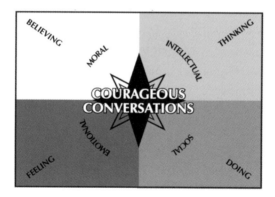

### 3. Challenge yourself to be vulnerable and uncomfortable, but respect others' decision not to engage.

Sharing your stories may require you to be at your most vulnerable. Courageously embrace any discomfort you feel, or even name your discomfort in the conversation.

Some people of color won't want to talk about race. For someone who is forced to talk or think about race constantly, choosing to not do it again can be an act of self-preservation (books such as *Why I'm No Longer Talking to White People About Race* by Reni Eddo-Lodge cover this exact topic). Respect that. We've also interviewed people of color who would rather share their *culture* than talk about race—be sure to differentiate between the two.

### 4. Ask open questions. Practice radical listening.

We always started our interviews with an open-ended question like, *"How has race, culture, or intersectionality impacted your life?"* (Find "intersectionality" explained in chapter 3.) As they responded, we would fully listen. (Read about the act of radical listening in the introduction to chapter 4.) If everyone follows this norm, no one should be speaking for too long and not giving others, especially people of color, space to speak.

Examples of open questions: Ask "How do you identify in terms of race and gender?" first, instead of "So, what's it like to be a Hispanic woman?" Or, instead of asking, "You were sad, right?" ask, "How did you feel?"

### 5. Speak *your* truth.

Don't speak on behalf of anyone but yourself. It's fine to recount something you heard or read, but be specific; avoid generalizing with statements like "The African Americans there thought that . . ." or "Everyone gets mad because . . ." The two of us have caught ourselves saying "Most Asian Americans struggle with . . ." when clearly all Asian Americans, Chinese Americans, or Indian Americans do not share the same struggle. Be honest about *your* experience, but resist the urge to make broader statements about other people's experiences.

## 6. Acknowledge your positionality and privilege.

Be mindful of *positionality*: How are your experiences "markers of relational positions rather than essential qualities"? Scholar john a. powell said, "The slick thing about Whiteness is that you can reap the benefits of a racist society without personally being racist." White people should not talk about race without explicitly recognizing White privilege. Importantly, though, privilege can show up in many other forms, such as: family income, skin lightness (within or across different races), education, body size, ability, and access to role models and opportunities. Everyone should acknowledge not just the plights but the privileges they have. This shouldn't be a matter of guilt, but, rather, responsibility; as James Baldwin wrote, "Guilt is a luxury

we can no longer afford. I know you didn't do it, and I didn't either, but I am responsible for it because I am a man and a citizen of this country, and you are responsible for it, too, for the very same reason . . ."

## 7. Affirm rather than invalidate experiences.

Don't invalidate a person's feelings or their memory of an event. At a lecture we attended in October 2016, Professor Eddie S. Glaude Jr. said, "Being Black in this place called America is constantly having to convince White folks that what happens to us is real. And then we always have to endure the surprise, the shock of horror." Avoid telling someone, "You're wrong" or "That couldn't have happened." If you doubt something, ask open questions.

For privileged people: note that being defensive can make people feel like you're invalidating their experience. Don't act on your urge to make yourself relevant. Firmly accept your privilege or another's story by saying "yes" without a "but," acknowledging (again) that you can't ever fully understand another person's experience.

## 8. Place personal experience in systemic context.

Always keep systems in mind. In a family conversation about conflict between immigrant parents and first-generation children in Chinese-American households, Winona noted that it was not her parents or the kids who culturally "act wrong," but rather a *cultural gap* between the White culture that Winona grew up in, and the Chinese culture that her parents grew up in. Another example: Priya noticed that her parents' hesitation to interact with non-Indian-American families was not because of personal animosity, but because of a language barrier. Without removing necessary blame from individual actions, we must nevertheless understand that the systems that often result in our stories and statistics are much more insidious and powerful than each of us alone.

### 9. Call in rather than call out. Check in rather than check out.

We all make mistakes. Be *fully* accountable for them. In some cases, all we have to do is acknowledge, apologize, and do better next time. If we have to communicate what others did wrong, we could try "calling in" instead of "calling out." That means reacting constructively with patience and compassion rather than angry public shaming (although the latter can sometimes be justified). While we should recognize that impact matters, someone with genuine intent would apologize and seek to do better. Ngọc Loan Trân wrote,

I picture "calling in" as a practice of pulling folks back in who have strayed from us. It means extending to ourselves the reality that we will and do f*** up, we stray, and there will always be a chance for us to return. Calling in as a practice of loving each other enough to allow each other to make mistakes; a practice of loving ourselves enough to know that what we're trying to do here is a radical unlearning of everything we have been configured to believe is normal.

To prevent uncommunicated hurt feelings, also try occasionally checking in by saying something like, "I just wanted to check in, how are you feeling? Should we continue? Can I be doing something better?" If tense moments arise, give each other moments to breathe.

### 10. Focus on solutions.

Actions matter as much as words, and what you do *after* the conversation matters as much as your initial intention. Did you really listen? If you made a mistake, how will you act differently than before? (There is a big difference between messing up once or twice, and continuing something repeatedly without thought.) How can you find an ally or be an ally to issues that were mentioned? How have you or your relationships changed because of this conversation?

Remember: You should never have engaged in these conversations about race if you only wanted to feel less guilty or check off that you appear nonracist. Most likely, you genuinely wanted to understand and support someone else better, and that doesn't stop at one conversation.

# ACKNOWLEDGMENTS

The smartest thing we've ever done is ask for help. This book was an idea made alive by the vision and hard work of so many people. It is rooted in years of support from our mentors who, whenever we called out for help, were always there. Our mentors have given us immeasurable strength and direction. We would've accomplished *nothing* without their belief in us and in CHOOSE, our racial literacy organization. One day in 2014, while randomly interviewing, we tapped the shoulder of Protim Adhikari; it is because of Protim that we began to imagine ourselves not as short-lived high school club leaders, but as strong, passionate, lifelong activists. Around the same time, we first met with Not in Our Town: Princeton—over a dozen role models who so generously guided us as we wobbled through the very first steps of our racial literacy journey. As Princeton Professor Ruha Benjamin drilled confidence and consciousness into our bones, we took her every word as, essentially, the CHOOSE gospel. Nishat and Pieter Ruiter welcomed us into their home, where, over many cups of tea, we gulped up their wisdom and, because of them, have never forgotten to stay grounded in our purpose. While traveling, we pretty much had Betsy and Stuart "Beef Stu" Scolnik on speed dial; they unfailingly mentored us on every topic imaginable while Betsy took over as our manager-mom. Just as we couldn't include every story or moment inside this book, we cannot acknowledge every person who has shaped our journey, or every way that our mentors have shaped us—please know that we value and treasure you all, and all you have done for this book. We've called many of our mentors randomly on the road, desperate to discuss a difficult interview that just struck our hearts. We've been saved by their texts, e-mails, and letters, asking us, for example, "Have you two done any self-care recently?" They've stayed late after work, came (de facto) out of retirement, counseled us, been patient with us, and indulged in our crazy ideas. CHOOSE was born during our meetings in their homes. They've done so much more than was ever listed in the "Professional Advisory Board" member description. Thank you (in first-name alphabetical order here and below) as well to Allison Bland, Eduardo Cadava, Ethan Frisch, Harini Subrahmanyam Frederickson, Howard Stevenson, Jennifer Lea Cohan (who introduced us to the incredible photographer Robin Resch),

Jocelyn Jimenez, John Anagbo, John Cutsinger, John Steele, Julie Meyers, Kareen and Sara Coyoca, Karen Griffin, Kristina Donovan, Linda Oppenheim, Liz Vogel, Marie Deangelo, Martha Sandweiss, Neha Shah, Nipurna Shah, Roberto Schiraldi, Shirley Satterfield, Simona Brickers, Steve Cochrane, Thomas Safian, Timothy Campbell, Timothy Charleston, Wilma Solomon, and all our other advisors. We could write an essay about how CHOOSE would be wildly different without each of you. We love you all, and are beyond grateful.

In room 142 of Princeton High School, before the first bell rang, during lunch, and long after the school day ended, you could find us and three other students huddled together, on the—as we call it—"CHOOSE grind." Ayesha Qureshi specialized in creating artistic pieces about current events for CHOOSE's social media and website, Hamza Nishtar in interviewing dozens of local Princetonians, and Abby Emison in managing our student team. All three contributed greatly to our last book, *The Classroom Index*. After graduating, we met Yasna Vismale, a Columbia University student who helped us ideate ways to involve students across the country. And, while on the road, Brian Li, a student at Duke University, tirelessly maintained our website. This whole time, we have informally employed our siblings— Michaela Guo, Ethan Vulchi, and Daniel Guo—to help us with way too many odd

tasks. You all were the OG team. You had our backs. Thank you.

Our core team member, and current Cambridge University student, Marie Louise James, deserves a ginormous thank you as well. Her artistic skills were legendary in our high school, so, one day in 2017, we asked her: "How can we creatively display our interviewees' fun facts on their photos?" In a heartbeat, she responded with several jaw-dropping samples. We immediately asked her to join our team. She agreed and, since then, has been in charge of CHOOSE's visuals, creating and inspiring the design of hundreds of breathtaking fun-fact illustrations featured on our social media and website.

We came to know the most extraordinary people during our gap year. As we traveled, we met over five hundred people through interviews ranging from four minutes to four hours. We are humbled by how they trusted us with their stories, and by their courage in sharing the most vulnerable parts of themselves with the world. Although we are excited to highlight many more stories on our organization's social media platforms, we wish we could've included more of those significant and striking voices in this book.

All of those interviews amounted to tens of thousands of transcribed words. From all across the globe, these people, many of them high schoolers, were responsible for those transcriptions: Aly Buonocore, Amy Huang, Anna Cincotta, Anne Jackson,

Brenna Miller, Cassia Cai, Connie Cai, Darya Tahvildar-Zadeh, Deeja Qureshi, Eric Holdhusen, Fedlyne Cleophat, Gabrielle Myers, Haley Palumbo, Izzy Nuñez, Jasmine Lyte, Jennifer Nguyen, Johana Pineda-Angon, Kiara Kunnes, Kimi Kobayashi, Lee Linde, Malik Jaff, Marina Curchitser, Mckim Jean-Pierre, Michaela Guo, Najma Dayib, Nancy Wilson, Natalie Marinides, Nayha Zahid, Priyanka Nanayakkara, Raisa Rubin-Stankiewicz, Rin Nagano, Sabrina Roberts, Shane Spring, Tabitha Rucker, Taylor Whittington, Trisha Pickelhaupt, and Yoselin Hernandez. Without all of you, this book would be filled with empty pages. Another thank you to all the other young people who have so enthusiastically supported this work—Sage Adams, Morgan Awner, Samuel Weinglass, Trent Kannegieter, Jordan Collins, our siblings, again, to name just a few. To young people everywhere—you keep us going. Our voices matter, and our generation must lead the way for change, together.

Occasionally, while traveling, we'd run into someone whose expertise would blow us away. We asked many of these people to join our Content Review Team. We firmly believe they're greater than any squad ever assembled before—definitely more impressive (and way more diverse) than the Justice League or the Avengers. Annah Kuriakose, Corrine Sanchez, Dione King, Eran DeSilva, Hunter Taylor, Karen Barss, Linda Oppenheim (who edited our many drafts up to the very last one), Marie Deangelo, Neha Shah, Ophelia Hu Kinney, Protim Adhikari, Sara Fairley, and Sybil Hampton, you're our review team superheroes. In addition, we were lucky to have Ahyoka Youngdeer, Andrew Bentley, Brian Fong, Dejon Jordan, Ethan Frisch, Jocelyn Jimenez, John Kirk, Kelcy Bentley, Milton Reynolds, Nikko Viquiera, Nina Trivedi, and Victor Cirilo review our content too. A big thank you goes out to Meghan Stevenson, who helped us edit our chapter introductions, and Sue Carswell, our fact checker.

Many people ask us, "How did your parents allow you two young girls to travel alone to all fifty states?" The answer is: our hosts. Our hosts made sure we were safe, cared for, and loved. Many we didn't meet until the day of; others were close friends and family. They took days off work to drive us over state borders, fed us delicious Persian, Indian, and Hawaiian food (to name a few), welcomed us into their churches and temples, and even held up our hair as we threw up from food poisoning (sorry, Suchitra and the Harshbargers!). For some of these "hosts," we didn't stay in their home, but they significantly curated our local experience by introducing us to so many interviewees. Every single state was a memorable experience because of them. In Alabama, many, many thanks to the King family; in Arizona, Sarvesh Karra; in Arkansas, Sybil Hampton; in California, Ritesh and Hannah Rae Paspulati, the Vaddi family,

Gena Casillas and Paul Glen, and Betsy and Stuart Scolnik; in Colorado, the Nuñez family; in Connecticut, the Alaparthi family; in Florida, the Vargas family (the first of many on this list from the Baha'i community!); in Georgia, the Pulakanam family; in Hawai'i, Mollie and Mark Sperry, and Miranda Linsky; in Idaho, Ron and Wanda Mills, and Bridgette Kelling; in Kansas, Vindhya Rao and Abhinav Reddy; in Illinois, Cynthia Barnes Slater and Sai Anudeep Kllipara; in Massachusetts, Monisha Vulchi; in Michigan, Dinesh and Gayathri Cyanam, and Sallie and Stephen Campbell; in Minnesota, the Shoemaker family; in Mississippi, the Taylor family, and Annah Kuriakose; in Montana, the Harshbarger family; in Nebraska, Katja Starkey, Priti Agrawal, Prakash Kukreja, and family; in Nevada, Suchitra Reddy; in New Mexico, Martha Sandweiss; in North Carolina, Arch and Phyllis Montgomery; in North Dakota, the McManamon family; in Ohio, the Rajshekar family; in Oklahoma, Sam Hedrick and Haley Myers-Brannon; in Pennsylvania, the Pakulath family; in South Dakota, the Bentley family; in Texas, the Kourosh family; in Utah, the Zehner family; in Vermont, the Brubaker family; in Virginia, Glo Felicia; in Washington, the Pellerin family, Yasna, and Chi Amy; in Washington, D.C., Kareen and Sara Coyoca; and, finally, in West Virginia, thank you to Bradley Wilson, Cynthia Gorman, and family. If you weren't already, we consider you all our family.

Another question we get: "How did you fund this trip?" In 2017, we started a GoFundMe page. Since then, over one hundred people donated, setting our idea in motion. One cold e-mail and a few more phone calls later, Airbnb became our primary sponsor, and we are hugely grateful for their persistence in supporting our mission. Thank you, Airbnb—and more specifically Franchesca Hasim—for believing in us. We especially can't forget to recognize Princeton University's Department of African American Studies and the Princeton Education Foundation for funding our last book, which first experimented with our heart–mind model of racial literacy.

You are able to hold *Tell Me Who You Are* in your hands because of the publishing team at TarcherPerigee and Penguin Random House. Our wonderful team includes, among many others, Casey Maloney, Emily Fisher, Linda Rosenberg, Lindsay Gordon, Marian Lizzi, Megan Newman, Rachel Ayotte, Sara Carder (our editor!), Sara Johnson, and Tiffany Estreicher. Guiding us through this entire process has been our badass literary agent, Lynn Johnston, who we met through the wonderful Tara Parker-Pope.

Again, there are so many other people in this world to credit for guiding CHOOSE's journey, or for shaping the two of us into who we are today. Angelica Agishi from Gibson Dunn, your relentless patience leaves us in awe. Brian Lai, we will forever remember your continued tremendous kindness. Our NYC and TED and TED Residents 5 family—wow, each of you are such beloved pieces of our heart. Our teachers from Princeton High School, Chapin School, and Princeton Friends School, our friends who know our fullest selves yet still manage to make our hearts more full, all those who have offered undisguised critique of our work, our role models who lavish us with unforgettable wisdom, organizations who have recognized or invested in our work, strangers e-mailing with the kindest words . . . the list goes on! You know who you are—thank you for enriching our lives with your love.

Finally, our parents. If there's one group we have to acknowledge most here, it would be you all. To Mama Vulchi, Mama Fan, Papa Guo, and Papa Vulchi—we love you so much. We can never fully understand what you've endured and sacrificed for us to be here. We wrote this book because of something you told us: that, "as children of immigrants, you must give back to your country." Thank you for always being a reminder that we have so much to be grateful for. Who we are is because of you.

# SOURCES

## INTRODUCTION

3 **Intersectionality**: Matthew Desmond and Mustafa Emirbayer, *Racial Domination, Racial Progress: The Sociology of Race in America* (New York: McGraw-Hill Education, 2010).

6 **Racial Homogeneity**: https://www.washington post.com/news/wonk/wp/2014/08/25/three -quarters-of-whites-dont-have-any-non-white -friends/?noredirect=on&utm_term=.e038e83 1660.

7 **Racial Social Networks**: https://www.prri. org/research/poll-race-religion-politics -americans-social-networks.

8 **Indigenous Population**: Matthew Desmond and Mustafa Emirbayer, *Racial Domination, Racial Progress: The Sociology of Race in America* (New York: McGraw-Hill Education, 2010).

## CHAPTER ONE: RACE IMPACTS EVERYTHING

### *Introduction*

13 **Pregnancy**: Jacqueline Howard, "Childbirth is killing black women in the U.S., and here's why," CNN, Nov. 15, 2017, https://www.cnn.com/2017/ 11/15/health/black-women-maternal-mortality/ index.html.

### *Alexa, Justin P., and Jennifer L.*

15 **Racially Divided Cities**: William H. Frey, "Census Shows Modest Declines in Black White Cities," Brookings Institution, Dec. 8, 2015, https://www.brookings.edu/blog/the -avenue/2015/12/08/census-shows-modest -declines-in-black-white-segregation/.

15 **Model Minority**: Kat Chow, "'Model Minority' Myth Again Used as a Racial Wedge Between Asians and Blacks," Code Switch, NPR, April 19, 2017, https://www.npr.org/sections/code switch/2017/04/19/524571669/model -minority-myth-again-used-as-a-racial-wedge -between-asians-and-blacks.

16 **Race-Related Definitions**: "Glossary," Racial Equity Tools, http://www.racialequitytools.org/ glossary.

16 **Median Household Income**: Matthew A. Painter, Malcolm D. Holmes, Jenna Bateman, "Skin Tone, Race/Ethnicity, and Wealth Inequality among New Immigrants," *Social Forces* 94, no. 3 (March 2015): 1153–85, https://academic .oup.com/sf/article/94/3/1153/2461532.

16 **Stereotypes**: Laura Green, "Negative Racial Stereotypes and Their Effects on Attitudes Toward African-Americans," Virginia Commonwealth University, https://ferris.edu/HTMLS/ news/jimcrow/links/essays/vcu.htm.

18 **Plyler v. Doe**: "Immigrant Students' Rights to Attend Public Schools," Intercultural Development Research Association (2017), http://www .idra.org/wp-content/uploads/2017/08/eBook -Immigrant-Students%E2%80%99-Rights-to -Attend-Public-Schools-2017-August.pdf.

### *Queen Esther*

22 **Enslaved Women and Birth**: Dorothy E. Roberts, *Killing the Black Body: Race, Reproduction, and the Meaning of Liberty* (New York: Penguin Random House, 1997).

23 **Texas Textbook**: Diana Ozemebhoya Eromosele, "Texas Makes Changes to History Textbooks: No Mention of KKK Or Jim Crow, and the Civil War Was Fought over States' Rights, Not Slavery," The Root, July 8, 2015, https:// www.theroot.com/texas-makes-changes-to -history-textbooks-no-mention-of-1790860433.

23 **Zora Neale Hurston**: Zora Neale Hurston, "How It Feels to Be Colored Me," *The World Tomorrow* (May 1928), http://www.casa-arts.org/ cms/lib/PA01925203/Centricity/Domain/50/ Hurston%20How%20it%20Feels%20to%20 Be%20Colored%20Me.pdf.

### *Justin E.*

26 **Africa**: Matthew Desmond and Mustafa Emirbayer, *Racial Domination, Racial Progress: The Sociology of Race in America* (New York: McGraw-Hill Education, 2010).

26 **Post Traumatic Slave Syndrome**: Joy DeGruy, *Post Traumatic Slave Syndrome: America's Legacy of Enduring Injury and Healing*

(Baltimore: Uptone Press, 2005), https://www
.nasmhpd.org/sites/default/files/SAMHSA
%20-%20Impact%20of%20Historical%20
Trauma%20on%20Communities.pdf.

### Nick

29 **Treaties**: Helen Oliff, "Treaties Made, Treaties Broken," Partnership With Native Americans (blog), posted March 3, 2011, http://blog.native partnership.org/treaties-made-treaties-broken/.

29 **Equity Definition**: Race-Related Definitions: "Glossary," Racial Equity Tools, http://www .racialequitytools.org/glossary.

### Vic

32 **Chinatown**: "The Story of Chinatown," Chinatown Resource Guide, Public Broadcasting Service, http://www.pbs.org/kqed/chinatown/resourceguide/story.html.

32 **Chinese Exclusion Act**: David W. Dunlap, "135 Years Ago, Another Travel Ban Was in the News," *New York Times*, March 17, 2017, https:// www.nytimes.com/2017/03/17/insider/chinese -exclusion-act-travel-ban.html.

32 **Positionality**: Mary K. Thompson Tetreault, "Positionality and Knowledge Construction," in James A. Banks, ed., *Encyclopedia of Diversity in Education* (n.d.), doi: http://dx.doi.org/ 10.4135/9781452218533.n542.

### Melina

35 **White Racial Identity Development Model**: Janet E. Helms, "Toward a model of White racial identity development," in J. E. Helms (ed.), *Black and White Racial Identity: Theory, Research and Practice* (Westport, CT: Greenwood Press, 1993), pp. 44, 49–66.

37 **White Privilege**: Cory Collins, "What is White Privilege, Really?" *Teaching Tolerance*, 2018, https://www.tolerance.org/magazine/fall -2018/what-is-white-privilege-really.

### Rylee, Marley, and Parker

40 **Cultural Appropriation**: Jamé Jackson, "3 Hairstylists on Braids, Cultural Appropriation and Media's Erasure of Black Women," Fashionista, Jan. 2, 2018, https://fashionista .com/2018/01/black-hair-braids-cultural -appropriation-media-erasure.

40 **Reparations**: "Reparations," International Center for Transitional Justice, https://www .ictj.org/our-work/transitional-justice-issues/ reparations.

### Liz

43 **Black Travel**: Fabiola Fleuranvil, "Black Travel Dollars Matter," *Huffington Post*, May 23, 2017, https://www.huffingtonpost.com/entry/ black-travel-dollars-matter_us_59243d84e 4b07617ae4cbf8e?guccounter=1.

43 **Double-Consciousness**: W. E. B. Du Bois, *The Souls of Black Folk* (1903), available online: https://www.gutenberg.org/files/408/408 -h/408-h.htm.

### Ed

45 **Emancipation**: Jim Downs, *Sick From Freedom: African-American Illness and Suffering During the Civil War and Reconstruction* (New York: Oxford University Press, 2012).

45 **Meteorological Society**: Dayvon Hill, et al., "Why Aren't More African Americans Drawn to the Atmosphere Sciences?" paper presented at the annual meeting of the American Meteorological Society, Jan. 8, 2018, Austin, TX.

### Chef Tu

47 **Ethnic Groups**: "Ethnic Groups in Vietnam," Socialist Republic of Viet Nam Government Portal, http://www.chinhphu.vn/portal/page/ portal/English/TheSocialistRepublicOf Vietnam/AboutVietnam/AboutVietnam Detail?categoryId=10000103&articleId= 10002652.

47 **Vietnamese War**: C. N. Trueman, "Vietnamese Boat People," History Learning Site, Sept. 2018, https://www.historylearningsite.co.uk/ vietnam-war/vietnamese-boat-people/.

## CHAPTER TWO: THE PAST IS THE PRESENT

### Introduction

52 **Desegregation**: Aria Bendix, "A Mississippi School District Is Finally Getting Desegregated," *The Atlantic*, March 14, 2017, https:// www.theatlantic.com/education/archive/ 2017/03/a-mississippi-school-district-is -finally-getting-desegregated/519573/.

53 **Racism Is Still Alive and Well**: https:// qz.com/726245/more-black-people-were -killed-by-us-police-in-2015-than-were -lynched-in-the-worst-year-of-jim-crow.

### Susan

55 **Charlottesville**: "Charlottesville Attack: What, Where and Who?," Al Jazeera News, Aug. 17,

2017, https://www.aljazeera.com/news/2017/08/charlottesville-attack-170813081045115.html.

55    **Racially Homogeneous**: Barrett A. Lee, John Iceland, Gregory Sharp, "Racial and Ethnic Diversity Goes Local: Charting Change in American Communities over Three Decades," US2010 Project of Brown University and the Russell Sage Foundation, Sept. 2012, https://s4.ad.brown.edu/Projects/Diversity/Data/Report/report08292012.pdf.

### Autumn

58    **Alcatraz Takeover**: Evan Andrews, "Native American Activists Occupy Alcatraz Island, 45 Years Ago," History.com, Nov. 20, 2014, https://www.history.com/news/native-american-activists-occupy-alcatraz-island-45-years-ago.

58    **Seven Generations**: David E. Wilkins, "How to Honor the Seven Generations," Indian Country Today, June 18, 2015, https://newsmaven.io/indiancountrytoday/archive/how-to-honor-the-seven-generations-0UNiIfbN5UOL36SXV6rIiQ/?full=1.

### Ronnie M.

60    **Three-Fifths Compromise**: "What Was the Three-Fifths Compromise?" Constitution, "Laws," https://constitution.laws.com/three-fifths-compromise.

### Jackie

63    **Creoles and Cajuns**: Sylvie Dubois and Barbara M. Horvath, "Creoles and Cajuns A Portrait in Black and White," *American Speech* 78, no. 2 (Summer 2003): 192–207, https://pdfs.semanticscholar.org/2565/2c357339f0efb33f6a4a2ea98c95b89f3769.pdf.

63    **Blood Law**: Frances Frank Marcus, "Louisiana Repeals Black Blood Law," *New York Times*, July 6, 1983, https://www.nytimes.com/1983/07/06/us/louisiana-repeals-black-blood-law.html. See also F. James Davis, *Who Is Black? One Nation's Definition*, (University Park, PA: Penn State University Press, 1991), quoted in part at *Frontline*, https://www.pbs.org/wgbh/pages/frontline/shows/jefferson/mixed/onedrop.html.

63    **Racial Passing**: Karen Grigsby Bates, "'A Chosen Exile': Black People Passing in White America," National Public Radio, "Code Switch," Oct. 7, 2014, https://www.npr.org/sections/codeswitch/2014/10/07/354310370/a-chosen-exile-black-people-passing-in-White-america.

### Archibald

66    **First Amendment**: John Villasenor, "Views among college students regarding the First Amendment: Results from a new survey," Brookings, Sept. 18, 2017, https://www.brookings.edu/blog/fixgov/2017/09/18/views-among-college-students-regarding-the-first-amendment-results-from-a-new-survey/.

### Ashley

69    **Crime**: "Race and Poverty," Equal Justice Initiative, https://eji.org/death-penalty/race-and-poverty.

69    **Ku Klux Klan**: "Grant, Reconstruction and the KKK," *PBS: American Experience*, from the collection, "The Presidents," http://www.pbs.org/wgbh/americanexperience/features/grant-kkk/.

69    **Confederate Ghosts**: Alison Kinney, "How the Klan Got Its Hood," *New Republic*, Jan. 8, 2016, https://newrepublic.com/article/127242/klan-got-hood.

### Juanenna

71    **KKK**: Megan Trimble, "KKK Groups Still Active in These States in 2017," *U.S. News & World Report*, Aug. 14, 2017, https://www.usnews.com/news/best-states/articles/2017-08-14/the-kkk-is-still-based-in-22-states-in-the-us-in-2017.

### Rhonda

73    **Indian**: Desmond and Emirbayer, *Racial Domination, Racial Progress*, p. 57.

### Konnor and Aaron

75    **Desegregation and Integration**: William Raspberry, "The Difference between Desegregation and Integration," *Washington Post*, Dec. 1, 1980, https://www.washingtonpost.com/archive/politics/1980/12/01/the-difference-between-desegregation-and-integration/7af50057-1ae1-4f30-8fd7-96e025ac39b0/?utm_term=.9dd930cf6f3a.

### Jo

77    **"Retarded" Term**: Dan Barry, "Giving a Name, and Dignity, to a Disability," *New York Times,* May 7, 2016, https://www.nytimes.com/2016/05/08/sunday-review/giving-a-name-and-dignity-to-a-disability.html.

78    **Lynching**: Andrew Belonsky, "How the NAACP fought lynching by using the racists' own pictures against them," *The Guardian*, April 27, 2018, https://www.theguardian.com/us-news

/2018/apr/27/lynching-naacp-photographs
-waco-texas-campaign.

### Lisa

80   **Sharecropping**: "Sharecropping," History.com, accessed Sept. 21, 2018, https://www.history .com/topics/black-history/sharecropping.

80   **Whistling Vivaldi**: "'Whistling Vivaldi' and Beating Stereotypes," *Talk of the Nation,* interview with author Dr. Claude M. Steele, National Public Radio, April 12, 2010, https://www.npr.org/ templates/story/story.php?storyId=125859207.

## CHAPTER THREE: OUR RICHNESS, RACE AND BEYOND

### Introduction

85   **Intersectionality**: "What is intersectionality, and what does it have to do with me?", YW Boston, March 29, 2017, https://www.ywboston.org/ 2017/03/what-is-intersectionality-and-what -does-it-have-to-do-with-me/.

85   **Beyond Race**: Eduardo Bonilla-Silva, *Racism Without Racists,* (Guilford, CT: Rowman & Littlefield, 2003).

85   **Marsha P. Johnson**: "Marsha P. Johnson," Biography, https://www.biography.com/people/ marsha-p-johnson-112717.

85   **Joan Baez**: "Joan Baez," Biography, https://www. biography.com/people/joan-baez-9195061.

### Lauren

87   **NYC Subways**: Emily Nonko, "The NYC subway has an accessibility problem—can it be fixed?," Curbed New York, Sept. 21, 2017, https://ny.curbed.com/2017/9/21/16315042/ nyc-subway-wheelchair-accessible-ada.

### Ahyoka

90   **Two-Spirit**: "Two-Spirit Community," Researching for LGBTQ Health, http://lgbtq health.ca/community/two-spirit.php.

90   **Cherokee Language**: David Goldberg, Dennis Looney, and Natalia Lusin, "Enrollments in Languages Other Than English in United States Institutions of Higher Education, Fall 2013," Modern Language Association, 2015, https:// apps.mla.org/pdf/2013_enrollment_survey.pdf.

### Barry and Omar

93   **Refugees' PTSD**: Elisa E. Bolton, "PTSD in Refugees," U.S. Department of Veterans Af-

fairs, Feb. 23, 2016, https://www.ptsd.va.gov/ professional/trauma/other/ptsd-refugees.asp.

### Hamza, Ayesha, and Saboor

96   **Hate Crimes**: Scott Malone, "U.S. anti-Muslim hate crimes rose 15 percent in 2017: Advocacy group," Reuters.com, April 23, 2018, https://www.reuters.com/article/us-usa-islam -hatecrime/u-s-anti-muslim-hate-crimes-rose -15-percent-in-2017-advocacy-group-idUSKB N1HU240.

96   **Qur'an**: https://www.islamreligion.com/articles/ 523/prophet-muhammad-last-sermon/.

97   **Palestine**: "The Human Cost of the Conflict," Israel-Palestine Timeline, last updated Aug. 11, 2018, https://israelpalestinetimeline.org/charts/.

### Shermaine

100   **STEM PhD**: "The STEM Pipeline," Inside Higher Ed, Boston University Center for Teaching & Learning, Feb. 2015, https://www.bu.edu/ stem/files/2015/02/The-STEM-Pipeline -booklet1.3-36.pdf.

100   **Interracial Couples**: Columbia Business School, "Gender and race: How overlapping stereotypes affect our personal and professional decisions," Science Daily, Dec. 3, 2012, https:// www.sciencedaily.com/releases/2012/ 12/121203131702.htm.

101   **The National Science Foundation**: "Women, Minorities, and Persons with Disabilities in Science and Engineering," National Science Foundation data, updated June 2018, http:// www.nsf.gov/statistics/wmpd/.

### Butler

103   **Rosa Parks**: Justin Taylor, "No, Rosa Parks Was Not Sitting in the White Section of the Montgomery Bus—And Four Other Myths," The Gospel Coalition, Dec. 1 2016, https://www .thegospelcoalition.org/blogs/evangelical -history/no-rosa-parks-was-not-sitting-in -the-white-section-of-the-montgomery-bus -and-four-other-myths/.

104   **Jo Ann Robinson**: Dwayne Mack, "Robinson, Jo Ann (1912–1992)," BlackPast.org, http:// www.blackpast.org/aah/robinson-jo-ann -1912-1992.

### Deb

107   **Mental Illness**: Doris A. Fuller et al., "Overlooked in the Undercounted: The Role of Mental Illness in Fatal Law Enforcement Encounters,"

Office of Research & Public Affairs, Dec. 2015, http://www.treatmentadvocacycenter.org/ storage/documents/overlooked-in-the-under counted.pdf

### Deja

109 **Cisgender and Transgender**: Trans Student Educational Resources. http://www.trans student.org/definitions/.

109 **Sex Trade**: Erin Fitzgerald, Sarah Elspeth Patterson, Darby Hickey, and Cherno Biko, "Meaningful Work: Transgender Experiences in the Sex Trade," Harper Jean Tobin National Center for Transgender Equality, Dec. 2015, http:// www.transequality.org/sites/default/files/ Meaningful%20Work-Full%20Report_FINAL_ 3.pdf.

### Keah

112 **Disability**: "Fact Sheet on Persons with Disabilities," United Nations Enable, http://www .un.org/disabilities/documents/toolaction/ pwdfs.pdf.

### Tracye

114 **Great Migration**: "Great Migration," History .com, https://www.history.com/topics/black -history/great-migration.

115 **Police**: Jeremy Ashkenas and Haeyoun Park, "The Race Gap in America's Police Departments," *New York Times*, Sept. 3, 2014, https://www .nytimes.com/interactive/2014/09/03/us/the -race-gap-in-americas-police-departments.html.

### Vaughn

119 **Incarceration**: Jake Flanagin, "Native Americans are the unseen victims of a broken US justice system," Quartz, April 27, 2015, https://qz .com/392342/native-americans-are-the-unseen -victims-of-a-broken-us-justice-system/.

120 **Boarding Schools**: Cheryl Easley and Kanaqlak (George P. Charles), "Boarding School: Historical Trauma among Alaska's Native People," National Resource Center for American Indian, Alaska Native and Native Hawaiian Elders, Jan. 2006, https://www.uaa.alaska.edu/academics/ institutional-effectiveness/departments/center -for-advancing-faculty-excellence/_documents/ boarding-school-historical-trauma-among -alaska-s-native-people.pdf.

## CHAPTER FOUR: OUR BEST FRIENDS ARE STILL STRANGERS

### Introduction

122 **Landlords and Leasing Agents**: Nikole Hannah-Jones, "Portland housing audit finds discrimination in 64 percent of tests; city has yet to act against landlords," *The Oregon*, May 19, 2011, https://www.oregonlive.com/portland/index.ssf/ 2011/05/a_portland_housing_audit_finds.html.

122 **Suspensions**: Laura Frazier, "Portland expels, suspends fewer students, but still disciplines African American students at higher rates," *The Oregon*, Feb. 16, 2017, https://www.oregonlive .com/portland/index.ssf/2015/02/portland_ expels_suspends_fewer.html.

122 **KKK Membership**: George Will, "George Will: Oregon and the Klan," *Daily Freeman*, Aug. 11, 2018, https://www.dailyfreeman.com/news/ george-will-oregon-and-the-klan/article_ a65bb599-762a-541d-823f-c971b785f2f6.html.

122 **Whitest City of Its Size**: Alana Semuels, "The Racist History of Portland, the Whitest City in America," *The Atlantic*, July 22, 2016, https:// www.theatlantic.com/business/archive/ 2016/07/racist-history-portland/492035/.

### Burton and Shelley

125 **Special Education**: Paul L. Morgan and George Farkas, "Is Special Education Racist?," *New York Times*, June 24, 2015, https://www .nytimes.com/2015/06/24/opinion/is-special -education-racist.html.

### Rosa

128 **Undocumented Immigrants**: Crosby Burns, Ann Garcia, and Philip E. Wolgin, "Living in Dual Shadows: LGBT Undocumented Immigrants," Center for American Progress, March 2013, https://www.americanprogress .org/wp-content/uploads/2013/03/LGBT UndocumentedReport-5.pdf.

### TJ and Cecil

130 **Gender vs. Sex**: John Staughton, "What Is the Difference between Sex and Gender?," Science ABC, 2016, https://www.scienceabc.com/ eyeopeners/what-is-the-difference-between -sex-and-gender.html.

### William

133 **Founding Director**: National Center for Race Amity, "About," https://raceamity.org/about/, accessed September 11, 2018.

### Sandra

135 **Intergenerational Trauma**: Amy Wenzel, ed., *The SAGE Encyclopedia of Abnormal and Clinical Psychology*, vol. 4, I (Thousand Oaks, CA: SAGE Publications, 2017), p. 1861.

### John and Lydia

137 **Implicit Bias**: Lois James, "The Stability of Implicit Racial Bias in Police Officers," *Police Quarterly* 21, no. 1 (2018), https://doi.org/10.1177/1098611117732974. See also "Understanding Implicit Bias," Ohio State University Kirwan Institute for the Study of Race and Ethnicity, http://kirwaninstitute.osu.edu/research/understanding-implicit-bias/.

### Tyler W.

141 **Suicides**: Rachel A. Leavitt et al., "Suicides Among American Indian/Alaska Natives—National Violent Death Reporting System, 18 States, 2003–2014," Morbidity and Mortality Weekly Report, Centers for Disease Control and Prevention, March 2, 2018, https://www.cdc.gov/mmwr/volumes/67/wr/mm6708a1.htm.

141 **Drugs**: "Fighting Alcoholism and Substance Abuse in the Native American Community," FATE (Fighting Addiction Through Education), https://www.fate.org/programs/native-fate/.

### Laureen and Cara

144 **Diaspora**: Rogers Brubaker, "The 'diaspora' diaspora," *Ethnic and Racial Studies*, Vol. 28 No. 1, pp. 1–19 (Taylor & Francis Ltd, Jan 2005), http://www.sscnet.ucla.edu/soc/faculty/brubaker/Publications/29_Diaspora_diaspora_ERS.pdf.

## CHAPTER FIVE: THE WORDS WE USE MATTER

### Introduction

145 **Joe Louis and Max Schmeling Fight**: Boxing's greatest, "Joe Louis vs Max Schmeling—1st Round Knockout," YouTube, Sept. 4, 2009, https://www.youtube.com/watch?v=2LNzWHuygpw.

145 **Joe Louis Fist**: Jer Staes, "The Real Story Behind Detroit's Giant Joe Louis Fist," July 10, 2015, *Daily Detroit*, http://www.dailydetroit.com/2015/07/10/the-real-story-behind-detroits-giant-joe-louis-fist/.

146 **Mellody Hobson**: Poppy Harlow and Haley Draznin, "Mellody Hobson on race: we must be 'color brave,'" CNN Business, Jan. 22, 2018, https://money.cnn.com/2018/01/22/news/mellody-hobson-boss-files/index.html.

146 **Martin Luther King, Jr.**: Mary Frances Berry, "Vindicating Martin Luther King, Jr.: The Road to a Color-Blind Society," *The Journal of Negro History*, Association for the Study of African American Life and History, University of Chicago Press, Vol. 81, no. 1/4 (1996): https://www.jstor.org/stable/2717613?seq=1#page_scan_tab_contents.

147 **Michigan Avenue**: Aaron Mondry, "Michigan's highway: The history of Michigan Avenue, our state's most important road," Model D, March 06, 2017, http://www.modeldmedia.com/features/michigan-avenue-pt1-030617.aspx.

147 **Underground Railroad**: "Underground Railroad," Detroit Historical Society, https://detroithistorical.org/learn/encyclopedia-of-detroit/underground-railroad.

### Hunter

152 **Segregation Academies**: American Sociological Association, "With Racial Segregation Declining Between Neighborhoods, Segregation Now Taking New Form," press release, July 28, 2015, http://www.asanet.org/sites/default/files/savvy/documents/press/pdfs/ASR_August_2015_Lichter_News_Release.pdf.

### Treniya

155 **Callbacks**: German Lopez, "Study: anti-Black hiring discrimination is as prevalent today as it was in 1989," Vox.com, Sept. 18, 2017, https://www.vox.com/identities/2017/9/18/16307782/study-racism-jobs.

### Jasmine and Karli

158 **Reservations**: Sierra Crane-Murdoch, "On Indian Land, Criminals Can Get Away with Almost Anything," *The Atlantic*, Feb. 22, 2013, https://www.theatlantic.com/national/archive/2013/02/on-indian-land-criminals-can-get-away-with-almost-anything/273391/.

158 **Affirmative Action**: Madison Trice, "The Affirmative Action Lawsuit against Harvard Isn't Really about Fairness," Refinery29.com, Aug. 20, 2018, https://www.refinery29.com/harvard-affirmative-action-lawsuit.

### AJ

161 **Gender Identity**: "Sexual Orientation and Gender Identity Definitions," Human Rights Campaign, https://www.hrc.org/resources/sexual

-orientation-and-gender-identity-terminology
-and-definitions.

161 **Gender Pronouns**: Steven Petrow, "Gender-neutral pronouns: When 'they' doesn't identify as either male or female," *Washington Post*, Oct. 27, 2014, https://www.washingtonpost.com/lifestyle/style/gender-neutral-pronouns-when-they-doesnt-identify-as-either-male-or-female/2014/10/27/41965f5e-5ac0-11e4-b812-38518ae74c67_story.html?utm_term=.50d1cde48742.

### Amanda

164 **Race and Gender:** Columbia Business School, "Gender and race."

164 **Bamboo Ceiling**: Stefanie K. Johnson and Thomas Sy, "Why Aren't There More Asian Americans in Leadership Positions?," *Harvard Business Review*, Dec. 19, 2016, https://hbr.org/2016/12/why-arent-there-more-asian-americans-in-leadership-positions.

### Aleksa and John M.

167 **"Illegal" Immigrants**: Jose Antonio Vargas, "The Immigration Debate: The Problem with the Word *Illegal*," *Time*, Sept. 21, 2012, http://ideas.time.com/2012/09/21/immigration-debate-the-problem-with-the-word-illegal/.

167 **Teachers' Rights**: Alexander Wohl, "The Extent and Limitations of Teachers' Rights," *Human Rights* 32, no. 2 (Fall 2005), https://www.americanbar.org/publications/human_rights_magazine_home/human_rights_vol32_2005/fall2005/hr_Fall05_teachersrights.html.

### Lita

170 **N-Word**: Marc Bain, "Ta-Nehisi Coates Gently Explains Why White People Can't Rap the N-Word," *Quartzy*, Nov. 13, 2017, https://qz.com/quartzy/1127824/ta-nehisi-coates-explains-why-White-hip-hop-fans-cant-use-the-n-word/.

### Brontë

172 **Broadway**: Robert Viagas, "Coalition Releases Report on Diversity in NY Theatre," *Playbill*, May 3, 2016, http://www.playbill.com/article/coalition-releases-report-on-diversity-in-ny-theatre.

### Newzad

174 **Kurdish state**: "Kurdish Diaspora," The Kurdish Project, 2015, https://thekurdishproject.org/kurdistan-map/kurdish-diaspora/.

174 **Nashville Kurdish population**: Ariana Maia Sawyer, "Who are the Kurds, and why are they in Nashville?," *Tennessean*, June 22, 2017, https://www.tennessean.com/story/news/local/2017/06/23/who-kurds-and-why-they-nashville/97706968/.

## CHAPTER SIX: WE NEED TO STOP FIGHTING AMONG OURSELVES

### Mareo

179 **Willie Lynch Syndrome**: "The Willie Lynch Letter: The Making of a Slave!" (Dec. 25, 1712), Internet Archive, https://archive.org/stream/WillieLynchLetter1712/the_willie_lynch_letter_the_making_of_a_slave_1712_djvu.txt.

179 **Tulsa Race Riot**: "1921 Tulsa Race Riot," Tulsa Historical Society & Museum, https://tulsahistory.org/learn/online-exhibits/the-tulsa-race-riot/.

180 **Oklahoman Private Prisons**: Curtis Killman and Cary Aspinwall, "Private prisons contribute thousands to Oklahoma political campaigns," *Tulsa World*, Jan. 6, 2014, https://www.tulsaworld.com/news/private-prisons-contribute-thousands-to-oklahoma-political-campaigns/article_f5ddca24-72e5-5c81-849b-031ac6c7c978.html. Elizabeth Hinton, *From the War on Poverty to the War on Crime* (Cambridge, Mass.: Harvard University Press, 2016).

### April

183 **The Shriver Report**: HuffPost, "Women in the U.S. Are Still Second-Class Citizens: Not Interested? You Should Be," blog entry by Samantha Paige Rosen, March 24, 2014, https://www.huffingtonpost.com/samantha-paige-rosen/women-in-the-us-are-still-wage-gap_b_5018490.html.

183 **Transgender Hate Crimes**: "Violence Against the Transgender Community in 2018," Human Rights Campaign, 2018, https://www.hrc.org/resources/violence-against-the-transgender-community-in-2018.

184 **Disability Rights**: Wendy Taormina-Weiss, "Rights of Persons with Disabilities in America," editorial, Disabled World, Feb. 27, 2012, https://www.disabled-world.com/editorials/6786854.php.

### Jason

189 **Anti-Semitic Incidents**: Anti-Defamation League, "Anti-Semitic Incidents Surged Nearly

60% in 2017, According to New ADL Report," Feb. 27, 2018, https://www.adl.org/news/press -releases/anti-semitic-incidents-surged-nearly -60-in-2017-according-to-new-adl-report.

189 **Leo Frank Lynching**: David Grubin, *The Jewish Americans*, "Anti-Semitism in America," Public Broadcasting Service, accessed Sept. 22, 2018, https://www.pbs.org/jewishamericans/ jewish_life/anti-semitism.html.

190 **Bengali Genocide and Congolese Genocide**: http://genocidewatch.net/2015/05/27/other -20th-century-massacres-that-go-ignored; https://www.theguardian.com/world/2002/ jul/18/congo.andrewosborn.

### Renee

192 **"Machismo"**: Definition of "machismo," Cambridge Dictionary online, https://dictionary .cambridge.org/us/dictionary/english/ machismo.

192 **"Chicana" and "Chicana Feminism"**: Leah Jackson, Michael Newman, Brittany Price, "Exploring the Chicana Feminist Movement," University of Michigan, Fall Semester, 2007, http:// umich.edu/~ac213/student_projects07/latfem/ latfem/whatisit.html.

192 **"Mestizo" and "Mulatto"**: Ana Gonzalez-Barrera, "'Mestizo' and 'Mulatto': Mixed-race identities among U.S. Hispanics," FactTank, Pew Research Center, July 10, 2015, http:// www.pewresearch.org/fact-tank/2015/07/10/ mestizo-and-mulatto-mixed-race-identities -unique-to-hispanics/.

### Howard and Delores

195 **Colorism**: David Knight, "'What's "Colorism"?' How Would Your Students Answer This Question?," *Teaching Tolerance* magazine 51 (Fall 2015), https://www.tolerance.org/magazine/ fall-2015/whats-colorism.

196 **Native Slaveholding Practice**: "America's 2nd Largest Indian Tribe Expels Blacks," *Tell Me More*, National Public Radio, Sept. 20, 2011, https://www.npr.org/2011/09/20/140630565/ americas-2nd-largest-indian-tribe-expels -blacks.

### Lisa E.

200 **Jewish Stereotype Origins**: Ophir Yarden, "Anti-Semitic Stereotypes of the Jewish Body," My Jewish Learning, https://www.myjewish learning.com/article/anti-semitic-stereotypes -of-the-jewish-body/.

201 **Audre Lorde**: Writing on Glass, "How to Combat Racial Injustice, According to Audre Lorde," blog entry by Stephanine Newman, Aug. 1, 2019. http://www.writingonglass.com/content/ audre-lorde-on-police violence. Also https:// www.goodreads.com/quotes/1337733-some -problems-we-share-as women-some-we-do -not.

### Patience, Lee'Najah, and Tarlice

204 **Bisexuality**: "Bisexuality: Myths and Realities," Cleveland State University, Cleveland, OH, https://www.csuohio.edu/sites/default/ files/bisexuality.pdf.

204 **Bisexuality Statistics**: "Understanding Bisexuality," American Psychological Association, http://www.apa.org/pi/lgbt/resources/ bisexual.aspx.

### Robert

206 **White and Native Multiracial Identity**: Pew Research Center, *Multiracial in America: Proud, Diverse and Growing in Numbers,* "Chapter 3: The Multiracial Identity Gap" (Washington, DC: Pew Research Center, June 2015). http://www .pewsocialtrends.org/2015/06/11/chapter -3-the-multiracial-identity-gap/.

206 **Traditional Indigenous Medicine**: Emory Keoke and Kay Porterfield, *American Indian Contributions to the World* (New York: Checkmark Books, 2003).

207 **"Red Power Movement"**: Duane Champagne, "Self-Determination and Activism among American Indians in the United States 1972-1997," *Cultural Survival* magazine (June 1997), https://www.culturalsurvival.org/publications/ cultural-survival-quarterly/self-determination -and-activism-among-american-indians.

### José

209 **Latino and Catholic Identity**: Pew Research Center, *The Shifting Religious Identity of Latinos in the United States*, May 7, 2014, http:// www.pewforum.org/2014/05/07/the-shifting -religious-identity-of-latinos-in-the-united -states/.

## CHAPTER SEVEN: WE ARE ALL "NORMAL"

### Safia

215 **Burkini**: Aheda Zanetti, "I created the burkini to give women freedom, not to take it away," *The*

*Guardian*, Aug. 24, 2016, https://www.theguardian.com/commentisfree/2016/aug/24/i-created-the-burkini-to-give-women-freedom-not-to-take-it-away.

215 **Corporate Colorism**: Maliha Rehman, "Getting Rich from the Skin Lightening Trade," Business of Fashion, Sept. 27, 2017, https://www.businessoffashion.com/articles/global-currents/profiting-from-the-skin-lightening-trade.

## Ronnie B.

217 **Black Father Absenteeism**: HuffPost, "No, Most Black Kids Are Not Fatherless," blog entry by Josh Levs, July 26, 2016, https://www.huffingtonpost.com/josh-levs/no-most-black-kids-are-no_b_11109876.html.

217 **Incarceration Trends**: NAACP, "Criminal Justice Fact Sheet," 2018, http://www.naacp.org/criminal-justice-fact-sheet/.

217 **Racial Profiling**: "Racial Profiling," American Civil Liberties Union, 2018, https://www.aclu.org/issues/racial-justice/race-and-criminal-justice/racial-profiling.

## Standing Alone

219 **Utah LDS Population**: "Utah Population 2018," World Population Review, 2018, http://worldpopulationreview.com/states/utah-population; https://history.lds.org/timeline/historic-sites/wyoming/us-migration-mormon-emigration-and-the-handcart-experiment?lang=eng.

## Claudette

222 **Restaurant Industry Diversity**: Soleil Ho, "The Restaurant Industry Is Very Diverse—But It's White Chefs Who Win Most of the Awards," bitchmedia.org, March 15,2016, https://www.bitchmedia.org/article/restaurant-industry-very-diverse—-its-white-chefs-who-win-most-awards.

223 **Use of "Ethnic"**: Sherina Ong, "4 Reasons Why We've Got to Stop Using 'Ethnic' to Describe People of Color," Everyday Feminism, July 21, 2016, https://everydayfeminism.com/2016/07/stop-using-ethnic-to-describe-poc/.

## Gerry

225 **Right-Leaning Media and Commentators**: Pew Research Center, Political Polarization and Media Habits, Oct. 2014, http://www.pewresearch.org/wp-content/uploads/sites/8/2014/10/Political-Polarization-and-Media-Habits-FINAL-REPORT-7-27-15.pdf.

## Eryn

228 **Dreadlocks Stereotypes**: Victoria Uwumarogie, "Don't Be Like Giuliana Rancic: 11 Assumptions People Make about Those Who Wear Locs That Don't Make Sense," Madamenoire, Feb. 25, 2015, https://madamenoire.com/514036/dont-like-giuliana-rancic-assumptions-people-locs-dont-make-sense/.

228 **Paulette Caldwell Quote**: Paulette Caldwell, "A Hair Piece: Perspectives on the Intersection of Race and Gender," *Duke Law Journal* 1991, no. 2 (April 1991): 365–96, https://www.jstor.org/stable/1372731?seq=1#page_scan_tab_contents.

228 **Black Women in Ballet**: Olivia B. Waxman, "'A Lot is Still So Much The Same': Misty Copeland on Decades of Racism and Ballet," Time.com, Jan. 16, 2018, http://time.com/5098808/misty-copeland-raven-wilkinson-book/.

## Jane

231 **Bombs in Marshall Islands**: Jon Letman, "Micronesians in Hawaii Face Uncertain Future," Al Jazeera News, Oct. 2, 2013, https://www.aljazeera.com/humanrights/2013/10/micronesians-hawaii-face-uncertain-future-201310191535637288.html.

## Natesho, Mohamed, and Hayat

234 **Muslim Attacks Coverage:** Kearns, E., Betus, A., and Lemieux, A. (n.d.) "Why Do Some Terrorist Attacks Receive More Media Attention Than Others?" Social Science Research Network (SSRN), https://papers.ssrn.com/sol3/papers.cfm?abstract_id=2928138.

## Neda

237 **Childhood Racial Development**: Kristin Pauker, Nalini Ambady, and Evan P. Apfelbaum, "Race Salience and Essentialist Thinking in Racial Stereotype Development," *Child Development* 81, no. 6 (Nov/Dec 2010): 1799–1813, doi: 10.1111/j.1467-8624.2010.01511.x.

## Shoghi

240 **Xenophobia**: David Haekwon Kim and Ronald R. Sundstrom, "Xenophobia and Racism," *Critical Philosophy of Race* Vol. 2 No. 1, The Pennsylvania State University, 2014, https://philpapers.org/archive/KIMXAR.pdf.

241 **Police Killings of African Americans**: Todd Beer, "Police Killing of Blacks: Data for 2015, 2016, 2017, and First Half of 2018," "Sociology

Toolbox," The Society Pages, updated Aug. 24, 2018, https://thesocietypages.org/toolbox/police-killing-of-blacks/.

### Louise

244 **Interned Japanese-American Citizenry**: National Archives, "Japanese Relocation During World War II," "Teaching with Documents," accessed Sept. 22, 2018, https://www.archives.gov/education/lessons/japanese-relocation.

245 **Alaskan Native Internment**: John Smelcer, "The Other WWII American-Internment Atrocity," *Code Switch*, National Public Radio, Feb. 21, 2017, https://www.npr.org/sections/codeswitch/2017/02/21/516277507/the-other-wwii-american-internment-atrocity.

245 **Japanese-American Loyalty**: Library of Congress, "Defiant Loyalty: Japanese-American Internment Camp Newspapers," blog entry by Malea Walker, May 9, 2017, https://blogs.loc.gov/loc/2017/05/defiant-loyalty-japanese-american-internment-camp-newspapers/.

## CHAPTER EIGHT: DIVERSITY IS NOT THE GOAL

### Introduction

251 **NYC Racial Divides**: Ford Fessenden and Sam Roberts, "Then As Now—New York's Shifting Ethnic Mosaic," *New York Times,* Jan. 22, 2011, http://archive.nytimes.com/www.nytimes.com/interactive/2011/01/23/nyregion/20110123-nyc-ethnic-neighborhoods-map.html.

251 **NYC 4th Most Segregated**: Christian Bautista, "New York ranks as fourth-most segregated city in America," May 31, 2018, https://therealdeal.com/2018/05/31/new-york-ranks-as-fourth-most-segregated-city-in-america/.

### Aaron G.

253 **Mark of Cain**: HuffPost, "The Biblical Roots of Racism," blog entry by Karl Giberson, June 24, 2015, https://www.huffingtonpost.com/karl-giberson-phd/the-biblical-roots-of-racism_b_7649390.html.

### Isabella

257 **Ta-Nehisi Coates:** "Ta-Nehisi Coates Has an Incredibly Clear Explanation for Why White People Shouldn't Use the N-Word," Vox.com, Nov. 9, 2017, https://www.vox.com/identities/2017/11/9/16627900/ta-nehisi-coates-n-word.

### Katja and Gadisa

259 **Same-Race Teachers**: Seth Gershenson, Cassandra M. D. Hart, Constance A. Lindsay, and Nicholas W. Papageorge, *The Long-Run Impacts of Same-Race Teachers*, IZA DP No. 10630 (Bonn, Germany: IZA Institute of Labor Economics, March 2017), http://ftp.iza.org/dp10630.pdf.

259 **Redlining Maps**: Bruce Mitchell and Juan Franco, *HOLC "Redlining" maps: The persistent structure of segregation and economic inequality* (Washington, DC: National Community Reinvestment Coalition, Feb. 2018), https://ncrc.org/wp-content/uploads/dlm_uploads/2018/02/NCRC-Research-HOLC-10.pdf .https://ncrc.org/holc/.

### Students from Central High School

263 **Reverse Racism**: HuffPost, "4 'Reverse Racism' Myths That Need to Stop," blog entry by Zeba Blay, Aug. 26, 2015, https://www.huffingtonpost.com/entry/reverse-racism-isnt-a-thing_us_55d60a91e4b07addcb45da97.

263 **Dear White People**: *Dear White People* (2014) International Movie Database, "Quotes," https://www.imdb.com/title/tt2235108/quotes.

### Angela

266 **Bootstrap Culture:** John McDermott, "Pulling Yourself Up by Your Bootstraps Is Actually Impossible," MEL Magazine, January 19, 2018, accessed September 17, 2018, https://melmagazine.com/pulling-yourself-up-by-your-bootstraps-is-actually-impossible-464e0f916a6b.

266 **Representative Romero Information:** State of Utah, House of Representatives, "Rep. Angela Romero," http://house.utah.gov/rep/ROMERAY.

266 **Advocate**: Nancy DiTomaso, "White People Do Good Things for One Another, and That's Bad for Hiring," Harvard Business Review, January 9, 2014, accessed September 17, 2018, https://hbr.org/2014/01/white-people-do-good-things-for-one-another-and-thats-bad-for-hiring.

266 **Opportunity Hoarding**: Nancy DiTomaso, "The American Non-Dilemma: Racial Inequality Without Racism," Russell Sage Foundation (Jan. 17, 2013).

### Eric, Josiah, and Galen

270 **Montana White Supremacists**: Lois Beckett, "How Richard Spencer's Home Town Weathered a Neo-Nazi 'Troll Storm,'" *The Guardian*, Feb. 5, 2017, https://www.theguardian.com/us-news/2017/feb/05/richard-spencer-whitefish-neo-nazi-march.

### Patience K.

273 **Food Deserts**: "11 Facts About Food Deserts," DoSomething.org, https://www.dosomething.org/facts/11-facts-about-food-deserts.

273 **Racial Health Disparities**: "A Nation Free of Disparities in Health and Health Care," Department of Health and Human Services, 2011, https://www.minorityhealth.hhs.gov/assets/pdf/hhs/HHS_Plan_complete.pdf.

273 **Food Workers**: "Food Equity," Center for Social Inclusion, May 8, 2013, http://www.centerforsocialinclusion.org/our-work/our-programs/food-equity/.

274 **Black Farmers**: Bruce J. Reynolds, *Black Farmers in America, 1865–2000: The Pursuit of Independent Farming and the Role of Cooperatives*, RBS Research Report 194 (Washington, DC: U.S. Department of Agriculture, Oct. 2002), http://www.federationsoutherncoop.com/blkfarmhist.pdf.

274 **40 Acres and a Mule**: Henry Louis Gates, Jr., "The Truth Behind '40 Acres And a Mule,'" The Root, Jan. 7, 2013, https://www.theroot.com/the-truth-behind-40-acres-and-a-mule-1790894780.

### Sione

277 **Pacific Islander Student Challenges**: "How Pacific Islander Students Are Slipping through the Cracks," Asian America, *NBC News*, July 8, 2014, https://www.nbcnews.com/news/asian-america/how-pacific-islander-students-are-slipping-through-cracks-n144281.

### Matt

279 **Pine Ridge Statistics**: "Pine Ridge Indian Reservation Facts," Re-Member.org, https://www.re-member.org/pine-ridge-reservation.aspx.

### Jennifer M. and Felicia

282 **Cracker**: Gene Demby, "The Secret History of the Word 'Cracker,'" NPR, July 1, 2013, https://www.npr.org/sections/codeswitch/2-13/07/01/197644761/word-watch-on-crackers.

### CHAPTER NINE: IF YOU WANT TO HELP, HEAL

### Kimmy

288 **Hawaii Imprisonment**: David T. Johnson, Janet T. Davidson, and Paul Perrone, *Hawaii's Imprisonment Policy and the Performance of Parolees Who Were Incarcerated In-State and on the Mainland* (Honolulu, HI: Department of Sociology, University of Hawaii at Manoa and Department of the Attorney General, State of Hawaii, Jan. 2011), https://ag.hawaii.gov/cpja/files/2013/01/AH-UH-Mainland-Prison-Study-2011.pdf.

289 **Cherríe Moraga Quote**: Cherríe Moraga and Gloria Anzaldúa, *This Bridge Called My Back: Writings By Radical Women of Color*, 2nd ed. (New York: Kitchen Table, Women of Color Press, 1983), https://monoskop.org/images/e/e2/Moraga_Cherrie_Anzaldual_Gloria_eds_This_Bridge_Called_My_Back_Writings_by_Radical_Women_of_Color-Kitchen_Table_Women_of_Color_Press.pdf.

### Javier

292 **New Mexico Demographics**: "U.S. Census Bureau QuickFacts: New Mexico, 2017," https://www.census.gov/quickfacts/NM.

293 **Transgender Students and Bathrooms**: Danni/y Rosen, "Gender-Neutral Bathrooms Are Radical, but Not How You Think," Gay, Lesbian and Straight education Network (GLSEN), https://www.glsen.org/blog/gender-neutral-bathrooms-are-radical-not-how-you-think.

### Aubrey

295 **Asian Americans and Mental Health**: Laurie Meyers, "Asian-American mental health," *Monitor on Psychology* 37, no. 2 (Feb. 2006): 44, http://www.apa.org/monitor/feb06/health.aspx.

295 **Asian-American Women and Suicide**: Joel Schwarz, "U.S.-born Asian-American women more likely to think about, attempt suicide," University of Washington News, Aug. 17, 2009, https://www.washington.edu/news/2009/08/17/u-s-born-asian-american-women-more-likely-to-think-about-attempt-suicide/.

295 **Asian Americans and "Depression"**: Anna Gorman, "For Many Asian Americans, Depression Is an Unfamiliar Word," *Washington Post*, May 22, 2015, https://www.washingtonpost.com/national/health-science/for-many-asian-americans-depression-is-an-unfamiliar-word/2015/05/22/f186d140-e8f1-11e4-9767-6276fc9b0ada_story.html?utm_term=.c5c736b1d7b4.

### Evelyn

298 **The Projects and Residential Segregation**: Richard Rothstein, *The Color of Law: A Forgotten History of How Our Government Segregated*

*America* (New York: Liveright Publishing Corporation, a division of W. W. Norton & Company, 2017).

298 **High-Poverty Neighborhoods**: Paul Jargowsky, "Architecture of Segregation," The Century Foundation, Aug. 7, 2015, https://tcf.org/content/report/architecture-of-segregation/.

### Alok

301 **Alok News Coverage**: Ishani Duttagupta, "Soul Survivor: How Alok Madasani Is Picking Up the Pieces Three Months after Kansas Bar Attack," *Economic Times,* updated June 10, 2017, https://economictimes.indiatimes.com/nri/nris-in-news/soul-survivor-how-alok-madasani-is-picking-up-the-pieces-three-months-after-kansas-bar-attack/articleshow/59087987.cms.

301 **Just-World Bias**: Dhammika Dharmapala, Nuno Garoupa, and Richard H. McAdams, "Belief in a Just World, Blaming the Victim, and Hate Crime Statutes," University of Chicago Public Law & Legal Theory Working Paper No. 242, 2008, http://citeseerx.ist.psu.edu/viewdoc/download?doi=10.1.1.1030.5128&rep=rep1&type=pdf.

### Karen

304 **White Flight in Gary:** Erin Devorah Rapoport, "The Politics of Disinvestment and Development in Gary, Indiana," *Advocates' Forum* (2014): 20–26, https://www.ssa.uchicago.edu/politics-disinvestment-and-development-gary-indiana.

### Darren and Dom

307 **The Sun Dance**: Michael E. Melody, "The Lakota Sun Dance: A Composite View and Analysis," *South Dakota History* (1976): 433–55, https://www.sdhspress.com/journal/south-dakota-history-6-4/the-lakota-sun-dance-a-composite-view-and-analysis/vol-06-no-4-the-lakota-sun-dance.pdf.

307 **Sweat Lodges**: "Inipi—The Rite of Purification," Akta Lakota Museum and Cultural Center website, http://aktalakota.stjo.org/site/News2?page=NewsArticle&id=8671.

308 **Spiritual Native Healers**: Deborah Bassett, Ursula Tsosie, and Sweetwater Nannauck, "'Our Culture Is Medicine': Perspectives of Native Healers on Posttrauma Recovery among American Indian and Alaska Native Patients," *Permanente Journal* 16, no. 1 (Winter 2012): 19–27, https://www.ncbi.nlm.nih.gov/pmc/articles/PMC3327107/#i1552-5775-16-1-19-b12.

### Ophelia

310 **Third Space**: Homi K. Bhabha, "Cultural Diversity and Cultural Differences," *The Post-Colonial Studies Reader*, ed. B. Ashcroft, G. Griffiths, and H. Tiffin (New York: Routledge, 2006), pp. 155–57, accessed Sept. 22, 2018, http://monumenttotransformation.org/atlas-of-transformation/html/c/cultural-diversity/cultural-diversity-and-cultural-differences-homi-k-bhabha.html.

311 **It Got Better Project:** "Laverne Cox stars in powerful 'It Got Better' video," Rolling Out, accessed September 18, 2018, https://rollingout.com/2014/06/20/laverne-cox-stars-powerful-got-better-video/.

### Ples and Azim

313 **Child Gun Violence**: "Key Gun Violence Statistics," Brady Campaign to End Gun Violence, 2016, http://www.bradycampaign.org/key-gun-violence-statistics.

313 **Gang Homicides**: Arlen Egley Jr., J. Logan, and Dawn McDaniel, "Gang Homicides—Five U.S. Cities, 2003–2008," Morbidity and Mortality Weekly Report, Centers for Disease Control and Prevention, Jan. 27, 2012, https://www.cdc.gov/mmwr/preview/mmwrhtml/mm6103a2.htm.

314 **Crack Cocaine Usage**: "Who Uses Crack Cocaine, and Why?" Criminal Justice Policy Foundation, https://www.cjpf.org/who-uses-crack-cocaine-and-why/.

### Hermon

316 **Frederick Douglass:** "Speech: Frederick Douglass," *Hartford Courant*, Sept. 29, 2002, http://articles.courant.com/2002-09-29/news/hc-douglass.artsep29_1_anti-slavery-society-speech-rochester-ladies.

317 **Poll on Capitalism and Socialism**: "Harvard IOP Spring 2016 Poll: Clinton in Commanding Lead over Trump among Young Voters, Harvard Youth Poll Finds," Harvard Kennedy School, Institute of Politics, http://iop.harvard.edu/youth-poll/past/harvard-iop-spring-2016-poll.

317 **Poll on American Democracy**: "Institute of Politics Spring 2018 Youth Poll: Nearly Two-Thirds of Young Americans Fearful about the Future of Democracy in America," Harvard Kennedy School, Institute of Politics, http://iop.harvard.edu/spring-2018-poll.

## CHAPTER TEN: LET'S ALL GET TO WORK

### Ron W.

330 **Hawaiian History and Demographics**: Sara Kehaulani Goo, "After 200 Years, Native Hawaiians Make a Comeback," FactTank, Pew Research Center, April 6, 2015, http://www.pewresearch.org/fact-tank/2015/04/06/native-hawaiian-population/.

### Tiara

333 **NFL Player Protest Support**: "ESPN survey shows Americans interested, divided on NFL protests during national anthem," ESPN.com, Sept. 29, 2017, http://www.espn.com/nfl/story/_/id/20858557/espn-survey-shows-americans-interested-divided-nfl-protests-national-anthem.

333 **Sports Teams White Ownership**: Shaun King, "The Unbearable Whiteness of NFL Ownership," The Intercept, May 25, 2018, https://theintercept.com/2018/05/25/nfl-owners-white-kaepernick-protest-rule/.

### Lua and Family

337 **Racism in Child Welfare**: "Racial Disproportionality and Disparity in Child Welfare," Issue Brief, Children's Bureau (Nov. 2016), https://www.childwelfare.gov/pubPDFs/racial_disproportionality.pdf.

338 **Foster Care System Statistics**: "51 Useful Aging Out of Foster Care Statistics," National Foster Youth Institute, May 2017, https://www.nfyi.org/51-useful-aging-out-of-foster-care-statistics-social-race-media/.

### Protim

340 **Family Conflict**: Jo Ann M. Farver, Sonia K. Narang, and Bakhtawar R. Bhadha, "East meets West: Ethnic identity, acculturation, and conflict in Asian Indian families," *Journal of Family Psychology* 16, no. 3 (Sept. 2002): 338–50, http://dx.doi.org/10.1037/0893-3200.16.3.338.

341 **James Baldwin**: James Baldwin, "The Negro in American Culture," *Cross Currents* 11 (1961): 205, cited here: https://radicalscholarship.wordpress.com/2016/07/08/this-is-u-s-to-be-a-negro-in-this-country/.

### Danya

344 **Syrian War Death Tolls**: "Total Death Count," I Am Syria, http://www.iamsyria.org/death-tolls.html.

345 **9/11**: Sam Dolnick, "Visiting Ground Zero, Asking Allah for Comfort," *New York Times*, Sept. 9, 2010, https://www.nytimes.com/2010/09/10/nyregion/10muslim.html.

### Steph

347 **Women in Tech**: Catherine Ashcraft, Brad McLain, and Elizabeth Eger, "Women in Tech: The Facts, 2016 Update," National Center For Women & Information Technology, 2016, https://www.ncwit.org/sites/default/files/resources/womenintech_facts_fullreport_05132016.pdf.

### Suzi

350 **School-to-Prison Pipeline**: Marilyn Elias, "The School-to-Prison Pipeline," *Teaching Tolerance* magazine, 43 (Spring 2013), https://www.tolerance.org/magazine/spring-2013/the-schooltoprison-pipeline.

351 **White Savior**: Celia Edell, "Here's What a White Savior Is (And Why It's the Opposite of Helpful)," Everyday Feminism, June 20, 2016, https://everydayfeminism.com/2016/06/white-savior-problem/.

### Monique

353 **Sassy Black Woman**: American Advertising Federation and Zeta Phi Beta Sorority, "Reality TV: Entertaining . . . But No Laughing Matter," white paper, 2016, http://aaftl.com/wp-content/uploads/2016/02/AAF_WatchParty_Whitepaper.pdf.

354 **Women Onscreen**: "Women onscreen," Women and Hollywood, 2017, https://womenandhollywood.com/resources/statistics/2017-statistics/.

### Kao Kalia

356 **Vietnam War**: Taggart Siegel, dir., "The Split Horn" (documentary, 56 minutes), Public Broadcast Service, 2001, https://www.pbs.org/splithorn/story1.html.

357 **Hmong Population**: "Hmong in the U.S. Fact Sheet," Pew Research Center, Sept. 8, 2017, http://www.pewsocialtrends.org/fact-sheet/asian-americans-hmong-in-the-u-s/.

357 **Prisons**: Ashley Nellis, "The Color of Justice: Racial and Ethnic Disparity in State Prisons," The Sentencing Project, June 14, 2016, https://www.sentencingproject.org/publications/color-of-justice-racial-and-ethnic-disparity-in-state-prisons/.

# INDEX

Bold indicates source notes.

ableist, 87
abortion, 219
acceptance, 340–41
accessibility, 87–88, **373**
activists and activism
    advocacy as, 265–66
    anti-ageism, 85
    antilynching, 78
    Asian, 203, 248
    Black, 179–81, 253–54
    civil rights, 147
    disabilities and, 82, 88, 183–84
    fat, 84–85
    Hispanic, 192
    Japanese American, 248
    LGBTQ, 85
    Native American, 29, 58, 207, 279
    policing and, 126
    for racial literacy, 36, 321–23
    against racism, 115, 333–34, **382**
    resilience of, 285–86
    right words for, 147
    social justice, 225–26
    storm damage and, 45
    women of color as, 289
addiction. See substance abuse
adoption, 122, 126, 137–38, 142–43, 219,
    259–60, 288–89, 337
advocates, 266, **379**
affirmative action, 158–59, **375**
Africa, 26, 43, 93, 156, 240, **370**
African Americans. See also Blacks
    community and, 60, 217, 298, 305
    in Gary, 304–5
    hair of, 228
    hatred toward, 149, 168
    health of, 99
    Native Americans and, 158, 195–96
    and police, 137
    population of, 51
    survival behaviors of, 26, 80–81
    in Tulsa, 179–80
ageism, 85
Alabama, 68, 83, 102, 227
Alaska, 73
Alaskan Natives, 11–12, 73, 245, **379**
Alcatraz takeover, 58, **372**

Alcoff, Linda, 32
alcoholism. See substance abuse
Aleut Natives, 245, **379**
ally/allies
    intersectionality and, 85
    listening as, 67, 122–23, 153, 184–85
    term, 16
American dream, 29–30, 99–100
American Indian Movement, 29
American Jazz Museum, 60–61
*American Non-Dilemma* (DiTomaso),
    266
anti-Blackness, 203
Anti-Defamation League, 189
Antigua, 172
antiracist, 269–70
anti-Semitism, 189, **376–77**
*Apocalypse Now* (film), 33
Arizona, 186
Arkansas, 70–71, 142, 261–64, 324–27
Asheville, North Carolina, 65, 224–25
Asian Americans. *See also specific*
    *ethnicities*
    Blacks and, 203–4
    cultures and, 135, 310, 340, 358
    as feminine, 164
    identity of, 310
    incomes of, 16
    mental health and, 295, **380**
    as model minority, 15–16, 295, 342,
        357
    privilege of, 15, 32, 164, 347
    racism and, 203
    as success-driven, 294
    suicides of, 294–95, **380**
Asian women, sexualization of, 143, 164
assimilation, 94, 120
assumptions, avoiding, 359–60
Atlanta, Georgia, 154
authentic experience, 257, 311, 360–61
avoidance, 80–81
Baez, Joan, 85, **373**
Baháʼí faith, 133, 198, 253
Baldwin, James, 341, **382**
Baltimore, Maryland, 157
Bamboo Ceiling, 164, **376**
banjo, 22–23
becoming, 316
belonging, sense of, 213, 257

Benjamin, Ruha, 2
Bernstein, Patricia, 77
Bhabha, Homi K., 310
biases
    avoiding, 359–60
    in health care, 99
    implicit and explicit, 137, **375**
    racial, 337
Big Three systems, 36, 38
bipolar disorder, 107
biracial, 63, 109–10, 149–50, 206, 262,
    333–34, 350
Birmingham, Alabama, 203, 227
birth, of slave children, 22, **370**
bisexuality, 204, **377**
Black Feminist Theory, 85, 200–201
Black Lives Matter, 126, 153, 179, 196,
    253
Blackness
    of country music, 23–24
    experience of, 112, 114–15
    Whiteness and, 9, 23–24
Blacks. *See also* African Americans
    Asians and, 203–4
    avoidance of, 170
    country music and, 22
    inventions by, 22–23
    killed by police, 53, 357–58, **378–79**
    lynching of, 53, 77–78, 179, **372–73**
    mark of Cain on, 253, **379**
    as masculine, 164
    representation of, 60
    schools and, 350
    sentencing of, 69
    slave names of, 155
    special education and, 125
    travel and, 43, 71, 80
Black women
    bearing children, 22, **370**
    stereotypes of, 326–27, 353
blood
    Black, 63, **372**
    quantum, 175–76
boarding schools, 90–91, 120, 256, **374**
body shaming, 334
Bonilla-Silva, Eduardo, 85
bootstraps, 266, **379**
borderline personality disorder, 128
Boston, Massachusetts, 131, 346

"Eskimo" (term), 13
Española, New Mexico, 57
Ethiopian American, 234, 259–60
ethnic (term), **378**
ethnicity, 167, 223, 228
eugenics movement, 26
executions, 69
Executive Order 9066, 244
experiences
    authentic, 257, 360–61
    racial differences in, 15, 114
    of racism, 20
    validation of, 19–20, 361
explicit bias, 137, **375**
expulsions, 350
family conflict, 340, **382**
Fargo, North Dakota, 173, 214–15, 233
fathers, 183, 217, **378**
fear
    felt by police, 242
    of non-Whites, 279
    of police, 118, 203, 217, 240–41
feminism
    Chicana, 192
    Disney princesses and, 200
    divisions in, 200–201, 234
    Muslims and, 234
    as negative term, 87
filial piety, 310
Filipina/Filipino, 142–43, 211–13
First Amendment, 66–67, 167, **372, 376**
first-generation, 19, 43, 172, 277, 316
*First Waco Horror, The* (Bernstein), 77
*Fist, The* (monument), 145, 147, **375**
Florida, 129, 171, 239, 335
food, 47, 96, 135, 222–23
food deserts, 273, **380**
food equity, 273–74
food swamps, 273
food workers, 47, 222–23, **378**
forgiveness, 219–20, 290, 313–14
formerly enslaved, 45, 80
40 acres and a mule, 274, **380**
foster care, 114, 125, 336–37, **382**
Fourteenth Amendment, 60
Fox News, 333
François, Vernon, 40
Frank, Billy, Jr., 207
Frank, Leo, 189, **377**
free speech, 167
friendships, 6–7, 132, 281–82, 313–14.
    *See also* relationships
Fula (language), 93–94
full-blooded, 175–76, 330
Gambian American, 93
gangs, 19, 180, 217, 313–14, 351, **381**
Garner, Eric, 1
Garrett, Thomas, 132
Gary, Indiana, 303–5, **381**

gay, 115–16
gender
    in Cherokee language, 90
    consciousness of, 161
    pronouns, 161–62, **376**
    race and, **376**
    sexuality and, 161, **374**
    term, 130
gender identity, 161, **375–76**
gender-neutral bathrooms, 292–93
genderqueer, 161
generational curse, 288
genocide, 120, 189–90, 344, 358, **377**
gentrification, 32, 146–47, 217
Georgia, 154
Great Migration, 114, **374**
Green, Nearest, 22
Greenville, South Carolina, 166, 168
Grierson, Randy, 52–53
gun violence, 20, 174, 241, 301, 313–14,
    344, **381**
hair, **378**
handicapped (term), 88
*Harvard Business Review,* 266
hate crimes, 96, 183, **373, 376**
    hate speech, 66, 167 diversity of,
    231
    history of, 231, 329–31, 382
    prisons in, 287–88, 380
Hawaiian people, 40
Hawai'i, 39–41, 44, 197–98, 328
healing, 283–86
health care, 99, **380**
Heather Heyer Foundation, 55
Helms, Janet E., 35
Heyer, Heather, 5, 54–56
high-poverty neighborhoods, **381**
hijab, 234–35
Hindus, 341
Hispanics. *See also* Latinx
    categories of, 192–93
    ethnicity and, 167
    high-achieving, 256
    LGBTQ, 209–10, 292–93
Hispanic women, income of, 18
history
    of desegregation, 103–5, 262
    genocides in, 120, 189–90, 344, 358,
        **377**
    of Hawai'i, 231, 329–31, **382**
    inclusive, 132
    of indigenous peoples, 58, 158
    Kurdish, 174
    of racism, 152, 155, 174, 179, 320–21
Hitler, Adolf, 147
Hmong people, 356–58, **382**
Hobson, Mellody, 146, **375**
Holocaust, 189–90, 200
homicides, 313–14, **381**

Honolulu, Hawai'i, 39, 44, 197, 230, 287,
    328
housing, 259, 298, **360–61, 374, 379**
housing projects, 298, **380–81**
Human Rights Campaign, 183
Hurston, Zora Neale, 23, **370**
Hyderabad, India, 301
hyphenated identity, 97, 310, 316
Idaho, 140
identity. *See also* intersectionality
    of adoptees, 290
    of Asians, 341
    of biracial people, 262
    cultural, 94
    gender, 161, **375–76**
    hiding, 237
    hyphenated, 97, 310, 316
    of Jews, 190
    multiracial, 187, **377**
    Native, 330
    positionality and, 32–33
    religious, **377**
    Whiteness and, 35
ideology, 225, 317, **381**
illegal immigrants, 167, **376**. *See also*
    citizenship status; undocumented
Illinois, 14–15, 17, 19–20, 199, 297
immigrants. *See also* illegal immigrants;
    *names of nationalities;*
    undocumented
    in Hawai'i, 231
    LGBTQ, 128
    multiracial, 273, 316–18
    in Norway, 269
implicit bias, 137, **375**
imposter syndrome, 99
incarceration, 119, 217, 289, 314, **374,
    378**
income, 16, 18, 279, **370**. *See also* poverty
India, 301
Indian (term), 73, **372**
Indiana, 303–5
Indian Americans, 301, 340–42
Indian Reorganization Act of 1934, 177
indigenous peoples. *See also names of
    tribes and nations;* Native
    Americans
    acknowledging, 30
    before colonization, 12
    contributions of, 206
    medicines of, 206, **377**
    teaching about, 73
Indonesian, 164–65, 225–26
institutional racism, 10
integration
    desegregation and, 75, **372**
    of identity, 94
intellectual disabilities, 77
intergenerational trauma, 135, **375**

## ABOUT THE AUTHORS

**Priya Vulchi** and **Winona Guo** met in tenth grade, after Eric Garner's death prompted a conversation in history class—the first time either of them remembers any teacher initiating a discussion about race. They ended up co-founding CHOOSE and developing a 224-page racial-literacy textbook for teachers, which was recognized and funded by Princeton University, featured in *Teen Vogue*, and used in classrooms in over 40 states.

Instead of starting college in the fall of 2017, Winona and Priya convinced their parents to let them take a year off from school. After fundraising themselves primarily through sponsorships from companies like Airbnb, they traveled alone to all 50 states and listened to over 500 strangers talk about race and intersectionality. Along the way, they also became the youngest TED residents ever, giving another TED Talk in addition to speaking at TEDWomen in 2017 (their talk, "What It Takes to Be Racially Literate," has had over 1 million views), the United Nations' Girl Up Conference, and over a dozen K–12 schools nationwide. Winona and Priya are currently students at Harvard University and Princeton University, respectively.

To stay involved with CHOOSE's journey, follow them on social media: @chooseorg (Facebook), choose_org (Instagram, Twitter).